Iranian Cinema with Psychoanalysis

Combining Lacanian psychoanalytic theory, Iranian Shi'ite thought, and Islamicate sexualities, *Iranian Cinema with Psychoanalysis: The Interpreter of Desires* provides a groundbreaking analysis of the logic of desire and sexuality in key films of contemporary Iranian cinema, arguing that there is a profound, albeit surprising, correlation between post-revolutionary Iranian cinema and psychoanalysis that has remained unthought.

Looking through the prism of psychoanalysis, Farshid Kazemi argues that censorship on the representation and expression of sexual desire in Iranian films has, contrary to the desired effect, produced a *cinema of desire*. This book is the first to provide an analysis of the unconscious structure of desire and sexuality operative in post-revolutionary Iranian cinema, demonstrating that psychoanalytic literature is uniquely positioned to shed light on this aspect of film. Kazemi uncovers the hidden libidinal economy of Iranian cinema by exposing the fact that despite the State censor's desire to suppress desire, it has inadvertently inscribed desire in its formal structure. The book offers a compelling and innovative examination of Iranian cinema through a psychoanalytic lens, contributing significantly to the field of film studies.

Iranian Cinema with Psychoanalysis will be of great interest to academics and scholars of film studies, psychoanalytic studies, Lacanian theory, film theory, Iranian cinema, global cinema, Iranian studies, and Middle Eastern studies.

Farshid Kazemi is Lecturer in Film Studies at the School for the Contemporary Arts, Simon Fraser University, Canada. He holds a PhD in Islamic and Middle Eastern Studies from the University of Edinburgh. His research interests combine an interdisciplinary and theoretical approach to film and media studies, film theory, Iranian studies, and Islamic and Middle Eastern studies. His book on the film *A Girl Walks Home Alone at Night* was published by Liverpool University Press in 2021.

The LACK Book Series
Series editors: Jennifer Friedlander and Hilary Neroni

The LACK Book Series is devoted to the promotion and development of thought inspired by the tradition of Lacanian psychoanalytic theory. The series publishes work that engages the intersection of psychoanalysis with philosophy, politics, and contemporary culture. The books in the series demonstrate the unique explanatory power of psychoanalysis in addressing the pressing concerns of our day. These books deepen readers' engagements with Lacan by offering new insights and pushing Lacanian theory in novel directions. The series develops key psychoanalytic concepts (such as fantasy, desire, death drive, and repetition) in conjunction with the vital concerns of our day (the reappearance of fascism, the climate crisis, contemporary conceptions of gender and sexuality, the impact of racism, the shape of ideology, and many others). Additionally, it provides a space for psychoanalytic books that focus on film, television, and other forms of media. The LACK Book Series provides a forum for a diverse group of scholars from across a wide range of disciplines and from around the globe.

Iranian Cinema with Psychoanalysis
The Interpreter of Desires
Farshid Kazemi

"Cinema arrived in Iran around the same time it arrived in the rest of the world, but it gave birth to psychoanalysis (or its precursor) centuries before Freud invented it. This is at least what we can surmise from this fascinating book. Kazemi offers a rich and surprising history of the entanglement of Iranian thinkers – from the medieval ages to the editors of *Cahiers du cinema* and beyond – in matters psychic and cinematic. He also provides compelling analyses of films from both the New Iranian Cinema, which emerged with a good deal of fanfare in the 1990s, and a newer, eerie, weird cinema recently unleashed from the constraints of the former."

—**Joan Copjec,** *Brown University, USA*

"The book is a pioneering exploration of the intersection between Iranian cinema and psychoanalysis, filling a gap in the literature. It rests on a novel premise, arguing for a significant homology between post-revolutionary Iranian cinema and psychoanalysis relating to their joint concern with repressed sexual desire. Moreover, it demonstrates how despite – or because of – its concern with modesty, Iranian cinema has inadvertently inscribed desire into its formal structures."

—**Shohini Chaudhuri,** *Professor in the Department of Literature, Film and Theatre Studies, University of Essex, UK*

"Farshid Kazemi's *Iranian Cinema with Psychoanalysis* is the book that we've been waiting for. It's the first great work on the most important cinema in the world today—Iranian cinema. Kazemi not only reveals what's at work in key films of the Iranian cinematic wonder but also lays out with remarkable clarity how to think about films anew in psychoanalytic terms. For anyone with the remotest interest in contemporary film, this book is an absolute necessity."

—**Todd McGowan,** *Professor and Director of Film and Television Studies, University of Vermont, USA*

Iranian Cinema with Psychoanalysis

The Interpreter of Desires

Farshid Kazemi

R Routledge
Taylor & Francis Group

LONDON AND NEW YORK

Designed cover image: Shirin Neshat
Offered Eyes, 1993
RC print & ink (photo taken by Plauto)
40 x 60 inches
© Shirin Neshat
Courtesy of the artist and Gladstone Gallery

First published 2025
by Routledge
4 Park Square, Milton Park, Abingdon, Oxon OX14 4RN

and by Routledge
605 Third Avenue, New York, NY 10158

*Routledge is an imprint of the Taylor & Francis Group, an informa
business*

© 2025 Farshid Kazemi

British Library Cataloguing-in-Publication Data
A catalogue record for this book is available from the British Library

ISBN: 978-1-032-87129-5 (hbk)
ISBN: 978-1-032-87127-1 (pbk)
ISBN: 978-1-003-53102-9 (ebk)

DOI: 10.4324/9781003531029

Typeset in Times New Roman
by KnowledgeWorks Global Ltd.

Contents

Acknowledgments

This book began its life during my PhD candidacy at the University of Edinburgh (2014–2018) at the Department of Islamic and Middle Eastern Studies. I want to record my sincere gratitude to Nacim Pak-Shiraz, my primary supervisor and to my secondary supervisor, David Sorfa.

During my Postdoctoral Fellowship at the School for the Contemporary Arts at Simon Fraser University, Laura U. Marks, was and has been, a continued source of tremendous support and encouragement. It was during my Postdoctoral Fellowship that I was able to turn part of my PhD thesis into a short book, *A Girl Walks Home Alone at Night*, which was published by Liverpool University Press in 2021. The Fellowship also afforded me the time and opportunity to prepare the present manuscript for publication. For this and much more, I owe a profound debt of gratitude to Laura.

Finding an ideal home for a book is never an easy task, but I could not be more honored when Hilary Neroni kindly asked if I would be interested in submitting my manuscript to be considered for a new book series called LACK (on psychoanalysis and culture), to be co-edited with Jennifer Freidlander and published by Routledge. To evoke the Lacanian adage, "the letter always arrives at its destination." I am convinced that my book has finally arrived at its destination. A version of Chapter 2 was previously published in the journal *Camera Obscura: Feminism, Culture, and Media Studies* in 2018, and I am grateful to Homay King and the two anonymous reviewers of the article for their comments. My sincere thanks to Hilary Neroni and Jennifer Friedlander for their belief in this project and for including it as the inaugural book of what looks to be a fantastic series. I am especially grateful to Hilary Neroni and Todd McGowan for their kind support and intellectual camaraderie throughout the years since our first meeting at the LACK conference back in 2016. They have both been a source of inspiration to me and my scholarly work.

I would also like to record my thanks to Shohini Chaudhuri, who has provided me with various forms of academic support over the years and encouraged my work. Among Lacanian theorists the work of Joan Copjec has been a major source of inspiration, and I am grateful and honored for the kind words she has written for this book. Although I am not personally acquainted with Slavoj Žižek, yet his theoretical work has been inspirational, and its influence evident throughout this book.

I am also grateful to Shirin Neshat and the Gladstone Gallery for kindly granting me permission to reproduce the image that appears on the cover. The image is a photograph by the artist Shirin Neshat called *Offered Eyes* (1993). It is a striking image of an eye that captures in essence the logic of the gaze that I articulate in Chapter 1. The eye is inscribed with lines of a poem from the modernist poet and filmmaker Forough Farrokhzad (d. 1967), who was the first female poet to openly and courageously express female/feminine sexual desire in her poetry, despite cultural proscriptions and negative repercussions that attended her work and person.

It is a special pleasure to mention all the friends and colleagues who have played a significant role in encouraging and supporting me before, during and beyond my years as a PhD candidate: Novin Doostar, Juliet Doostar, Armin Eschraghi, Omid Ghaemmaghami, Dina Al-Kassim, Todd Lawson, Franklin Lewis, Catherine Nelson-McDermott, Todd McGowan, Nostratullah Mohammad-Hosseini, Moojan Momen, Iraj Sabet, Erfan Sabeti, Francesco Stermotich-Cappellari, Farzin Vejdani, Sooyeon Zacharias, and Jamen Zacharias.

Finally, I want to thank my immediate family and loved ones without whose love and support I could not have written the following pages. Thanks are due to my dear sister Parastoo and my brother-in-law Davood. My deepest thanks to my most beloved parents, Simin and Baitullah. It is their unfailing love and support that has given me the opportunity to realize my dreams. Last but not least, I want to record my heartfelt gratitude to Dianne Malone, whose unfailing support, belief in this project and love have meant the world to me over the years, and whose careful reading of major portions of this book has saved me from many editorial oversights. I am forever grateful to her.

A Note on Transliteration

I have used a simplified and modified version of the *International Journal of Middle Eastern Studies* (*IJMES*) transliteration system. For vowels in Persian, I have used the "e" in place of "i," and the short "o" instead of the "u." I have dispensed with all diacritical marks in the transliteration. Persian and Arabic terms that are common in English usage have not been transliterated or italicized. The transliteration system in cited sources has been retained in their original form.

Introduction

Iranian Cinema with Psychoanalysis (or Watching Iranian Movies with Lacan)

The introduction situates the book within two bodies of scholarship: the first dealing with first-wave psychoanalytic film theory (Christian Metz, Jean-Louis Baudry, and Laura Mulvey), and the second with second-wave psychoanalytic film theory (Joan Copjec, Slavoj Žižek and Tod McGowan), and outlines the book's main theoretical contribution. The introduction also brings out the surprising parallel histories of psychoanalytic theory and Iranian cinema, as well as the history of applying psychoanalytic theory in the study of Iranian cinema. Finally, the introduction foregrounds the unexpected ways in which insights of psychoanalysis are aligned with Islamicate (mystical) philosophy and Iranian thought.

The central question that grounds the inquiry of this book is: why couple psychoanalysis with Iranian cinema or Iranian cinema with psychoanalysis? What is at stake in reading Iranian cinema through the prism of psychoanalytic film theory? At first glance, the two seem like an unlikely couple, but as psychoanalytic theory reminds us, it is only through probing the gaps, ruptures, and fissures in the filmic text that the world of unconscious desires reveals itself. The argument of this book is that, in fact, there is a profound homology between Iranian cinema and psychoanalysis which can only be discovered through a short-circuiting reading of the two, where through a crossing of wires between them, unexpected sparks and theoretical insights come to light, which would otherwise remain unthought. The metaphor of short-circuiting as a method of critical reading is provided by Slavoj Žižek, "A short circuit occurs when there is a wrong connection in the network—wrong... from the standpoint of the smooth functioning of the network." The effectiveness of the short-circuit as a method of critical reading is to cross wires that usually do not touch, for instance, "to take a major classic (text, author, notion [or film]), and read it in a short-circuiting way, through the lens of a 'minor' author, text, or conceptual apparatus ('minor' should be understood here in Deleuze's sense: not 'of lesser quality,' but marginalized, disavowed by the hegemonic ideology, or dealing with a 'lower,' less dignified topic)." As Žižek states, "If the minor reference is well chosen, such a procedure can lead to insights which completely shatter and undermine our common perceptions."[1]

From this perspective, films in post-revolutionary Iranian cinema function as texts which when read in a short-circuiting way, through the "minor" conceptual apparatus of Freudo-Lacanian psychoanalysis (again "minor" in the sense intended

DOI: 10.4324/9781003531029-1

by Deleuze and Guattari as marginalized, disavowed, but also subversive and revolutionary),[2] which can completely shatter our common perceptions and conceptions, not only of Iranian cinema but of psychoanalysis itself. There is a radical political core inherent to this approach, since the crossing of wires between psychoanalysis and Iranian cinema can generate a theoretical short circuit that can uncover the unthought in the libidinal economy of the ruling ideology. Here it should be recalled that the concept of a "short-circuit" goes back to Surrealism as formulated by André Breton in "the Second Manifesto for Surrealism (1930)" apropos inspiration, in which through a "sort of short circuit it creates between a given idea and a respondent idea (written, for example). Just as in the physical world, a short circuit occurs when the two 'poles' of a machine are joined by a conductor of little or no resistance. In poetry and in painting, Surrealism has done everything it can and more to increase these short circuits."[3] Indeed, from the outset Breton considered the Freudian field (the unconscious, dreams, desire, etc.) as the very *raison d'être* of Surrealism itself (not to mention Lacan's own close association with the surrealist movement early on in his career),[4] as well as the importance of Hegel's dialectical thought (whose importance to Surrealism is often forgotten).[5]

In a talk given at the Freud Museum in London on her book, *Doing Psychoanalysis in Tehran*, Gohar Homayounpour says, "The Iranian government calls psychoanalysis, the enemy of the state."[6] Indeed, this statement from Homayounpour demonstrates that, psychoanalysis is seen as politically subversive by the hegemonic ideology of the Islamic Republic, by the state and its apparatuses (to use Louis Althusser's famous formulation), since it considers psychoanalysis to pose such an existential threat that it must be deemed an enemy of the state. The theoretical question to be asked here is: why should psychoanalysis pose such a threat to the Islamic Republic? To put it briefly: the threat that psychoanalytic theory poses to the theocratic state lies in the fact that psychoanalysis is concerned with what is deemed the terrain of the ruling Shi'i *'ulama* (clergy) and *fuqaha* (jurists), namely desire and sexuality or Eros and eroticism. The ruling Shi'i clerics are concerned with veiling over all expressions of (sexual) desire, especially feminine desire and female sexuality.[7] Indeed, desire and eroticism is the subject of psychoanalysis par excellence, since as Jacques Lacan states what "Freudian thought has placed at the center of our interest in the economy of the psyche, [is] namely, Eros and eroticism."[8] In another turn Lacan states, "Desire is indeed the essential base, the goal, the aim, and the practice too, of everything that is being announced here, in this teaching, on the Freudian message."[9] As we shall see throughout this book, it is in Shi'i jurisprudence (*fiqh*) that a whole set of legal theories were elaborated in order to delimit or repress the representation of masculine and feminine desire and sexuality in relation to the cinema, through the enactment of the logic of the veil or the system of modesty (*hejab* in its broadest sense). In this sense, the Islamic Republic and its legal theoretical apparatus was/is concerned with the repression of (sexual) desire not just in society, but its manifestation and articulation in the cinema. This is why the historicist approach to sexuality derived from Michel Foucault would fail in a proper analysis of post-revolutionary Iranian cinema (and Iranian society under the Islamic Republic for that matter), since as Joan Copjec states, "[historicism] refuses to believe in repression and proudly professes to be *illiterate in desire*."[10] Indeed, Foucault famously positions himself against what he calls "the repressive hypothesis" (of desire), in psychoanalytic theory.[11] In this sense, to read post-revolutionary Iranian cinema, we have to be able to read desire, to know that desire is almost always unconscious desire, to recognize that desire is never transparent, neither to the subject nor to society or its cultural texts, and that where desire is concerned it always requires *interpretation*.

This brings me to the question of how we might understand the relationship between the psyche and culture, or how universal elements interact with cultural particularities. To answer this question, we must look at the historical emergence of Freudian psychoanalysis itself. Indeed, if Freudian theory, in its original articulation, was appropriate to explain a certain cultural matrix and historical milieu in the West that relied on a Judeo-Christian ethics of sexual repression and control; then similarly, psychoanalysis fits well the structure of Iranian society in the aftermath of the 1979 Iranian Revolution, since Iranian society underwent a total Islamization where traditional Islamic ethics of sexual repression and control became operative in the wider culture and society. As the philosopher Byung-Chul Han puts it, "Freud's psychic apparatus is a repressive apparatus of domination and compulsion that operates with commands and prohibitions, that subjugates and oppresses." In this sense as Han rightly formulates it, "Freud's psychoanalysis is therefore possible only in repressive societies, such as the society of sovereignty or the disciplinary society, which base their organization on the negativity of prohibitions and commands."[12]

In this precise sense, Freudian psychoanalysis is possible in post-revolutionary Iranian society precisely because it is a repressive society, at once a society of sovereignty and a disciplinary society (a Shi'i theocratic state operating with an Islamic legal code), whose organization is structured on prohibitions and commands. This is why a psychoanalytic theoretical method fits well with the structure of the psyche operative in post-revolutionary Iranian society and its cinematic production, since the interaction of psyche and culture in this formulation is based on repression, domination, and compulsion.

The overall trajectory of this book is to demonstrate that Freudo-Lacanian psychoanalytic film theory, more than any other theoretical framework, is the privileged instrument through which we may draw out the structure of desire and sexuality operative in post-revolutionary Iranian cinema, that would otherwise remain repressed or disavowed. This book then stages a mutually productive encounter between Iranian cinema and Freudo-Lacanian psychoanalytic film theory, which goes beyond the first-wave psychoanalytic film theory of the 1970s and takes its place along Lacanian theorists such as Joan Copjec, Slavoj Žižek, and Todd McGowan (among others discussed below), who have initiated a new wave of Lacanian film theory. If this book may be said to have one central aim: it is to argue that in order to properly read the logic of desire in post-revolutionary Iranian cinema, we must become *the interpreter of desires*, to "become literate in desire" as Copjec puts it, in order to read what is unarticulable in these filmic texts, since it is *desire and its interpretation*[13] that is at the nexus of our reading of post-revolutionary Iranian cinema with psychoanalysis.

0.1 Iranian Cinema and Psychoanalysis: Parallel Histories

There is a fortuitous co-incidence or fateful conjunction in the historical appearance of psychoanalysis and Iranian cinema that has hitherto remained hidden, occulted as it were, the uncovering of which is the first step in drawing out the homology between the two through a psychoanalytic procedure. The relationship between the historical emergence of psychoanalysis and the cinema has long been noted in film theory and by film theorists, with several volumes that variously foreground the parallel histories of cinema and psychoanalysis.[14] In a volume of collected articles called, *Endless Night: Cinema and Psychoanalysis, Parallel Histories*, Stephen Heath in his introduction foregrounds the "Parallel Histories," between cinema and psychoanalysis and states that the title for the book is taken from a line spoken in Jim Jaramusch's *Dead Man* (1995). Heath seems to be unaware that these words come from the poetry of the radical mystic and Romantic poet William Blake in his poem, *Auguries of Innocence*: "Every Night & every Morn/Some to Misery are Born/Every Morn and every Night/Some are Born to sweet delight/Some are Born to sweet delight/Some are Born to Endless Night."[15] Nevertheless, Heath is correct in considering "*Endless Night*" to be an "appropriate designation for this collection of essays, since psychoanalysis and film theory, both, are drawn to the darkness in their quest for logics of meaning."[16] This fascination with darkness, or the darker side of human subjectivity (desire, death drive, etc.) is called *Nachtseite*, "the dark or night side" in German Romanticism, and it is what connects Freudian psychoanalysis to the heritage of German Romanticism and Idealism.[17]

It was in 1895 that Freud and Breuer first published their work *Studies on Hysteria* and in the same year the Lumière Brothers screened the magic art of moving pictures in Paris to an astonished audience. In a now-famous letter to his friend Wilhelm Fliess dated June 12, 1900, the significance of this date was registered by Freud, "Do you suppose that some day a marble tablet will be placed on the house inscribed with these words: 'In This House, on July 24th, 1895, the secret of Dreams was Revealed to Dr Sigm. Freud.' At the moment there seems little prospect of it."[18] However, this "secret of dreams" was not disclosed to the world until Freud's seminal publication, *The Interpretation of Dreams* in 1900.[19] (In a strange twist of fate, Lacan was also born in the same year on April 13, 1900). It is this book that Freud considered, even late in life, to contain the most important discoveries and insights of his career, as he states, "It contains, even according to my present-day judgment, the most valuable of all the discoveries it has been my good fortune to make. Insight such as this falls to one's lot but once in a lifetime."[20] It is in *The Interpretation of Dreams* that Freud provides his first psychoanalytic theorization of the unconscious, and the analysis of dreams, as he states, "The interpretation of dreams is the royal road to a knowledge of the unconscious activities of the mind."[21] It is in dreams and their interpretation therefore that we find a parallel between psychoanalysis and the cinema, since the cinema has long been considered as a form of public dreaming and a *dream factory* (an appellation that was first given to Hollywood cinema).[22]

It was in the same year, on August 18, 1900 (21 Rabi al-Thani 1318) that the first cinematic images were captured by an Iranian photographer. These images were shot by the Baha'i born Mirza Ebrahim Khan Akassbashi Sani al-Saltaneh (1874–1915), the court photographer of the Qajar king, Mozaffar al-Din Shah, who accompanied the king in his first visit to Europe.[23] It was during their visit to France while seeing the Exposition in Paris earlier in July that Mirza Ebrahim Khan Akassbashi was introduced to the "*Cinématographe*." The introduction of the cinematograph or film technology in Iran was a subversive event during the Qajar era, and created an uproar among the Shi'i *'ulama* (clergy), and was especially deemed a threat to the performers of Iran's religious dramatic art, *ta'ziyeh* or Shi'i passion play, such as Shaykh Hassan Shimr, Haji Barak Allah, Akbar Taziyeh Khan, Amr Allah Malmoos, and Ahmad Marmari.[24] The *Tekkiyah-ye Dowlat* (the Royal State Theater) was constructed by Nasir al-Din Shah (1831–1896)[25] specifically for the purpose of performing the passion plays, and many of these actors (*shabih khans*) orchestrated its performance to devout male Shi'i audiences, for whom witnessing the enactment of the tragic events of Karbala functioned as a form of religious purgation or catharsis.[26] As Mas'ud Mehrabi states in his history of Iranian cinema: "suddenly among the gifts Mozaffar al-Din Shah brought back from his visit to Europe (*farang*), a technology entered Iran that incited the influential voice of Shaykh Hassan Shimr and drew his powerful opposition to: The Magic Lantern (*cheraq-e jadoo*)"[27] (i.e., the cinema).

It was after seeing the films at the Paris Exposition that Mozaffar al-Din Shah became enamored with "this magical phenomenon," of the "*cinématographe*" and as he states, "We instructed Akkas Bashi to purchase all kinds of it [cinematographic equipment] and bring it to Tehran so God willing he can make some there and show them to our servants."[28] Hence on the order of Mozaffar al-Din Shah, Akkasbashi purchased two film cameras, one a Gaumont, including some film stock and a number of films to bring back to Iran.[29] Akkasbashi then was responsible for the introduction of film technology to Iran, and may be regarded as Iran's first filmmaker. It was before their return to Iran that Akkasbashi shot this film footage in Belgium while at the Festival of Flowers or Flower Parade in Ostend, and recorded the parade in which the Shah participated, where a group of (unveiled) women traveling on floats threw flowers and bouquets at the king, and he enthusiastically threw flowers back at them. This moment was not only the first images of movement captured on the Iranian cinema(tograph), but as Negar Mottahedeh notes, it was during the parade in 1900, that there was "an exchange, in effect a movement – a movement of desire between the shah and European women, who, unlike women on the streets of Tehran, were moving about unveiled."[30] In this way, at the beginning of the introduction of film technology into Iran, desire was inscribed and recorded on this technology, whereby the "mutual exchange (of glances) on the anticipatory eve of modernity was overwritten years later by the veiling of all women from the voyeurism of the gaze and the Islamization of desire for the contemporary Iranian screen."[31] Beyond the fascination and novelty of movement in the technology of the moving image, the cinema, there was the movement of desire.

At the heart of the Freudian discovery is the theory of the unconscious. The Freudian unconscious is not the site of human feelings or emotions, but rather the reservoir of desires and drives. In psychoanalysis the unconscious operates under a different logic that is incommensurable with the conscious mind, namely the logic of desire. Indeed, as McGowan notes, the most significant element that functions as a co-incidence between psychoanalysis and the cinema is that "Freud takes an interest in dreams because they unlock the unconscious and films, which share the structure of dreams, carry the same promise."[32] In this way, psychoanalysis and Iranian cinema are mutually connected not only because they originate in the same year (1900); but more significantly, because psychoanalysis makes its most important discoveries through dream analysis, and in this sense it resembles the cinema itself, since "the cinema remains a dream factory, a form of public dreaming."[33] But, as McGowan notes, there is a fundamental difference between films and dreams since a dream is the product of an individual subject, but a film is not made by a single director but through collaboration with hundreds of other individuals.[34] Nonetheless, what we encounter in films is our collective dreams or nightmares: it is in the cinema where we are confronted not only with our own innermost desires but the desire of the (social) Other.

0.2   Iranian Cinema with Psychoanalytic Film Theory

Psychoanalytic film theory may be delineated into two distinctive historical phases or waves.[35] The primary sources for both of which are the thought of the French psychoanalyst Jacques Lacan (1901–1981), and secondarily the father of psychoanalysis himself, Sigmund Freud (1856–1939). The first wave of psychoanalytic film theory also called *Screen* theory—since many of the film theorists associated with this wave published their work in the British journal *Screen* —began in the late 1960s and 1970s which emphasized Lacan's imaginary order (and to a lesser degree the symbolic order), in Lacan's ternary orders of psychic formation: the imaginary, the symbolic, and the real,[36] and was characterized by a critique of the operation of ideology and the role of the cinematic apparatus in purveying this process. The break with the first wave of 1970s Lacanian film theory, called by Todd McGowan "an Imaginary Lacan"[37] due to its emphasis on the imaginary register—also an allusion to its misunderstanding of Lacan by evoking the notion of illusion/fiction inhering in Lacan's concept of the imaginary—appears in the late 1980s and early 1990s with two important figures, namely Joan Copjec[38] and Slavoj Žižek.[39] In Iranian cinema studies many film scholars have tended to fall within the first wave of psychoanalytic theory, but my own theoretical contribution here will be to stage a mutually productive encounter between Iranian cinema and second-wave Lacanian psychoanalytic film theory, whereby both can mutually illuminate and enrich each other in a short-circuiting way.

One of the first Iranian film critics/theorists who employed psychoanalysis in his writings on film was the novelist, essayist, and film critic Fereydoun Hoveyda (1924–2006), the brother of the more famous Amir-Abbas Hoveyda, the prime minister of Iran under Mohammad Reza Shah Pahlavi (from 1965 to 1977).[40]

Hoveyda received his education at Sorbonne University and worked in Paris for UNESCO in the 1950s. While living in Paris, Hoveyda became part of the influential film critics at *Cahiers du cinéma* "who developed the *politique des auteurs* in the 1950s,"[41] and contributed regularly to the film journal from 1955 to 1965. Along his more famous colleagues who were to become the auteurs of the French New Wave (*La Nouvelle Vague*)—such as Jean Luc-Godard, François Truffaut, Claude Chabrol, Éric Rohmer, and Jacques Rivette—Hoveyda was one of the key figures in the elaboration of auteurism in *Cahiers*, particularly in foregrounding the role of *mise-en-scene*, as seen in his celebrated review (published in May 1960) of Nicholas Ray's *Party Girl* (1958): "What constitutes the essence of cinema is nothing other than *mise-en-scene*. It is through this that everything on the screen is expressed, transforming, as if by magic, a screenplay written by someone else and imposed on the director into something which is truly the film of an auteur."[42]

Apropos psychoanalytic theory, from the mid-1950s to the mid-1960s Hoveyda authored 52 articles in total in *Cahiers*, many of which alluded to Freud and Lacan or psychoanalytic concepts. In one particular reference to Lacan that is relevant for our purposes here, Hoveyda also highlights certain resemblances between the psychoanalyst and the function of the film critic/theorist. Hoveyda theorizes that in many ways the film critic, "resembles that of the psychoanalyst. Does he not, in effect, have to reconstruct through the film the discourse of the auteur (subject) in its continuity, bring to light the unconscious that underpins it and explain the particular way it is articulated?" Further elaborating the analogy between the psychoanalyst and the film theorist, Hoveyda evokes Lacan's formulation in which the unconscious is marked by a gap and the way in which it constitutes the censored sequence as it were, noting that just as in psychoanalysis, "the truth can [still] reveal itself; it is written not in the 'visible' sequence of the images, but elsewhere: in what we call the auteur's 'technique,' in the choice of actors, in the decors and the way actors and objects relate to these decors, in gestures, in dialogue, etc."[43]

This early reference to Lacan and psychoanalysis by Hoveyda in 1961 is quite startling[44] since it prefigured the semiotic inflected first-wave Lacanian psychoanalytic theory which was to be later developed by figures such as Christian Metz, especially in his 1965 essay in *Cahiers*, "On the Impression of Reality in the Cinema,"[45] and of course later fully developed in "The Imaginary Signifier" published in *Screen* in 1975.[46] Therefore, from the various references to Lacan and psychoanalysis in Hoveyda's oeuvre during his *Cahiers* period,[47] he may be regarded as one of the proto-psychoanalytic film theorist who was among the earliest figures that prefigured the advent of first wave of psychoanalytic film theory or *Screen* theory.

Although Hoveyda intermittently used psychoanalysis or Lacan in his film criticism in general, he never deployed psychoanalytic theory in relation to Iranian cinema, since he almost never wrote an analysis of any Iranian films, although he does refer to the cinema of Abbas Kiarostami in passing.[48] The first sustained and insightful engagement between Iranian cinema and psychoanalytic film theory, particularly feminist gaze theory, was Negar Mottahedeh's already classic text, *Displaced Allegories* (2008).[49] Mottahedeh's work is influenced by psychoanalytic film theory via Christian Metz's film semiotics and Laura Mulvey's critique of the male-gaze in her essay, "Visual Pleasure and Narrative Cinema," both of which are seminal figures of first-wave psychoanalytic film theory or *Screen* theory. Since I locate my own work here in second-wave psychoanalytic film theory, I engage with Mottahedeh's work in depth in the chapters on the gaze (Chapter 1) and voice (Chapter 2).

Another important figure is the film scholar Hamid Naficy, who although does not utilize Lacan often, yet on occasion refers to Lacan and psychoanalytic theory. For instance, Naficy states apropos the veil in Iranian cinema that, "the concept of the veil as a lure or masquerade can profitably be discussed through Lacan's theories."[50] This concept of the veil as a lure apropos masquerade is more related to first-wave psychoanalytic theory, indeed Naficy mentions the work of the first-wave feminist psychoanalytic film theorist Mary Ann Doan in the footnote as an example of the use of the veil.[51] More recently Naficy has used Lacan's concept of the imaginary and symbolic discussing the contradictory logic that emerges from a pre-modern "psychosocial configuration" that "produces an apparent contradiction between an inner private self and an outer public self..."[52] Naficy considers the Lacanian imaginary and symbolic to be operative in Iranian cinema and its representation of women. As he states, "This dual, collective, and hierarchical conception of the self produces tensions between individual subjectivity and collective identity that are widespread in Iranian cinema and in women's representation by it."[53] Naficy's reading of the Lacanian imaginary and symbolic into the filmic structure of post-revolutionary Iranian cinema and women's representation in it are generally correct, yet I demonstrate that in the examples of Iranian films I analyze there is an outburst or eruption of the Lacanian real that disrupts, transgresses, and destabilizes the imaginary in its construction of the subject and the symbolic order, where the realm of politics and social normativity resides. Here again by focusing on the imaginary and the symbolic, Naficy's brief use of Lacan falls under first-wave psychoanalytic film theory.

Indeed, when speaking of Lacan in relation to the cinema, Naficy often refers to the Lacan of first-wave psychoanalytic film theory or *Screen* theory. For instance, in his discussion of the various looks that cinema engenders/produces, he speaks of three looks, the first is voyeuristic and derived from Freud, the second is narcissistic and derived from Lacan, and the third is masochistic, referring to Deleuze's discussion of masochism[54] to derive the last conception of the look, which he particularly associates with post-revolutionary Iranian cinema.[55] This reference to Lacan's concept of the look and its relation to cinema is derived from *Screen* theory and has as its point of departure Lacan's early essay on the mirror stage where he developed the imaginary order in which the child's identification with its specular image creates the illusion of wholeness – hence the Lacanian *imaginary* signifies at once both image and illusion.

Hamid Dabashi has also written that, "Lacan's distinction among what he called the imaginary order, the symbolic order, and the real had always fascinated me,"[56] and goes on to apply Lacan's concept of the imaginary and symbolic in his reading of Kiarostami, where he considers that Kiarostami's "anarchic imaginary disorder" disrupts the symbolic order. However, this is a misreading of Lacan's concept of the imaginary, and Farhang Erfani rightly corrects Dabashi's misinterpretation and states that, "'anarchic disorder' is on the side of the real and not the imaginary."[57] Although Dabashi has written a number of books on Iranian cinema, his use of Lacan in this instance is based on a misunderstanding of the imaginary for the real, since it is only the eruption of the real that can disrupt the smooth functioning of the symbolic order.

Perhaps the most significant figure to have used Lacan in reading Iranian cinema is the Lacanian theorist, Joan Copjec. Copjec's deployment of Lacan in reading Kiarostami's film, *Bad ma ra khahaad bord* (*The Wind Will Carry Us*, Iran, 1999), especially through Lacan's concept of the object-gaze, may be considered to be the first serious attempt at deploying Lacanian film theory in reading Iranian films by a Lacanian theorist who is one of the founding figures of second-wave psychoanalytic film theory.[58] Copjec's work is dedicated to the study of Iranian cinema through a focus on perhaps the greatest auteur of the New Iranian Cinema, namely Abbas Kiarostami.[59] However, based on the contents of various articles published by Copjec on Kiarostami, she has become more engaged with Islamic philosophy as a theoretical framework for reading Kiarostami's cinematic universe, where Lacanian theory seems to have taken the theoretical back stage, although it is not absent.[60] Particularly inspired by the scholarship of the French philosopher and Islamo-Iranologist Henry Corbin (1903–1978)[61] and his elaboration of the concept *alam al-mithal* or the world of images in Islamicate philosophy and mysticism, famously translated by Corbin as "the imaginal world"[62] (from the Latin *mundus imaginalis*).[63] Copjec's work on Kiarostami is influenced by this Corbinian inflection, which was partially articulated earlier by Negar Mottahedeh in her work, arguing that the concept of the imaginal world is operative in post-revolutionary Iranian cinema, where drawing on the reservoir of Shi'ite mytho-history (the martyrdom of Imam Hosayn) and drama (*ta'ziyeh*), "the post-Revolutionary film industry in the Islamic Republic was to purify these [filmic] technologies and thereby articulate the Iranian nation as a this-worldly displacement of an imaginal world – in other words, to create a world beyond the commodified image world of Hollywood."[64] In fact, it is likely that in one of his lectures in 1974 where Corbin distinguishes between the "imaginary" and the "imaginal" he not only wished to distinguish it from the common understanding of the term imaginary as "being equivalent to signifying unreal, something that is and remains outside of being and existence," but also from Lacan's already famous formulation of the imaginary, as both image and illusion.[65]

One of the more sustained encounters between second-wave Lacanian theory and Iranian cinema is staged by Farhang Erfani in his book *Shooting Truth: Philosophy and Iranian Cinema*. Erfani uses Lacanian theory to read two well-known Iranian films: Abbas Kiarostami's *Nema-ye nazdik* (*Close-Up*, Iran, 1990), and Marzieh Meshkini's *Ruzi ke zan shodam* (*The Day I Became a Woman*, Iran, 2000). Indeed, in his reading of Kiarostami's *Close-Up*, Erfani employs Lacan's theory of the gaze and relies on the work of Joan Copjec who had already made "the connection between Lacan and Kiarostami…" and as Erfani states Copjec's "work is invaluable for my thesis in this chapter…"[66] The second film that Erfani reads via Lacanian psychoanalytic theory is Meshkini's *The Day I Became a Woman*, in which he deploys Lacanian ethics and the concepts of desire and jouissance (enjoyment). Erfani's book consists of an encounter between Iranian cinema and (Western) philosophy, but it is not clear or self-evident how Lacan as psychoanalyst is considered a philosopher. Indeed, Lacan called his teaching "anti-philosophy," and declared, "I rebel, if I can say, against philosophy."[67] Therefore the use of Lacan as a "philosopher" requires some justification, which Erfani does not provide. Another element that is missing in Erfani's reading of Iranian films and distinguishes it from my own approach here is the lexicon of film studies or the formal grammar of cinema that informs my analysis of the unique film form and aesthetics of Iranian cinema.

In Copjec and Žižek's work on Lacanian theory there is a shift in the emphasis from the register of the imaginary and the symbolic, to the real. The Lacanian real is not synonymous with "reality," it is a term that goes through several stages of development in Lacan's teaching, but it must be formulated in terms of negation or negativity since the Lacanian real cannot be articulated in positive terms, it is the failure of signification. As Paul Verhaeghe states apropos Lacan's concept of the real, a "difference [lies] between knowledge and something beyond knowledge, something that belongs to another register, other than the symbolic order.... [T]here is something that cannot be put into words, something for which words are lacking."[68] For Lacan, "the Real is beyond symbolization," it is not reducible to the order of the signifier (i.e., language). According to Lacan "truth" is different from "mere knowledge" in that "the essential characteristic of truth is that it confronts us with the ultimate point where knowledge about desire... can no longer be put into words.... This dimension beyond the signifier is the Lacanian real."[69] The real appears at the point where the signifier misfires, at the moment where signification fails to signify within the signifying system.

Thus, my own approach to Lacanian film theory in reading Iranian cinema will be grounded more on this second-wave rather than the first-wave, as I stage the radical disruption of the real into the Iranian imaginary and symbolic operative in the Islamic Republic, where desire and sexuality are foregrounded in the register of the real rather than the register of the imaginary apropos voyeuristic pleasure and ideological identification. It is the eruption of the real of desire in the filmic form and narrative, which as we shall see, often destabilizes the censorship codes and conventions that regulate Iranian cinema under the Islamic Republic.

0.3 The Interpreter of Desires: The Mystic or Saint, the Analyst, and the Film Theorist

In this section I foreground the significance of the title of the book through a short-circuiting conjunction of the figures of the mystic or saint, the analyst and the film theorist, since what they all have in common is that they are all *Interpreter of Desires*. In the first tale of Rumi's *Masnavi* called, the tale of the King and "The Healing of the Sick Slave-Girl," there is a figure who is linked to the Persian philosopher Ibn Sina, variously called "the invisible guest," "the divine physician," and "the pure and trustworthy one" (1/6, 7, 8), and particularly the "saint" (*wali*), who is brought by the King to heal the slave-girl that he loves but who has fallen mysteriously ill.[70] The saint in the tale functions like the psychoanalyst trying to interpret what is ailing the slave-girl. The saint begins to ask her various questions while holding her wrist with his fingers on her pulse, and the slave girl begins talking—like the psychoanalytic talking-cure—and as the saint asks her various questions about her family, her hometown, etc., he discovers that her pulse rises considerably faster as he closes on the city of Samarkand, and finally he discovers that the source of her ailment is the love that she secretly harbors for a goldsmith who lives there, and her separation from him is the cause of her illness. In a similar way, in 1974 in *Television*, Lacan makes a startling claim and posits the figure of the psychoanalyst "in relation to what was in the past called: being a saint." Lacan states, "The more saints, the more laughter; that's my principle, and it may even be the way out of capitalist discourse."[71] This correlation of the figure of the saint and the analyst in Lacan, is homologous to what we encounter in Rumi's tale, since the saint in the tale functions as the analyst who is called the "physician of the soul" or psyche, in other words, a psychoanalyst.[72]

Having already mentioned Henry Corbin earlier, it is important to note the influence of Corbin's work on Lacan,[73] especially through his book on the Andalusian Sufi mystic Ibn 'Arabi (d. 1240) called, *L'Imagination Creatrice dans le Soufisme d'Ibn 'Arabi*.[74] In his seminar VII on *The Ethics of Psychoanalysis*, 1959–1960, Lacan already mentions this book by Corbin, specifically in his discussion of courtly love.[75] Corbin discusses Ibn 'Arabi and many of the Sufis among the precursors of the tradition of courtly love, calling them the *Fedeli d'amore* or the faithful of love.[76] But what is significant here is another reference to Ibn 'Arabi by Lacan that is mentioned by Fethi Benslema, namely the event of the encounter between the Andalusian philosopher Ibn Rushd (d. 1198), known as Averroes, and Ibn 'Arabi. Benslema recounts that during a conference at the Facultes universitaires Saint-Louis (Brussels) in 1960, "Lacan recalls the episode of the meeting of and dialogue between Averroes and Ibn Arabi in Andalusia, and affirms that his position as a psychoanalyst is aligned with Ibn Arabi rather than the philosopher."[77] This encounter between Averroes and Ibn 'Arabi is recorded in Corbin's book, and it would have been the only place that Lacan could have learned of it.[78] However, what is significant for our purposes here is that Lacan aligns the position of the analyst with that of the mystic Ibn 'Arabi, instead of the philosopher, namely Averroes. This link between the psychoanalyst and the mystic can also shed light on what Badiou calls Lacan's "anti-philosophy" or Lacan as an "anti-philosopher," since by associating the psychoanalyst with Ibn 'Arabi vs. Averroes, Lacan is positioning himself against a certain type of philosophy exemplified by the figure of Averroes, namely Aristotelian or peripatetic philosophy, rather than philosophy as such. It should be recalled that Ibn 'Arabi himself was a philosophizing mystic or mystic philosopher, and deeply influenced by the tradition of Pythagorean, Platonic, and Neo-Platonic (Plotinus) philosophy, including Hermeticism as translated into Arabic in the great translation movement in Baghdad during the Abbasid caliphate.[79]

One of Ibn 'Arabi's theories that has a profound resonance with the position of the psychoanalyst is how the world is structured like a dream, a dream that requires interpretation. In the *Fusus al-Hikam* (The Bezels of Wisdom), while referring to the famous prophetic tradition (*hadith*), "All men are asleep; only when they die, do they wake up," Ibn 'Arabi states that "the Prophet [Muhammad] called attention by these words to the fact that whatever man perceives in this present world is to him as a dream is to a man who dreams, and that it must be interpreted."[80]

This correspondence between the position of the mystic and the analyst comes to the fore in the title of Ibn 'Arabi's collection of poetry entitled, *Tarjuman al-Ashwaq* or *The Interpreter of Desires*.[81] The term *shawq* (plural *ashwaq*), which can mean love, desire, passion, or longing in Arabic (as well as in Persian), is a central term in Sufism and in Ibn 'Arabi. As Sells notes, "Ibn 'Arabi's *shawq* is analogous to classical Greek *eros* as it was taken as a fundamental driving force within human life, art, and thought."[82] Ibn 'Arabi is said to have composed these poems after his encounter with the daughter of an Iranian family originally from Isfahan, named Nizam. She was called by Ibn 'Arabi and others, "*ayn al-Shams wa'l-Baha'*," "Eyes of the Sun and of Glory," or translated by Corbin as "Harmonia [Nizam], Eye of the Sun and of Beauty." Regarding her Corbin states, "the young girl who was for Ibn 'Arabi in Mecca what Beatrice was for Dante, was a real young girl, though at the same time she was 'in person' a theophanic figure, the figure of the *Sophia aeterna*."[83] The poetry of *Tarjuman* contained such sensual and erotic imagery that Ibn 'Arabi was castigated by the religious scholars (*'ulama*) to have only written of carnal desire and profane love in the guise of mystical poetry; Ibn 'Arabi was forced to write an extended interpretation of each poem articulating their esoteric (*batin*) and mystical allusions, lest his life become endangered at the wrath of the clerics (*'ulama*). It is in this title that we can discern the profound confluence of the position of the mystic and the analyst, since the entire function of the analyst like the mystic is to be the interpreter of desires, which is why as I previously mentioned, Lacan called one of his seminars: *Desire and its Interpretation*.

In the final analysis, it is here that we can discern that there is a certain homology between the figure of the mystic (Ibn 'Arabi) with that of the psychoanalyst (Lacan), and the status of the analyst may be correlated to the film theorist/critic, as perceptively posited by Fereydoun Hoveyda, insofar as they are all *Interpreter of Desires*.

0.4   The Structure of the Book

One of the principle axis around which this book is structured is the Freudian partial (sexual) objects to which Lacan added the gaze and voice—the others being the phallus, the scybalum, and the breast. Each chapter contains one of these partial objects, although in the case of the first two chapters the gaze and voice are positioned in the foreground, and in the case of the following three—the phallus, the feces, and the breast—remain in the background. In Chapters 3 and 4, the partial objects do not function as the main argument of the chapters but as their libidinal underside, but they do not form the central core or argument of the chapters, as they do with the gaze and voice. All of the partial objects are different forms of what Lacan calls *objet petit a* or object-cause of desire, since they all form an object that is imagined as an extension of the body, from which the subject must separate itself in order to constitute itself as subject. As Lacan states, "You know: the breast, the feces, the gaze, the voice, these detachable parts which are nevertheless entirely linked to the body - this is what is involved in the *objet a*."[84] Although Freud imagined the sexual objects in terms of the developmental phase of the child, namely the initial oral phase, the breast, and later followed by the anal object, the excrement. The phallic phase is the last phase where the relation to the phallus (as object) organizes the way sexual difference is constituted. The other innovation of Lacan was to reinterpret the phallus not as the anatomical penis, but as a signifier. In Lacan the *objet petit a* does not have a developmental structure, but it is the way a field is organized around that object, hence the *objet a* in the visual field is the gaze and in the aural field it is the voice.

The book is organized into two parts. Part I, *Desire between Gaze and Voice*, is structured around two chapters that theorize examples from the New Iranian Cinema that revolves around the axis between the (Lacanian) gaze and voice. Starting with Lacan's concept of the gaze Chapter 1, "A Cinema of Desire: Object-Gaze in the New Iranian Cinema," provides a close reading of Abbas Kiarostami's *Shirin* (2008), and Majid Majidi's *Baran* (2001) in light of the gaze. In the chapter I argue that contrary to Negar Mottahedeh's thesis, who argues that post-revolutionary Iranian cinema or New Iranian Cinema is the realization of the goals of feminist gaze theory, whereby the male gaze is absent, and hence can be conceived as a "women's cinema" or a "feminist cinema," I argue instead that what appears in the New Iranian Cinema is the Lacanian object-gaze, which makes this cinema, a cinema of desire, since the logic of desire is based on what is often beyond the visual sensorium, rather than what is reducible to it. I demonstrate that the logic of the averted gaze due the Shi'ite modesty system (*hejab*) that is operative in this cinema can be theoretically correlated to the logic of *looking awry* formulated by Žižek apropos Lacan; but unlike Mottahedeh and Naficy, who missed the Lacanian dimension of looking awry, I foreground it as an instance of the object-gaze in Lacan.

In Chapter 2, "The Object-Voice: The Acousmatic Voice in New Iranian Cinema," I theorize the structure of the voice in the New Iranian Cinema, especially through what Jacques Lacan calls the object-voice and the French film theorist Michel Chion calls *acousmêtre* or acousmatic voice, namely the disembodied voice. I focus on how the voice without the body, or acousmatic voice, in which the voice of a character is off frame detached from a particular body, is often operative within Iranian cinema, as a way to circumvent showing bodies, especially female bodies, in erotic configurations. This phantom-like voice without a body or *acousmêtre*, like a spectral presence, haunts the entire landscape of post-revolutionary Iranian cinema. I also focus on the male voice without a body, which acts to subvert the logic of veiling female bodies, since representing the acousmatic male voice without a body, critiques the foregrounding of the male subject as the privileged site of subjectivity. I analyze two films in light of the acousmatic voice, namely Mohsen Makhmalbaf's *Gabbeh* (1996) and Rakshan Banietemad's *The May Lady* (1999), and demonstrate that in both films the voice acts as an erotic signifier, and becomes a love-object, since the body cannot be displayed erotically on the screen the voice at times fills in the erotic void created by the censors.

Part II, *The Fright of Real Desires*, consists of two chapters that look at two different films that stage what may be termed the logic of "desiring otherwise," where the ambiguities in the pure texture of the filmic text open up possibilities for reading forbidden desires, forbidden because outlawed by the Islamic Republic. The traumatic dimension of desire, where the real of desire appears in all its ambiguity in the pure texture of the films. It is here in the final chapter that I articulate a new shift away from the New Iranian Cinema of the 1990s and 2000s by theorizing *Atomic Heart* as part of a new filmic movement that is structured around what I call, *Unheimlich between the Weird and the Eerie* (apropos Mark Fisher's formulation).

In Chapter 3, "From Femininity to Masculinity and Back: The Feminine 'No' in *Daughters of the Sun*," the idea that guides the analysis of this chapter is the Lacanian feminine "No" and feminine jouissance in reading Mariam Shahriar's neglected masterpiece *Daughters of the Sun* (*Dokhtaran-e Khorshid*, 2000). I provide a close textual analysis of the film's protagonist Amangol's gender re-signification from feminine to masculine by her father through the technique of shaving her hair and cross-dressing her as a boy. I argue that in the texture of the film a constellation of motifs emerges such as transgender, gender and sexual ambiguity, same-sex desire or homoeroticism, and cross-dressing or transvestism that provides Shariar with an opportunity to critique not only the imposition of the veil, but also the loss of feminine identity. Finally, I demonstrate that the Lacanian ethics of the feminine "No" and feminine jouissance are enacted by Amangol, through a radical suicidal act that entails the burning of the carpet-weaving sweat shop, whereby she sacrifices her imposed embodiment of masculinity. Thus, Amangol traverses from femininity to masculinity and back through the logic of the feminine "No," and the full reassertion of her feminine identity.

In Chapter 4, "Dreaming of a Nightmare in Tehran: The Fright of Real Desires in *Atomic Heart*," a close reading of Ali Ahmadzadeh's film *Atomic Heart* (2015) is provided, where I theorize the film through Mark Fisher's formulation of "the weird and the eerie," foregrounding *Atomic Heart* as an instance of the two modes of the *weird* and *eerie* and argue that the film belongs to this larger category (of the *weird and eerie*) that I consider to form part of a new transnational filmic movement. The film is structured into two halves with the first half apparently functioning as reality and the second half as surreality. I turn this double or two-part structure of the film around and deploying Lacan's theory of fantasy and desire, I argue that contrary to outward appearance, the first part of the film functions as the world of fantasy and the second part as the world of desire. It is in the second half, when reality loses its grounding in the world of fantasy, that we are confronted with the traumatic (Lacanian) real in all its horror in the figure of Toofan, whose link with totalitarian and dictatorial figures (Sadam, Hitler) represents the Islamic Republic, and the Iranian president Mahmud Ahmadinejad. I argue that the second part of the film stages Lacan's dictum of the enigma of the Other's desire, *Che vuoi*? where the question of what the Other's desire is remains an incessant mystery, namely what does the Other, as in Toofan, who symbolizes the State, want from the two female protagonists of the film. In the second part of the film Nobahar and Arineh's thinly veiled lesbian or homoerotic desire functions as the fright of real desires, since in the Islamic Republic same-sex desire is forbidden and may bring one into confrontation with the Law, exemplified in the figure of Toofan. It is this oppressive, sinister, and menacing atmosphere in Iran that this film so powerfully stages, and which is what all the films related to this emerging new movement have in common, and that I have theorized as revolving around the two modes of the weird and the eerie.

Finally, the book simultaneously makes several theoretical interventions in a number of related fields and/or theoretical approaches or discourses to cinema: first, it contributes to a Lacanian film theoretical approach to Iranian cinema and reconfigures the previous approach that was dominated by first-wave psychoanalytic film theory or *Screen* theory; second, it makes a case for the productivity of a Lacanian theoretical approach in studies of desire and sexuality in Iranian cinema (and in Iranian studies on desire and sexuality more generally); third, it contributes to the burgeoning discourse of the encounter between Lacanian psychoanalysis and Islam, especially (Iranian) Shi'ite Islamic culture and thought; finally, it theorizes that a new art cinema and genre bending film movement is emerging in Iranian cinema moving on from the New Iranian Cinema of the past, and also beyond the influence of a figure such as Asghar Farhadi. In all these areas the book seeks to either open up new avenues of theoretical enquiry or reconfigure older debates and discourses to questions of desire, gender and sexuality by enacting a theoretical break, through a Freudo-Lacanian psychoanalytic intervention.

Notes

1 The first book in the Short-Circut series was by Žižek himself, see Slavoj Žižek, *The Puppet and the Dwarf: The Perverse Core of Christianity* (Cambridge, Massachusetts: MIT Press, 2003), vii.

2 See Gilles Deleuze and Félix Guattari, *Kafka Toward a Minor Literature* (Minneapolis: University of Minnesota, 1986).

3 André Breton, *Manifestoes of Surrealism*, trans. Richard Seaver and Helen R. Lane (Michigan: The University of Michigan, 2010), 161.

4 "To be sure, Surrealism, which as we have seen deliberately opted for the Marxist doctrine in the realm of social problems, has no intention of minimizing Freudian doctrine as it applies to the evaluation of ideas: on the contrary, Surrealism believes Freudian criticism to be the first and only one with a really solid basis." Breton, *Manifestoes of Surrealism*, 160.

5 Breton states, "Whenever the Hegelian dialectic does not function, there is no thought, no hope for truth (1952)." Quoted in José Pierre, *An Illustrated Dictionary of Surrealism* (New York: Barron's, 1979), 54.

6 Homayounpouer goes on to state, "which I think they are right." See, "Doing Psychoanalysis in Tehran," The Freud Museum, London, January 2020, time 57 min., 40 sec., https://thefreudmuseum.podbean.com/e/doing-psychoanalysis-in-tehran/

7 This underlying fear and threat of psychoanalysis ascribed to the Islamic Republic's ruling ideology by Homayounpour may be traced back to one of the early ideologues of the
Iranian Revolution and vehement critics of the Pahlavi regime, namely the leftist Islam-
ist, Ali Shariati (1933–1977). Regarding Freud and psychoanalysis Shariati writes, "In
this new bourgeoisie, [he] armed himself against all moral and human values, against all
high and ascending manifestations of the human soul and called it realism… A prophet
of the bourgeoisie, whose religion was *sexualism*…. This prophet was named Freud.
His religion was sexuality; his temple, *Freudism*." In another instance, Shariati blames
psychoanalysis for the moral corruption of women, "… From *Freudism* [the bourgeoi-
sie] built a supposedly scientific and humane religion. From sexuality they built their
place of worship and created a powerful servant class. And the first sacrifice on the
threshold of this temple was women's human values." Ali Shariati quoted in Orkideh
Behrouzan, *Prozak Diaries: Psychiatry and Generational Memory in Iran* (Stanford,
California: Stanford University Press, 2016), 37–38. A history of psychoanalysis in Iran
is currently a desideratum. The main figure in Iran who has perhaps done most to try and
rehabilitate psychoanalysis from such blatant misreading is perhaps the British trained
psychoanalyst and psychiatrist Mohammad Sanati. See Mohammad Sanati and Arash
Javanbakht, "Psychiatry and Psychoanalysis in Iran," *Journal of The American Academy of Psychoanalysis and Dynamic Psychiatry*, 34, no. 3 (2006): 405–414. http://www.
mohammadsanati.net/1390/culturepsychoanalysisiran/580. See also, Nader Barzin, "La
pscychanalyse en Iran," *Topique* 1, pp. 157–71, 2010. I have dealt with some aspects of
psychoanalysis in Iran in a book chapter, see Farshid Kazemi, "The Repressed Event of
(Shi'i) Islam: Psychoanalysis, the Trauma of Iranian Shi'ism, and Feminine Revolt," in
Psychoanalytic Islam and Islamic Psychoanalysis, ed. Ian Parker and Sabah Siddiqui
(New York: Routledge, 2018), 70–87.
8 Jacques Lacan, *The Ethics of Psychoanalysis: The Seminar of Jacques Lacan: Book VII*, ed.
Jaques-Alain Miller, trans. Dennis Porter (London and New York: Routledge, 2008), 175.
9 Jacques Lacan, *Anxiety: The Seminar of Jacques Lacan, Book X*, ed. Jacques-Alain
Miller (Cambridge: Polity Press, 2014), 214.
10 Joan Copjec, *Read my Desire: Lacan against the Historicists* (Cambridge, Massachusetts: MIT, 1994) 14.
11 See Michel Foucault, *The History of Sexuality* (New York: Vintage Books, 1990),
10–12.
12 *Byung-Chul Han, Topology of Violence* (Cambridge, Massachusetts: MIT Press,
2018), 23.
13 Jacques Lacan, *Le séminaire: Livre VI, Le Désir et son interprétation*, (Paris: Editions
de la Martinière, 2013); cf. Jacques Lacan, *Desire and Its Interpretation: The Seminar
of Jacques Lacan Book VI*, trans. Bruce Fink (Cambridge: Polity, 2019).
14 Janet Bergstrom, ed., *Endless Night: Cinema and Psychoanalysis, Parallel Histories*
(Berkeley: University of California Press, 1999).
15 William Blake, *William Blake: Selected Poems* (Oxford: Oxford University Press,
2019), 80.
16 Stephen Heath, "Cinema and Psychoanalysis: Parallel Histories," in *Endless Night*, 25–56.
17 Sufficient proof of this is Freud's essay on The Uncanny (*das Unheimliche*), where
Freud refers to E. T. A. Hoffmann's short tale "The Sandman" and to F. W. J. Schelling in his theorization of the uncanny. See Sigmund Freud, *The Uncanny*, trans. David
McLintock with Introduction by Hugh Haughton (New York: Penguin Books, 2003).
Freud was also influenced by the imagined or fantasmatic "Orient" in the works of
Hoffmann and the German Romantics, see Joanna Neilly, *E.T.A. Hoffmann's Orient:
Romantic Aesthetics and the German Imagination* (Oxford: Legenda, 2016).
18 Sigmund Freud, *The Interpretation of Dreams* (I), trans. James Strachey, in *The Stand-
ard Edition of the Complete Psychological Works of Sigmund Freud*, vol. 4, ed. James
Strachey (London: Hogarth, 1953), 121n.

19 McGowan perceptively observes that the *Interpretation of Dreams* appeared at the end of 1899, but Freud asked his publisher to date the book 1900 to publish the manuscript, in order to signal the epochal character of the book. See Todd McGowan, *Psychoanalytic Film Theory and the Rules of the Game* (New York: Bloomsbury, 2015), 2.

20 Sigmund Freud, *The Interpretation of Dreams* (II), trans. James Strachey, in *The Standard Edition of the Complete Psychological Works of Sigmund Freud*, vol. 4, ed. James Strachey (London: Hogarth, 1953), 608.

21 Freud, *The Interpretation of Dreams* (I), trans. James Strachey, in *The Standard Edition of the Complete Psychological Works of Sigmund Freud*, vol. 5, ed. James Strachey (London: Hogarth, 1953), 608.

22 Vicky Lebeau, *Psychoanalysis and Cinema: The Play of Shadows* (New York: Wallflower Press, 2002), 6.

23 On the life and background of Ebrahim Khan Akassbashi see, Hamid Naficy, *A Social History of Iranian Cinema Volume 1: The Artisanal Era, 1897-1941* (Durham: Duke University Press, 2011), 44–50; see also, Farrokh Gaffary, "Akkas-Bashi." *Encyclopedia Iranica*, vol. 1, ed. Ehsan Yarshater, p. 719. London: Routledge and Kegan Paul, 1985. http://www.iranicaonline.org/articles/akkas-basi-ebrahim

24 Massoud Mehrabi, *Tarikh-e sinema-yi Iran: Az aghaz ta sal-e 1357* (The History of Iranian Cinema: From the Beginning to 1979) (Tehran: Film Publication, 1988), 14.

25 Abbas Amanat, *The Pivot of the Universe: Nasir Al-Din Shah Qajar and the Iranian Monarchy, 1831-1896* (London: I.B. Tauris, 2008) 435.

26 On the *ta'ziyeh* see Bahram Beyzaie, *Namayesh dar Iran* [Dram in Iran]. Tehran: Roshangaran va motale'at-e zanan, 2001); cf. Peter J. Celkowski ed. *Ta'ziyeh: Ritual and Drama in Iran* (New York: New York University Press, 1979).

27 Mehrabi, *Tarikh-e sinema-yi Iran*, 14.

28 Translation of the travelogue in Ali M. Issari, *Cinema in Iran 1900-1979* (Metuchen: The Scarecrow Press, 1989), 58–59.

29 Naficy, *A Social History of Iranian Cinema Volume 1*, 44.

30 Negar Mottahedeh, *Representing the Unpresentable: Images of Reform from the Qajars to the Islamic Republic of Iran* (Syracuse University Press, Syracuse, 2008), 209. It is interesting that one of the earliest short films made by Akkasbashi in Iran, is a film shot of Iranian women wearing their long veils (*chador*) with their face veils (*rubandeh* or *charchoq*), which may index his modernist Baha'i views by highlighting the status and condition of women in Iran in juxtaposition to their unveiled European counterparts as seen and shot by him in his European tours with the shah, exemplified by the Flower Parade. See, Mehrdad Zahedian's *Lost Reels* (*Halqehha-ye Gomshodeh*, 2004). Film.

31 Mottahedeh, *Representing the Unpresentable*, 210.

32 McGowan. *Psychoanalytic Film Theory*, 2.

33 Ibid., 1.

34 Ibid., 2.

35 Here I follow Todd McGowan's delineation of the two waves of psychoanalytic film theory. See Todd McGowan, "Introduction." In *Lacan and Contemporary Film*. Ed. Todd McGowan and Sheila Kunkle (New York: Other Press, 2004); cf. the introduction in *The Real Gaze: Film Theory after Lacan* (Albany: SUNY Press, 2007), xi–xxix.

36 Lacan never capitalized the ternary order of the imaginary, symbolic, and real in the original French, and throughout this book all references to Lacan's orders will be uncapitalized. However, whenever they appear in quotes from the work of other authors, they are left as they are in the original.

37 McGowan, *Lacan and Contemporary Film*, xiii.

38 Joan Copjec, *Read my Desire: Lacan against the Historicists* (Cambridge and Massachusetts: MIT, 1994) 19. See especially chapter 2,. 15–38.

39 Slavoj Žižek, *The Fright of Real Tears: Krzysztof Kieślowski Between Theory and Post-Theory* (London: BFI Publishing, 2001).

40 Hoveyda was accused of being a Baha'i by the Shi'ite clergy in order to discredit the Pahlavi regime since their father, Habib Allah, had come from a Baha'i family, although there is evidence that he had grown distant from the Baha'i faith, and did not bring up his children in the religion. In the biography of Amir Abbas Hoveyda, *The Persian Sphinx*, Abbas Milani refers to an account from Fereydoun Hoveyda that states, "I was fourteen years old when I first heard the word 'Baha'i' and learned what it meant from a friend." See Abbas Milani, *The Persian Sphinx: Amir-Abbas Hoveyda and the Riddle of the Iranian Revolution* (Mage Publishers, 2000), 47; cf. also see, Abbas Milani, "Hoveyda, Amir-Abbas," *Encyclopaedia Iranica*, Vol. XII, Fasc. 5, 543–50. http://www.iranicaonline.org/articles/hoveyda-amir-abbas

41 Robert Lang, "An interview with Fereydoun Hoveyda," *Screen* 34:4 Winter 1993, p. 392.

42 Lang, "An interview with Fereydoun Hoveyda," 392.

43 Fereydoun Hoveyda, "Self-Criticism" ("Autocritique," *Cahiers du Cinema* 126, December 1961) in *Cahiers du Cinéma Volume 2. 1960–1968: New Wave, New Cinema, Re-evaluating Hollywood*, ed. Jim Hillier (London: Routledge, 1986), 261.

44 Jim Hillier writes, "Fereydoun Hoveyda's 1961 'Self-Criticism,' noting the general imprecision of critical language, makes manifest the desire to find a more 'scientific' critical language and gives some sense of this 'opening up': his main points of reference are Saussure, Merleau-Ponty and the nature of signification in language, Marx on literature, Lévi-Strauss and anthropology, Lacan and psychoanalysis. This may be a startling array of references for an essay dated 1961, when *Cahiers* was generally reckoned to be thoroughly obsessed with American cinema, authorship and *mise-en-scene*!" See, *Cahiers du Cinéma Volume 2. 1960–1968: New Vave, New Cinema, Re-evaluating Hollywood*, ed. Jim Hillier (London: Routledge, 1986), 226.

45 See "On the Impression of Reality in the Cinema" in Christian Metz, *Film Language – A Semiotics of Cinema* (New York: Oxford University Press, 1974).

46 Christian Metz, "The Imaginary Signifier" *Screen*, 16, no. 2 (1 July 1975): 14–76.

47 In another essay in *Cahiers* in 1961 Hoveyda refers to Lacan and psychoanalysis, while interpreting Jean Rouch's film *Chronique d'un été* (1961). See Fereydoun Hoveyda: *Cinéma vérité*, or Fantastic Realism' (*Cinéma vérité ou realism fantastique*', *Cahiers du Cinema* 125, November 1961), in *Cahiers du Cinéma Volume 2. 1960–1968*, 252.

48 Fereydoun Hoveyda, *The Hidden Meaning of Mass Communications: Cinema, Books, and Television in the Age of Computers* (Westport, Connecticut/London: Praeger Publishers, 2000), 27, 71.

49 Negar Mottahedeh, *Displaced Allegories: Post-Revolutionary Iranian Cinema* (Durham: Duke University Press, 2009).

50 Hamid Naficy, "Veiled Vision/Powerful Presences," in *Life and Art: The New Iranian cinema*, ed. Rosa Issa and Sheila Whitaker (London: British Film Institute, 1999), 63.

51 Naficy states, "For a relevant application of these to cinema, see Mary Anne Doane, *The Desire to Desire: The Women's Films of the 1940s* (Bloomingdale: Indiana University, 1987)."

52 Naficy, *A Social History of Iranian Cinema Vol. 4*, 102.

53 Ibid., 102.

54 Gilles Deleuze, *Masochism: Coldness and Cruelty & Venus in Furs*, trans. Jean McNeil (New York: Zone Books, 1991).

55 Naficy, *A Social History of Iranian Cinema Vol. 4*, 107.

56 Hamid Dabashi, *Masters & Masterpieces of Iranian Cinema* (Mage Publishers, 2007), 283.

57 Farhang Erfani, *Iranian Cinema and Philosophy: Shooting Truth* (Palgrave Macmillan, 2011), 88.

58 Joan Copjec, "The Object-Gaze: Shame, Hejab, Cinema," *Filozofski Vestnik* (Ljubljana), vol. XXVII, no. 2 (2007): 161–83.

59 Joan Copjec's forthcoming book is on Kiarostami, provisionally titled: *"Cloud": Between Paris and Tehran*, to be published by MIT Press.

60 For these studies see, Joan Copjec, "The Fate of the Image in Church History and the Modern State," *Politica Comun: A Journal of Thought*, 1, no. 2 (November 2012), Mexico: 17, Instituto de Estudios Criticos/TAMU/ Aberdeen/ Universita degli Studio Salerno; cf. Joan Copjec, "The Censorship of Interiority," *Umbr(a)*, special issue on "Islam," Spring 2009. Joan Copjec, "Cinema as Thought Experiment: On Movement and Movements," *differences* (2016) 27 (1): 143–75.

61 For a critical appraisal of the work of Corbin, see Steven M. Wasserstrom, *Religion After Religion: Gershom Scholem, Mircea Eliade, and Henry Corbin at Eranos* (Princeton University Press, Princeton, 1999); also, Vahid Brown, "A Counter-History of Islam: Ibn 'Arabi within the Spiritual Topography of Henry Corbin," *Journal of Ibn Arabi Society*, Volume XXXII, Autumn 2002. For a response to some of the critiques of Corbin, see Maria E. Subtelny, "History and Religion: The Fallacy of Metaphysical Questions (A Review Article)." *Iranian Studies*, 36, no. 1 (March 2003): 91–101. Also, Nile Green, "Between Heidegger and the Hidden Imam: Reflections on Henry Corbin's Approaches to Mystical Islam," in M.R. Djalili, A. Monsutti and A. Neubauer, *Le monde turco-iranien en question, coll. Développements*, (Paris, Karthala; Genève, Institut de hautes études internationales et du développement, 2008), pp. 247–59.

62 Joan Copjec, "The Imaginal World and Modern Oblivion: Kiarostami's Zig-Zag," *Filozofski Vestnik*, XXXVII, no. 2 (2016): 21–58.

63 This linking of Islamic philosophy and mysticism with the cinema of Abbas Kiarostami is already treaded ground, see especially Sussan Shams, *Le cinéma d'Abbas Kiarostami: Un voyage vers l'Orient mystique* (Paris: Editions L'Harmattan, 2011).

64 Mottahedeh, *Displaced Allegories*, 8.

65 Henry Corbin, "Mundus imaginalis ou l'imaginaire et l'Imaginal," *Cahiers internationaux de Symbolisme* 6 (June 1964); Henry Corbin, "*Mundus Imaginalis* or The Imaginary and the Imaginal," trans. Leonard Fox in *Swedenborg and Esoteric Islam* (Pennsylvania: Swedenborg Foundation, 1995). Also available online: https://www.amiscorbin. com/bibliographie/mundus-imaginalis-or-the-imaginary-and-the-imaginal/

66 Farhang Erfani, *Iranian Cinema and Philosophy: Shooting Truth* (London: Palgrave Macmillan, 2011), 88.

67 Lacan cited in Adrian Johnson, "This Philosophy which is Not One: Jean-Claude Milner, Alain Badiou, and Lacanian Antiphilosophy," *S: Journal of the Jan van Eyck Circle for Lacanian Ideology Critique* 3 (2010): 137. For a discussion of the debates surrounding the meaning of Lacan's anti-philosophy and how he may be considered a philosopher also see Alain Badiou's seminar on the notion of Lacan as anti-philosopher, *Séminaire Lacan : L'antiphilosophie 3, 1994–1995* (Paris: Fayard, 2013); cf. Alain Badiou, *Lacan: Anti-Philosophy 3* (New York: Columbia University Press, 2018); see also, Justin Clemens, *Psychoanalysis is an Antiphilosophy* (Edinburgh: University of Edinburgh, 2013), especially the introduction.

68 Paul Verhaeghe, *Beyond Gender. From Subject to Drive* (New York: Other, 2001) 38.

69 Ibid., 39.

70 Jalal al-Din Rumi, *The Masnavi, Book One*, trans. Jawid Mojaddedi (Oxford: Oxford University Press, 2004), 6–18.

71 Jacques Lacan, *Television: A Challenge to the Psychoanalytic Establishment*, ed. Joan Copjec, trans. Denis Hollier, Rosalind Krauss, and Annette Michelson (New York: Norton, 1990), 16.

72 See Omina El Shakry, *The Arabic Freud: Psychoanalysis and Islam in Modern Egypt* (Princeton: Princeton University Press, 2017); Also more recently, see Mehdi Touraj, "Lacan and Sufism: Paths for Moving Beyond Pre- and Postmodern Subjectivities," in *Esoteric Lacan*, ed. Philipp Valentini and Mahdi Tourage (London, New York: Rowman & Littlefield Publishers, 2019), 59–76.

73 For the influence of Corbin on Lacan see, Elisabeth Roudinesco, *Jacques Lacan: An Outline of a Life and History of a System of Thought* (Cambridge: Polity, 1999).

74 Henry Corbin, *L'imagination créatrice dans le soufisme d'Ibn 'Arabi* (Paris: Flammarion, 1958); translated from the French by Ralph Manheim as *Creative Imagination in the Sufism of Ibn Arabi* (Princeton: Princeton University Press, 1969).

75 Lacan, *The Ethics of Psychoanalysis*, 183.

76 Corbin states that what "we group as the *Fedeli d'amore...* [are] dominated by two great figures: Ibn 'Arabi, the incomparable master of mystic theosophy, and Jalaluddin Rumi, the Iranian troubadour of that religion of love whose flame feeds on the theophanic feeling for sensuous beauty. *Fedeli d'amore* struck us as the best means of translating into a Western language the names by which our mystics called themselves in Arabic or Persian (*'ashiqun, muhibbun, arbab al-hawa*, etc. [lovers, the loving ones, lords of desire', etc.]) Since it is the name by which Dante and his companions called themselves, it has the power of suggesting the traits which were common to both groups and have been analyzed in memorable works." Henry Corbin, *Alone with the Alone: Creative Imagination in the Sufism of Ibn 'Arabi* (Princeton: University of Princeton Press, 1998), 110. The term *arbab al-hawa* by which these mystics referred to themselves significantly means "the lords of desire" and appears in the first poem of Ibn 'Arabi's *Tarjuman al-Ashwaq*, and which Michael Sells translates as "the lords of love." See Michael Sells, *The Transaltor of Desires: Poems by Ibn al-'Arabi* (Princeton: Princeton University Press, 2021), 2–3.

77 Fethi Benslama, *Psychoanalysis and the Challenge of Islam* (Minneapolis: University of Minnesota Press, 2009), 220.

78 What is interesting to note is that the Ibn 'Arabi we encounter in Corbin's book is a thoroughly Persianized figure, and Lacan's encounter with Ibn 'Arabi therefore, is through Corbin's Persianizing prism. This is one of the elements that Vahid Brown foregrounds in his critique of Corbin's reading of Ibn 'Arabi, as he states, "Examples of Corbin's essentialist characterizations of Iran, Iranian spirituality, or events and personalities somehow related historically to Persian culture could be multiplied for pages, as they appear constantly throughout his many works. It will be seen to have been a constant theme in Corbin's visionary rearrangement of the facts of the life-history of Ibn al-'Arabi in his efforts to fit the latter into his own esoteric 'counter-history'." See Brown, "A Counter-History of Islam," 50.

79 For the translation movement see Dimitri Gutas, *Greek Thought, Arabic Culture: The Graeco-Arabic Translation Movement in Baghdad and Early 'Abbasaid Society (2nd-4th/5th-10th c.)* (New York: Routledge, 1998).

80 Toshihiko Izutsu, *Sufism and Taoism* (Los Angeles, CA: University of California Press, 1983), 8.

81 Michael Sells translates it as *The Translator of Desires*. See also an earlier translation by Reynold Nicholson, *The Tarjumán al-Ashwáq: A Collection of Mystical Odes by Muhyiddīn Ibn al-'Arabī* (London: Royal Asiatic Society, Oriental Translation Series, New Series xx, reprinted by the Theosophical Publishing House, Wheaton, Illinois, 1981).

82 Sells, *The Translator of Desires*, xv.

83 Corbin, *Alone with the Alone*, 100–101.

84 For a provisional translation of this seminar, see Cormac Gallagher, Jacques Lacan, Seminar the *Logic of Fantasy*, Seminar XIV (1966-1967), 4. Translation modified. http://www.lacaninireland.com/web/wp-content/uploads/2010/06/THE-SEMINAR-OF-JACQUES-LACAN-XIV.pdf. For the unpublished French version, see Jacques Lacan, *Logique du Fantasme*, Seminar XIV (1966-1967), 9. http://www.valas.fr/IMG/pdf/S14_LOGIQUE.pdf.

Part I

Desire between Gaze and Voice

Chapter 1

A Cinema of Desire

The Object-Gaze in *Shirin* and *Baran*

In this chapter, I theorize the deployment of the gaze in the New Iranian Cinema, especially through what Lacan calls the object-gaze (*l'objet regard*). As it will be seen, the gaze, according to Lacan, is not on the side of the subject looking or the camera, as it was theorized by *Screen* theory where the camera's look represented the male gaze, but rather on the side of the object. In this way, the gaze is that obscure stain or blot in the image that when looked upon (either by the character in the film or the spectator watching the film) returns the gaze. I will argue that the Lacanian gaze often appears within the New Iranian Cinema as the result of censorship restrictions that impose the rules of the modesty system (*hejab*) on the cinema and enjoined the practice of the averted gaze, as a way to purify or cleanse the visual sensorium in order to contain the male gaze. In this way, the New Iranian Cinema inadvertently or paradoxically becomes the site of the Lacanian gaze rather than the site of feminist gaze theory as proposed by Negar Mottahedeh. This pervasive presence of the object-gaze in the New Iranian Cinema renders it the *locus classicus* of the *cinema of desire* (as theorized by Todd McGowan in relation to Italian Neorealism and the French New Wave), since it is what is often invisible rather than visible in the field of vision that structures the formal logic of this cinema. In this sense, the New Iranian Cinema is the cinema of desire at its purest.

I will look at two filmic instances in which the object-gaze appears in the New Iranian Cinema which implicates the spectator's desire by removing our ability to see, by staging what cannot be reducible to the visual field, and by removing the ability of direct vision from the spectator, focusing thereby on Kiarostami's *Shirin* (2008) as well as Majid Majidi's *Baran* (2001). In Kiarostami's cinema, the gaze appears through the lack or absence in the visual field, which activates the spectator's desire, that is, the desire of the viewer is accounted for through what cannot be seen in the screen image or what remains invisible from the scopic field. I will argue that with *Shirin*, Kiarostami reaches the apotheosis of the gaze in which the film itself returns the gaze. In *Baran*, as it will be seen, the gaze appears not where it is expected, in Latif's voyeuristic act of looking as theorized by *Screen* theory, but in the opacity of the window, which blots the picture, and behind which is the silhouetted feminine figure of Baran. In this sense, it will be argued that the New Iranian Cinema is one of the exemplary sites of the (Lacanian) gaze, since it relies

DOI: 10.4324/9781003531029-3

on absences and lack in the cinematic form and narrative, and in this way, it is linked to other film movements such as Italian Neorealism and the French New Wave as exemplary instances of the cinema of desire.

1.1   The Gaze in Lacan: From *Screen* Theory to the Object-Gaze

In the introduction, I briefly articulated the difference between the first-wave and second-wave psychoanalytic film theory and gestured toward the difference that lies between the two, namely the gaze and the cinematic apparatus and their interconnection. Here, I foreground their differences in the deployment of the gaze and mark the difference between Lacan's object-gaze from the way the gaze operates in feminist gaze theory in first wave psychoanalytic film theory. The first phase or wave of psychoanalytic film theory, also called *Screen* theory, began in the late 1960s and 1970s and emphasized Lacan's imaginary order and to a lesser degree the symbolic order in Lacan's ternary registers of psychic formation (i.e., imaginary, symbolic, and real). It was characterized by a critique of the operation of ideology and the role of the cinematic apparatus in purveying this process. In this first phase of psychoanalytic film theory, such figures as Jean-Louis Baudry[1] located this ideological interpolation of the subject (apropos Louis Althusser's notion of ideological interpolation) in the cinematic apparatus rather than the filmic narrative.[2] According to this phase of psychoanalytic film theory, as articulated by Baudry and Metz, the gaze functions as a way to ideologically construct the spectator as a subject, since it purveys the illusory impression of control and mastery over the visual field. This is then developed by other theorists such as Jean-Pierre Oudart[3] and Christian Metz,[4] and especially Metz whose influential study *The Imaginary Signifier* was the first full length study to deploy psychoanalytic theory to articulate the ideological work of the (dominant) cinema as a sign system.

The feminist iteration of this conception of the gaze was theorized by Laura Mulvey, where following Baudry and Metz, she argues that Hollywood cinema or dominant cinema is intrinsically voyeuristic and based on the logic of the "male gaze" that positions the female character in the filmic diegesis as an object of what she calls "to-be-looked-at-ness," not only for the spectator but also within the film world itself.[5] In *Screen* theory, the gaze is conceptualized as an ideological problem that must be overcome, whereby a cinema in which the male gaze is absent can become possible as part of a feminist emancipatory struggle to overcome privileging the male subject. Mulvey deploys Lacan's mirror stage essay as a way to equate the male spectators look at the female character in the screen image with the child's look into the mirror. The child's gaze into the mirror bestows an illusion of wholeness on the fragmented body, whereby the child misrecognizes the seen object (i.e., its body in the mirror).[6] Therefore, Mulvey conceives the cinema screen as mirror and the gaze as a form of violence enacted on the female body, and in this way, the gaze functions as the modus operandi of classical cinema and thereby functions as

the site of the dominant ideology (patriarchy) and must be critiqued and disman-
tled. It is here that the misunderstanding of Lacan's notion of the gaze and the logic
of the look in *Screen* theory becomes visible, since for Lacan, the gaze is not on the
side of the looking subject nor does it have anything do with mastery and control,
but rather on what destabilizes and disrupts our control or mastery in our vision or
when we look,[7] as Lacan states, "the gaze is not the vehicle through which the subject masters the object, but a point in the Other that resists the mastery of vision."[8]
Therefore, *Screen* theory erroneously conceives the cinematic screen as a mirror,
and in so doing, as Joan Copjec aptly puts it, "it operates in ignorance of, and at
the expense of, Lacan's more radical insight, whereby the mirror is conceived as
screen."[9]

This conception of the gaze has been influential in theorizing the visual structure
of the New Iranian Cinema, particularly in Negar Mottahedeh's use of feminist
gaze theory in her book, *Displaced Allegories*, which is particularly indebted to
Laura Mulvey, and is operative under the sign of first wave psychoanalytic film
theory or *Screen* theory. Mottahedeh's argument rests on the premise that due to the
Shi'ite laws of the modesty system (*hejab*), post-revolutionary Iranian cinema, at
the level of form, is the enactment of the goals of feminist film theory and is therefore "the apotheosis of 1970s feminist gaze theory." She states, "In the attempt to
cleanse its technologies, the post-Revolutionary Iranian film industry came to produce a cinema that I will argue is the apotheosis of 1970s feminist gaze theory."[10] In
this reading, contra Hollywood cinema, the male gaze is absent in Iranian cinema,
since through the logic of the veil the spectator is no longer positioned in a voyeuristic or fetishistic spectatorial position. In this sense, Mottahedeh derives her theory
of visuality operative in the New Iranian cinema from *Screen* theory that influenced
feminist film theorists (Mulvey, Doane, and Silverman), a psychoanalytic film theory based on a misconception of Lacan's concept of the gaze and its relation to the
imaginary order, identifying the gaze with the camera and the voyeuristic (heterosexual) male gaze which rendered female bodies into objects of to-be-looked-at-
ness. In this sense, Mottahedeh's deployment of feminist gaze theory inherits some
of the misconceptions and misunderstandings of Lacan's theory of the gaze from
Screen theory as she applies them to post-revolutionary Iranian cinema.[11]

The misconception of the gaze in *Screen* theory is not only based on what Copjec
has aptly termed "a Foucauldianization" of the gaze but also on the Sartreanization
of the gaze, where the "look" is conceptually confused with the Lacanian notion of
the gaze.[12] It should be noted that the confusion lies in the difference between early
and later versions of the gaze in Lacan, where later Lacan himself clearly distinguishes his notion of the gaze from Sartre's. Indeed, it must be recalled that Lacan's
early formulation of the gaze owes much to Jean-Paul Sartre's analysis of "the
look," since in his first seminar "Freud's Papers on Technique" (1953–1954), Lacan's concept of the gaze is almost indistinguishable from Sartre's, although there
is still a discernable kernel of difference between them (in fact the term "look,"
which is often translated for Sartre's works in order to distinguish it from Lacan's
gaze, is the same term in French: *le regard*). Sartre's interpretation of the gaze/look

is what makes the subject to acknowledge the Other also as subject, which (like Lacan) is clearly influenced by Hegel's dialectic of the master and the servant in the *Phenomenology of Spirit* (1807). For Sartre, the possibility of being seen by the Other is what constitutes our connection with the Other-as-subject.[13]

It is in his Seminar XI, *The Fundamental Concepts of Psychoanalysis* (1964), that Lacan develops his full theory of the gaze as object in which the gaze is no longer on the side of the subject in the act of looking but on the side of the object. In this sense, Lacan divests the term "gaze" from its common sense meaning or dictionary definition and invests it with a new theoretical significance that disturbs our normal subject and object relations, wherein the gaze is no longer on the side of the subject looking (or cinematic spectator) but appears outside (in the filmic image), where the object looked upon returns the gaze. It is here that the gaze as object acts as the agent that causes our desire in the visual field, and thereby becomes what Lacan calls *l'object petit a* or the object-cause of desire as he states, "The *objet a* in the field of the visible is the gaze."[14] The locution *objet petit a* signifies that the object at issue here has no positive substantiality but appears only as a gap or void in the scopic field. It is not located in the subject's act of looking at the object but appears in the fissure or hole within the subject's seeming look of mastery over the visible. This lacuna in our act of looking signals the moment at which our desire becomes manifest in the very thing that we see in the order of the visible (i.e., the screen image).[15] This is the point at which our desire distorts the visual field, and this distortion is registered by us through the gaze as *objet petit a*. As Žižek puts it, "the object *a* is an object that can be perceived only by a gaze 'distorted' by desire...."[16] In this sense, the object manifests itself in the visual field only through a gaze "distorted" by desire. Therefore, the gaze as the object-cause of desire is this distortion of the visual field through the subject's desire.

In Lacan, the gaze is an eyeless gaze, it does not derive from a subjective eye(s) that look(s), but from a gaze without an eye, which is why Lacan says there is a split between the eye and the gaze.[17] Apropos the gaze, in French, there is an expression that exemplifies Lacan's notion of the gaze, namely *jeter l'oeil*, which has a less than satisfactory counterpart in English, to "cast a glance."[18] The term literally means "to throw an eye," as though it is on the obverse side of where the eye is, the eye literally is never cast or thrown but remains fixed in its place on our head, in their sockets, but in this throwing as it were, the eye is outside as an object, as Lacan states, "...outside, is the point of gaze."[19]

In his seminar *Les non-dupes errent* (The Non-Duped Err) (1973–1974), Lacan asks himself a rhetorical question as to what he invented apropos psychoanalysis, and he states that it is the "*objet (a)*."[20] Lacan often insisted that the term always remain in French as *objet a* or *objet petit a*, so that it may signal its non-coincidence with the social order or the big Other (*grand l'Autre*), the world of language and signification.[21] The *objet petit a* is an element which the subject must separate itself from in order to constitute itself as subject in the process of entering the world of language and signification (the symbolic order),[22] which is why the *objet petit a* is not any *thing* that exists as such but exists only in so far as it is lost. The loss of the *object a* is only posited retroactively after the subject's entrance into language, since it does not exist before it is imagined as lost. This is where the constitutive lack inhering in the subject emerges, since the loss of the object gives rise to the desiring subject, the subject emerges as desiring insofar as it lacks the (desired) object. In this way, the *objet petit a* is the object-cause of desire rather than the actual desired object. The *objet petit a* is the unattainable object of desire, always eluding the subject's reach, which is why desire always circulates around this privileged object without ever attaining it. This is what in psychoanalysis is called the drive (*Terib*) and where the split between the eye and the gaze manifests itself.[23]

Since the gaze functions as the *objet petit a* in the visual field, it is through the gaze that this field is ordered. When something within the visual field provokes the subject's desire, the gaze appears there beyond the sensorium. The gaze attracts our look, as it seems to offer us access to what is unseen, the obverse side of what is visible. The gaze is the point at which we recognize that we are co-implicated in what we are seeing and the moment in which what is seen appears to take our desire into account.[24] The object-gaze occurs therefore when the visual field or the screen image in the cinematic fiction implicates the desire of the viewing subject. In this way, the gaze is on the side of Lacan's register of the real (as with all the other instances of *objet petit a*) rather than the imaginary or symbolic, whereas in *Screen* theory, the gaze was formulated in light of Lacan's mirror phase, and hence it was on the side of the imaginary, which is why the screen was conceived as a mirror that did the work of ideological or imaginary identification. The gaze as an instance of the real rather than the imaginary "marks a disturbance in the functioning of ideology rather than its expression."[25] In this sense, the Lacanian gaze has a political dimension that functions as a critique of ideology, unlike the (male) gaze in *Screen* theory, which is part of the dominant ideology.

In his book, *The Real Gaze*, Todd McGowan provides a theorization of the cinema of desire based on the way the gaze appears in this cinema. He states, "In the experience of desire, the gaze remains a motivating absence: it triggers the movement of desire but remains an impossible object in the field of vision. Visually, desire concerns what we don't see, not what we see...."[26] McGowan distinguishes between the way in which desire and the gaze function in what he calls the cinema of fantasy, exemplified by Hollywood cinema as the cinema of fantasy, from the way it manifests in the cinema of desire, "Whereas the cinema of fantasy renders the gaze manifest through a distortion of the filmic image, the cinema of desire sustains the gaze as a structuring absence and an impossibility."[27] Contrary to the cinema of fantasy that seeks to resolve the tensions of desire through the creation of a fantasy scenario, "the cinema of desire offers spectators the opportunity of recognizing and embracing their position as desiring subjects."[28] In this sense, the New Iranian Cinema and its apotheosis in the cinema of Kiarostami is the cinema of desire, since its logic is based on absence and lack or what remains invisible in the visual field, and thus what causes us (the spectator) to desire is the structuring absence in the order of the visible. Therefore, the filmic image reveals the gaze as *objet petit a*, through what remains unseen in the field of vision.

In the chapter dedicated to the cinema of desire, McGowan considers two film movements, Italian neorealism and the French *nouvelle vague* (and a couple of individual directors such as Orson Welles and Claire Denis), to be examples of the cinema of desire.[29] To this, we may add New Iranian Cinema as another film movement that can be theorized as the cinema of desire and Kiarostami as its exemplary practitioner, since it is based on absence in the cinematic form and narrative that is distinctive to this cinema, and in this respect, it bears a close resemblance to these film movements. Indeed, the New Iranian Cinema and many of its directors have been variously associated with the influence of the two above-mentioned movements, and Kiarostami himself has acknowledged the influence of Italian neorealism on his cinematic universe.[30] However, I would argue that this link is not based on what has often been characterized as their similarity (rural settings, nonprofessional actors, realist technique, etc.), but rather on the specific deployment of the gaze operative in their filmic structure and in the way Kiarostami's cinema for instance always contains, both at the level of form and narrative, what remains invisible and unseen in the visual field or is irreducible to this field. In this sense, Kiarostami's cinematic world, emblematic of the New Iranian Cinema, can be designated as an exemplary instance of the cinema of desire.

1.2   The Averted Gaze as *Looking Awry*: An Islamic Theory of the Gaze

The advent of the 1979 revolution brought about a radical transformation of the cinema in Iran, which was nothing short of "the Islamization of film culture in Iran,"[31] as Naficy puts it. In 1982, the "Ministry of Culture and Islamic Guidance" (*Vezarat-e Farhang va Ershad-e Islami*) was instituted in order to ensure that films made in Iran were produced according to the codes and conventions of an Islamic "system of modesty"—veiling or *hejab* in its broadest sense. These guidelines were instituted to control the ways in which women's bodies were to be represented on screen. Women were to be portrayed wearing veils, headscarves, and loose-fitting clothing that obscured the contours of their bodies. The rules were to ensure that women's movements on the screen would not frame their bodies in an erotically charged manner. The guidelines also sought to proscribe the visual field by the "commandments of looking" (*ahkam-e negah kardan*), which was to ensure that unrelated men and women do not glance at each other on screen with a desiring gaze—hence the logic of the averted gaze. The logic of the averted gaze prohibited the direct relay of the female gaze either toward a male character on-screen or into the camera lens. A female character gazing into the camera—thus transgressing the prohibition—allowed the presumed heterosexual male spectator to become the subject of the female character's gaze and vice versa. This linking of gazes would make the female character available to this presumed spectator's desire and allow the spectator to identify with the male character. In other words, the logic of the averted gaze directly undermines the process of suture as it operates in classic Hollywood cinema.[32] These restrictions were related to the "purification" (*pak-sazi*) of the sensorium, so that it may be aligned to an Islamic system of modesty or veiling.

In post-revolutionary Iranian cinema, the female body becomes the emblematic site of heterosexual erotic desire. The female body must be veiled from the male gaze both on screen and in the theater. The Islamic modesty system proscribes close-ups of women or point-of-view shots prevalent in dominant or Hollywood cinema that create the cinematic illusion in which unrelated men and women directly look at each other on screen. The eye-line matches or the shot-reverse-shot techniques that are the constituent elements of the system of suture (the invisible stitching of the spectator into the filmic narrative) in the filmic grammar of dominant cinema are often absent as they represent "a threat to male piety, in relation to a female body in which, in Islamic culture, heterosexual desire itself is said to reside."[33] This censorship of visuality or veiling of the visual sensorium hinges upon the Shi'ite logic of the veil, which was to ensure that the male gaze would be contained or controlled through the modesty system, and the female figure would not be staged on screen in a way that would arouse male desire. In an Islamic jurisprudential theory of the gaze, there are strict laws that regulate the gaze (negah)[34] and the voice (seda).[35] The concept of averting the gaze has its origin in the Qur'an, where it states that God has set the limits (hodud Allah) of what is permissible and impermissible: "Say to the believers to cast down their eyes and guard their private parts; that is purer for them. God is aware of the things they work" (24: 30–31).[36] Such statements are further elaborated in Islamic law (fiqh) and tradition (sunnah), where an elaborate set of prescriptions set limits on what is a "'lawful look' (al-nadhar al-mubah')."[37] As Bouhdiba has perceptively noted, the corpus of Islamic traditions functions as a veritable super-ego injunction over the Muslim community.[38] For example, in a controversial oral tradition (hadith) ascribed to prophet Muhammad, he states, "The zina [adultery], of the eye is the gaze."[39] In her discussion of sexuality within a Muslim framework, Fatema Mernissi has argued that the eye "is undoubtedly an erogenous zone,"[40] and in some jurisprudential sources, the logic of the veil is prescribed as a way to impede "zina al-'ayni," namely adultery of the eye or visual adultery.[41]

In the context of Islamic legal theory (fiqh), the direct gaze is part of what is called 'awra which variously means nakedness or one's private bodily parts, especially a women's body and hair which is to be veiled or covered before all non-related men (na-mahram).[42] As Haeri states, "In the context of the Perso-Arab Muslim society, a woman is perceived as 'aura, or 'aurat in its Persian usage, though the meaning of the term is not understood exactly same in the two cultures. The Arabic term 'arua is complex and multifaceted, meaning, among other things, both woman and genitalia."[43] The term 'awra has a profoundly rich root in Arabic, and as Bouhdiba notes, it also signifies the "loss of the eye." Bouhdiba notes that it is here that a powerful and culturally significant association between the gaze, the sexual organ, and the logic of women as 'awra become co-incident.[44] There are several ahadith (oral traditions) according to Bouhdiba that "bear witness to the canonical and oneiric importance of 'aura." For instance, "The man who looks with concupiscence at the attractions of a woman who is not his will have lead poured into his eyes on the Day of Judgment."[45]

Now in Iranian Shi'i legal theory, in general, there are limits set on both men and women's gazes, and a distinction is made between what is considered "a lustful gaze (*raybe*), and an innocent look."[46] While the former is completely forbidden, the later has been a source of constant debate among religious scholars (*'ulama*).[47] As noted earlier, in Shi'ite law, a whole system of guidelines were constituted called *ahkam-e negah*, which formed an elaborate set of prohibitions on the gaze. For instance, one of the clerics, Ayatollah Khoe'i states: "Gazing at the body of a *namahram* [non-related] woman is forbidden for a man, whether it does or does not invoke feelings of pleasure."[48] Ayatollah Khomeini contends, "It is best, *ihtiyat-i vajib*, not to look at a woman's body, face and hands, even if it does not provoke pleasure. Likewise, it is forbidden for a woman to look at a man except for his face and hands."[49] This is why Khomeini was against the Pahlavi state, since it allowed women to appear unveiled in the cinema. Khomeini states, "By means of the eyes they [the Shah's government] corrupted our youths. They showed such and such women on television and thereby corrupted our youth."[50] This is why the logic of the averted gaze as related to the modesty system (*hejab*) was enacted in relation to post-revolutionary Iranian cinema.

Naficy makes an important link between Žižek's concept of "looking awry"[51] and the averted gaze as it appears in Iranian cinema; he writes, "Like the 'looking awry' that Slavoj Žižek formulated, the averted look theorized here is anamorphic, as it makes the power relations at work in the game of veiling clearer: anamorphic looking is charged, and distorted, by the *voyeuristic* desires and anxieties of the lookers and by the regulations of the system of modesty" [emphasis added].[52] Mottahedeh also uses the term "looking awry," gesturing toward Žižek's formulation (but without mentioning his name or citing him), and similarly links it to the averted gaze stating that Iranian cinema's adoption of the modest or averted gaze "in embodying the look of the veiled subject, also emphasizes the spectator's vulnerability vis-à-vis the inscription of *voyeurism* in cinematic codes, as his look identifies mimetically with the look of the camera." Therefore, Mottahedeh contends that Iranian cinema's "post-Revolutionary camera *looks awry* in a gesture of purification, not only in self-defense against the subject's loss of mastery, in its becoming image, but also to produce a different relation to time and space in film beyond the commodified image."[53]

However, although I agree with the theoretical link that Naficy and Mottahedeh have made between the averted gaze and Žižek's looking awry, they nonetheless blur the notion of looking awry with first-wave psychoanalytic theory's concept of the gaze and link it to *voyeurism* on which their work is largely based, and thereby miss the radical Lacanian dimension of Žižek's formulation of looking awry. As Žižek states, "if we look at a thing straight on, i.e., matter-of-factly, disinterestedly, objectively, we see nothing but a formless spot; the object assumes clear and distinctive features only if we look at it 'at an angle,' i.e., with an 'interested' view, supported, permeated, and 'distorted' by desire."[54] Here Žižek's formulation of looking awry is precisely related to Lacan's concept of the gaze as *objet petit a*, which he derives from Lacan's reading of a painting. In *Seminar XI*, Lacan provides an instantiation of the gaze in Hans Holbein's painting *The Ambassadors* (1533). The painting is a representation of two world travelers and the wealth they have acquired in their journeys. However, at the bottom of the painting, there appears a distorted image, which the viewer is unable to make out at first, and which functions as a disruption in the painting. This image is an *anamorphosis* (a distorted projection), an anamorphic figure which when looked at directly nothing is clearly seen, but once we look at the figure from an angle and to the left, *looking awry* as it were, the image of a skull comes into focus—a *memento mori*. It is here that for Lacan, the anamorphic figure of the skull functions as the site where the gaze appears in the image.[55] This is why Lacan states, "We… see emerging on the basis of vision… the gaze as such, in its pulsatile, dazzling and spread out function, as it is in this picture [i.e., Holbein's *The Ambassadors*]."[56] The anamorphic figure of the skull in the image thereby acts as a blot or stain in the image which when looked at awry takes the viewing subject into account and returns the gaze. In this instance, it is *death* that returns the gaze.

This logic of looking awry or viewing sideways has the structure of the averted gaze or the sideways glance in the Islamic system of modesty in which the female subject is not to be directly looked upon in a frontal direct way nor is she to look directly at the male subject—hence in this paradoxical way, the averted gaze, far from reducing or diminishing the cause of desire, on the contrary becomes the object-cause of desire, the Lacanian *objet petite a*.[57] In other words, the object of desire (either the male or female) only properly becomes the desired object by being viewed sideways or by looking awry—this is the paradoxical logic of the averted gaze, it does not suppress your desire, but rather causes you to desire.

Recall for instance the first moment in Alfred Hitchcock's *Vertigo* (1958), where Scottie sees the fake Madeline in the restaurant. While sitting at the bar in the restaurant, Scottie waits to get a glimpse of Madeline, and once she passes by, he glances at her sideways, this is done through the camera by a lack of a subjective point of view shot, and in this non-subjective shot, his look is effectively averted so as not to draw attention to himself by *looking awry* rather than directly at her. It is precisely at this moment that Madeline becomes the object-cause of Scottie's desire, as she enters the coordinates of his desire by entering his frame of fantasy. This is why fantasy is "the *mise en scène* of desire,"[58] as Jean Laplanche and J. B. Pontalis put it. Žižek clearly states that the status of the object-cause of desire is that of an anamorphosis: "a part of the picture which, when we look at the picture in a direct frontal way, appears as a meaningless stain, acquires the contours of a known object when we change our position and look at the picture from aside." According to Žižek, Lacan's point is even more radical for "the object-cause of desire is something that, when viewed frontally, is nothing at all, just a void—it acquires the contours of something only when viewed sideways."[59] In this sense, the averted gaze that governs the visual regime of Iranian cinema is linked to the logic of looking awry and is co-incident with the Lacanian gaze. In this quite formal sense, the way the averted gaze functions in the formal structure of New Iranian Cinema is precisely how the (Lacanian) gaze becomes manifest as the object-cause of desire.

In his discussion of Islamic prohibitions on the gaze regulating relations between the sexes, Bouhdiba makes a fascinating connection to Sartre's conception of the look and writes, "The confrontation of the sexes, as conceived by Islam, transforms each sexual partner into '*être-regard*', being-as-a-look, to use Sartre's term."[60] Here, I would go further than Bouhdiba and contend that the relation between the sexes as conceived in Islam renders each sexual partner susceptible to what Lacan calls *l'objet regard* or the object-gaze. For instance, as the religious scholar Daylami states, "Never go into water without clothing for water has eyes...."[61] This recalls Lacan's notion of the gaze as object, since such descriptions take on an uncanny dimension where even water (an object) can return the gaze. In this way, a short-circuiting reading becomes possible where there is an uncanny homology between the Lacanian gaze and the Shi'i Islamic theory of the averted gaze. In order to contain the "male gaze" as it were, through the injunction of the modesty system's averted gaze, the New Iranian Cinema paradoxically became the exemplary site of the Lacanian gaze and thereby a cinema of desire.

1.3   The Film Returns the Gaze: Abbas Kiarostami's *Shirin*

Upon his untimely death, Abbas Kiarostami (d. 2016) was one of the most renowned *auteurs* of Iranian cinema. For more than three decades, he created a unique form of cinematic art that mesmerized the world and left an indelible mark in the history and language of cinema. It is perhaps a testament to this profound influence on the formal language of cinema that no less of a figure than Jean Luc-Godard said of him, "Film begins with W.D. Griffith and ends with Abbas Kiarostami."[62] The cinema of Kiarostami garnered world-wide critical praise for its poetic beauty and for its formal complexity and narrative simplicity, and won major awards in prestigious film festivals around the world including the Palme d'Or at the Cannes Film Festival for *Ta'm-e gilas* (*Taste of Cherry*, 1997), the first ever to be given to an Iranian director.

It is little wonder than that among all the Iranian filmmakers of his generation, it is Kiarostami's cinema that has received the greatest critical attention by some of the most renowned film critics, scholars, and theorists who have each strived to distill the essence of his cinema by describing its unique formal and narrative structure. The cinema of Kiarostami has variously been designated as the cinema of "delay and uncertainty,"[63] the "cinema of questions,"[64] of "ellipsis and omission,"[65] an "unfinished" or "half-finished cinema,"[66] "cinema as thought experiment,"[67] the cinema of "an open image,"[68] and "a cinema of silence."[69] Many of these scholars have often noticed and noted both the aural and visual absences in Kiarostami's cinema, yet no one has fully theorized the significance of these absences. Indeed, it is in Kiarostami's cinema that we can witness the proper tension between gaze and voice: the axis around which the art of cinema revolves.[70] This is why I argue that the cinema of Kiarostami is "the cinema of desire" par excellence, since the (Lacanian) gaze (and voice) is ubiquitous in his cinematic universe. It is through an analysis of Kiarostami's film *Shirin* (Iran, 2008) that the logic of the gaze that produces this cinema of desire will be analyzed. It is perhaps no coincidence that more than any other auteur of New Iranian Cinema, it is the cinema of Kiarostami that has attracted the gaze of psychoanalytic film theorists.

Psychoanalysis and Kiarostami's cinema see through a similar lens as it were and Kiarostami himself notes this uncanny co-incidence in a foreword to a book on psychoanalysis in Tehran and states that, "the psychoanalytic lens closely resembles what I see through my camera."[71] One of the loci where these two lenses converge and come together is through the logic of the gaze. Although the gaze has been theorized to a degree in film theoretical work on the New Iranian Cinema, it has largely been in the form of first wave psychoanalytic film theory or *Screen* theory (i.e., the absence of the male gaze).[72] For instance, Sara Saljoughi has theorized that Kiarostami's *Shirin* returns a female gaze, which has largely remained non-existent in post-revolutionary Iranian cinema.[73] In Mary Ann Doane's reading of *Shirin,* what is foregrounded is the close-up and the way in which the film "offers an intensive study of the faces of women as screens and as facing the screen."[74] For Doane, the significance of such films as *Shirin* lies in the way that "women's faces are not simply a kind of privileged content of the cinema but instead are bound up in, implicated in the technology and techniques of the cinema and its apparatuses—the screen, the celluloid, the camera, the spectator."[75]

It was the philosopher Jean-Luc Nancy in his now classic book on Kiarostami, *L'évidence du film* (2001), who described Kiarostami's cinema as the cinema of the gaze (the French *le regard,* is often translated in the book into English as "look"), as he states, "Kiarostami mobilizes the look (*le regard*): he calls it and animates it, he makes it vigilant."[76] But, although Nancy's formulation of the gaze in relation to Kiarostami's cinema was influential on subsequent attention on the way the gaze functions in Kiarostami's cinema, it bears slight relation to Lacan's concept of the object-gaze, since Nancy's use of the look/gaze is on the side of the subject (spectator) looking or what the camera shows, it is still related to the looking subject rather than a split between the eye and the gaze. Indeed, it is only more recently that there have been instances of a direct engagement with the Lacanian gaze in light of Abbas Kiarostami's cinema, and this section is an effort to theorize the way the object-gaze appears in *Shirin.*[77]

Shirin is the apotheosis of Kiarostami's experiment with what is unseen in the screen image, and if we accept his own assessment that he would like *Shirin* in some ways to be regarded as his last film, we can well understand that what this film achieved at its purest, was a common motif that ran through all his films, namely "their play with what's not shown on screen."[78] *Shirin* consists mostly of single close-up shots of a group of 113 women in the foreground (with a few men partially visible in the background), who are presumably in a darkened movie theater watching the film-within-a-film about the life of a princess named Shirin based on the 13th-century poet Nezami Ganjavi's romance *Khowsrow and Shirin.*[79] Throughout the film, we never see the film-within-a-film but hear its narrative story on the soundtrack as a seemingly diegetic sound, and gleams of reflected light are presumably cast on the actresses faces from the off-screen film.[80] All we can see as viewers is the reaction and the emotions writ large on the faces of these women (consisting of mostly famous actresses in Iranian cinema, including the French actress Juliette Binoche) who are presumably moved by the power of this love story that is being enacted and heard through music, sound effects, and the actors' voices. The women at times appear to look into the camera at the viewer, but more often they appear to be looking at an invisible point, presumably the cinematic screen. This, in short, is the entirety of the 85 minutes that make up *Shirin*.

In order to render visible, the structure of the gaze in *Shirin*, I will deploy Lacan's reading of a famous painting by Diego Velázquez, *Las Meninas* (1656), as there is a profound co-incidence between the way the gaze functions in this painting and its formal operation in the film. The painting depicts a scene in an expansive room in the Royal Alcazar at the court of the Spanish King Philip IV, with several figures notably the young Infanta Margaret Theresa at the center, the king's youngest surviving daughter, surrounded by maids of honor, a chaperone, a bodyguard, a dwarf, a child, and a dog. At the left hand of the painting, Velázquez has portrayed himself engaged in the act of painting on a large canvas. Several of the figures including Velázquez and Margaret Theresa, directly look outward beyond the space of the painting toward where the viewing subject would be standing. There is a mirror at the back of the painting, which reflects in a medium shot (to use a cinematic term) the figures of the king and queen, who seem to be positioned outside the pictorial space possibly in the position of the viewing subject. Finally, just to the right of the mirror, there is another figure, a man standing by an open door, who looks back toward the scene just as he is about to exit the room.

In his unpublished Seminar XIII, *l'Objet de la Psychanalyse* (*The Object of Psychoanalysis*) (1965–1966),[81] Lacan provides a brilliant reading of *Las Meninas* (against Foucault's reading in his book *The Order of Things*).[82] In this seminar, Lacan argues that the "the painting functions as a trap for the gaze, [and] its imagery incites the spectator's desire and does something with this desire."[83] For Lacan, there are several ruses operative in the painting, which many interpreters are taken in by (such as Foucault), namely the mirror in the back of the painting where the image of the king and queen appear. According to Lacan, such a reading occludes the question of the desire of the looking subject or the desire that divides the subject. As Aaron Schuster notes, the overall thesis of Lacan "is that the subject is not only the spectator who looks at the picture, but the picture in a way looks back, it looks back at the subject and frames it in its own manner, the subject's gaze is inscribed in the picture as something separated from it, as an object, an object that is the subject."[84] In this sense, the subject is not only outside the painting, looking at it from a safe distance but is effectively drawn into the painting, and as Lacan puts it, is "caught like a fly in glue"[85] and appears there as an uncanny object. As Schuster notes, this "synthesis of the divided subject with a partial object, in this case the gaze, defines the structure of fantasy," since for Lacan *Las Meninas* "provides a brilliant illustration of the visual structure of fantasy."[86] Hence, Lacan argues that the painting is not a "representation of representation" (as it is for Foucault) but an instance of the Freudian "representative representation" (*Vorstellungsrepräsentanz*), which signifies a representation of the scopic derive.[87]

It is here that we can turn to *Shirin*, since in the film, the gaze formally functions in the same way as it does in Lacan's interpretation of *Las Meninas*. Like *Las Meninas*, *Shirin* functions as a trap for the gaze, the images on screen evoke the spectator's desire, and it does something with this desire. The first ruse at work in *Shirin* is the film-within-a-film, which we can hear on the soundtrack and observe the women watching it but remains unseen and invisible. The spectator's desire is thereby aroused, since we want to see the invisible film-within-the-film that the women are watching. While watching the film, we are taken in by the trick that these women are watching a film, but they were never watching a film. All the women were shot separately, in small groups sitting in Kiarostami's living room. Similarly, the trick of the film is to make us think that they are responding to a real film, but no such film exists, the actresses were told to just look at a few dots above the camera. The supposed film was a radio play performance of *Khosrow and Shirin* that was used later by Kiarostami and added on the soundtrack in the editing process, matching the various emotions of the actresses to the development of plot points in the story. In this way, the spectator looking at the film, all of a sudden has the uncanny feeling that the film returns the gaze, and thereby divides the subject, the subject's gaze becomes inscribed in the film as a separated object, an object that functions as the subject. In this sense, the spectator is no longer outside the film looking at it from a safe distance but is drawn into the film and appears there as an uncanny object. This division of the subject from the partial object, namely the gaze, is what characterizes the logic of fantasy, and following Lacan's reading of *Las Meninas*, it may be said that *Shirin* is a cinematic visualization of the structure of fantasy.

In Lacan's reading, *Las Meninas* is not about the play of mirror reflections (as it is for Foucault) but a window, "the window or the frame of fantasy."[88] Lacan argues that the mirror functions as a sort of trap in the painting and that the true key for understanding the painting is the window or frame.[89] Indeed, the logic of the frame, or the frame of fantasy is exactly what is at work in *Shirin*. Kiarostami himself was fully aware of this function of the frame, as he states in the trailer of his final and most experimental film *24 Frames* (2017), "I've often noticed that we are not able to look at what we have in front of us, unless it's inside a frame."[90] From this perspective, each shot of one of the actresses in the film functions as a frame or the frame of fantasy. The other ruse in the painting is the question of the canvas, namely the mystery of the painting within the painting and what Velázquez is painting there. Many interpreters (such as Foucault) are taken in by this trick of the painting, but Lacan suggests that perhaps there is nothing on the canvas at all and that "the question of what's on the canvas is the wrong question to ask. The very question is a trap. The painting wants us to wonder about what's on the other side of the canvas."[91] This is the trick of *Shirin*, since the film wants us to wonder about the contents of the mysterious film-within-the-film, which does not exist. *Shirin* is perhaps the only film in which the film-within-the-film is itself completely fictional and non-existent.[92] In an interview, Kiarostami states, "Someone who had seen the movie told me, and I quote, 'when I was watching the film, I just wanted to see the things they were watching.' Do I want to see what they were watching, I asked myself? The answer was no way, no way."[93] In other words, for Kiarostami, what they are watching is a ruse, what we should be watching is the cinematic screen itself.

Now following Lacan, what we must do here is to analyze how this trick operates in the film rather than be taken in by it. Lacan argues that the way the canvas functions in the painting is to stage "the painting's completely fictional status," as Schuster states, since for Lacan "The point is not merely to create an illusion, but to make illusion appear as illusion, or to make appearance appear as appearance."[94] This is what is formally operative in *Shirin*, Kiarostami has not just created a cinematic illusion through the film-within-the-film, but has made illusion appear as illusion, namely to make cinema appear as cinema. In order to draw out this fictional status of the painting as a way to make illusion appear as illusion, or how the painting within the painting functions, Lacan makes an illuminating link between another painting, namely René Magritte's *The Human Condition* (1933) as a way to understand what is at work in *Las Meninas*.

Although Kiarostami's cinema has mostly been read as a form of self-reflexivity (films about the process of making film) and as the symbiosis of documentary and narrative fiction, but what Kiarostami's cinema reveals is not self-reflexivity or *mies-en abyme* but what it does is to question our very conception of reality itself. Jean Luc-Nancy is correct when he states that "[Kiarostami] is not interested in the film about the film or in the film, he is not investigating the *mise-en-abyme*."[95] The achievement of *Shirin* as cinematic art is rather to make us discern the fictional structure of reality itself, that is, the realization that reality would cease to exist without the fictions or the fantasmatic support that sustains it. As Žižek formulates it: "The ultimate achievement of film art is not to recreate reality within the narrative fiction, to seduce us into (mis)taking a fiction for reality, but, on the contrary, to make us discern the fictional aspect of reality itself...."[96] This is what Kiarostami's cinema reveals and which *Shirin* stages at its most radical form. *Shirin*, like *Las Meninas* (and Magritte's *The Human Condition*), is not about the representation of reality by reproducing it as representation cinematically, but it reveals that reality itself can only be viewed through the window of fictions, through the frame of fantasy; this is the elementary lesson of fantasy in psychoanalysis: without the fictions that sustain reality, there would be no reality, since reality is always already mediated by fictions (i.e., fantasies). Such is the truly radical core of Kiarostami's cinema, it does not give us the reality of fiction but the fiction of reality itself. This is cinematic art at its purest, what it reveals to us through the cinematic fiction is the realization that we never get to the bare-naked reality without the fantasies that sustain it. In this formal sense, *Shirin* stages the fictional structure of reality itself.

In *Shirin*, therefore, the story of the invisible film-within-the-film on the soundtrack is a ruse that incites the subject's desire to see this invisible film, but as Kiarostami states, "I believe if you dare let go of the story [of Shirin], you will come across a new thing which is the Cinema itself. In fact, I suggest you let go of the story and just keep your eyes on the screen."[97] By letting go of the story and keeping our eyes on the screen what we come to realize as spectators is that it is not only we who look at the film or the screen but in a way it is the film or the screen itself that looks back at us. In this precise sense, the screen returns the gaze. Even an avowed post-theorist such as David Bordwell recognized that what is going on in *Shirin* is that "the movie looks back at us."[98] But since Bordwell lacks the theoretical terms to articulate the gaze as a cinematic object, he is unable to recognize that when an object, such as the movie-screen looks back at the viewer, what we get is precisely the object-gaze. Therein lies the profound significance of *Shirin* since it is one of the few masterpieces in the history of cinema where the film itself returns the gaze.

1.4   The Fantasized Gaze in *Baran*

Majid Majidi's *Baran* (2001) is one of the post-revolutionary films produced in Iran that received world-wide critical attention and was distributed in the US by Miramax Films. The film represents an example of "poetic cinema" (an appellation that Majidi himself endorsed in relation to his films), which came to be associated with the New Iranian Cinema at international film festival circuits.[99] *Baran* fits well into what Blake Atwood has theorized as a set of "reformist aesthetics" that he argues are unique to films produced in the reformist era under president Mohammad Khatami (1997–2005), such as the motif of "mystic love."[100] Like many of Majidi's films, *Baran* often draws on Sufi mystical discourse, such as the mystical allegory of the voyage of the soul toward the divine Beloved, as found in the works of classical Persian poets, such as Sana'i, 'Attar, Rumi, and Jami.[101] In this way, most of Majidi's cinematic oeuvre, including *Baran*, have often been read in light of the mystico-philosophical motif of "the Voyage and the Messenger" (*Le motif du voyage et du messager*), to borrow a phrase from a title essay in Henry Corbin's book.[102]

Baran (literally meaning "rain" in Persian) is effectively a story of youthful love between an illegal Afghani worker and an Azari construction worker. The Azari youth, Latif (Hossein Abedini), works at a construction site for Memar (Mohammad Amir Naji), doing simple jobs such as grocery shopping and serving tea to the workers. During a work accident, an Afghan worker named Najaf breaks his leg, and his fragile looking son Rahmat is brought in as replacement for his father by an elderly Afghan family friend, Soltan, so that the poor family may survive. Once Rahmat appears, Latif suddenly feels threatened by him, as he immediately loses his work in the kitchen to him, forced to engage in heavy work instead. His initial hatred is transformed into amorous desire when he finally discovers that the fragile androgynous boy is in fact a girl named Baran (Zahra Bahrami), who had cross-dressed as a boy in order to work at the construction site. During a raid by authorities, the illegal Afghanis, including Baran, run away and she is reduced to working at a nearby village lifting large heavy stones from the river to support her family. Latif discovers her plight and buys crutches for her father, Najaf, and entrusts his year of wages to Soltan to give to Najaf, as a way to compensate for his disability pay. In similar poverty, Soltan instead takes the money and returns to Afghanistan, promising in a note to pay the boy back. Desperate to help Baran and her family, Latif sells his identity papers and gives the money to Najaf under the pretext that it is from Memar, but in a twist of fate, Najaf uses the money to go back to Afghanistan. In the final scene, just as they are about to leave, Baran drops some fruits on the floor and Latif helps her pick them up and for a moment she looks at him, before flipping the *burqa* (Afghani face-veil) over her head to leave on the back of the truck, but her shoe gets stuck in the mud, and Latif takes the shoe and holds it as she puts it back on her foot. The last shot of the film is of rain (*baran*) filling the footprint left behind by Baran, which will shortly wash away all traces of it.

The emblematic scene where we get the imagined, fantasized gaze is perhaps the most beautifully shot scene in the entire film. The scene begins with a shot of Latif about to carry a heavy cement bag, and as he moves toward the camera, a rush of rustling wind blows a fog of debris across the screen that agitates Latif's eyes, causing him to momentarily lose his sight. The sound of the rustling leaves and wind and thunder in the background, all of a sudden turn his attention toward the kitchen where the curtain covering the kitchen door is being blown open lightly by the wind, which almost inexorably draws Latif toward the kitchen area. At the same time as we hear wind blowing and the sounds of thunder, we can hear the faint sound of a female humming on the soundtrack. As Latif's blinking stops, the camera pulls toward him in a medium close-up, and we get a reverse shot of the curtain slowly blowing in the wind and as the camera pulls closer for a moment, we get a glimpse of the silhouette of a female figure behind an opaque window-frame combing her hair. The camera stays in medium shot by the curtain, and we see Latif enter the frame with his back to the camera as he approaches the curtain. Latif slowly pulls the curtain partially open, and we get a reverse shot of Latif looking through the crack of the semi-opened curtain, his eyes widening at the full revelation of what he is seeing. Then in a reverse shot, which is a subjective point of view shot of Latif, we see the silhouette of Baran behind an opaque window-frame brushing her long hair, presumably humming to herself (although the voice seems to be extra-diegetic, yet the implication is that the source is Baran). The logic of the modesty system is maintained by having Baran framed behind an opaque window which functions as a veil that separates the look of Latif and that of the spectators from seeing her unimpeded, and the backlighting creates a strong contrast where she becomes a shadow cast on a screen (a cinematic screen even). The scene ends when suddenly Latif hears the sound of footsteps and realizes that she is about to come out, which makes him run away in panic and hide behind the stack of cements, as he spies on her leaving, dressed as a boy with a tray of tea in her hands.[103]

This scene where Latif is effectively a peeping Tom or voyeur is a perfect instantiation of the fantasized or imagined gaze, and the power of fascination in this entire scene resides in the fact that it traverses from the Sartrean gaze to the Lacanian gaze. In the scene, at first, you have the classic description of the gaze in Sartre's *Being and Nothingness* regarding the voyeur peeping through a keyhole. For Sartre, the gaze emerges not only from the organ of sight but is evoked through the sound of rustling leaves, which startles the voyeur. According to Sartre, what usually manifests a look is the convergence of "two ocular globes" in our direction, but that "the look will be given just as well on occasion when there is a rustling of branches, or the sound of a footstep followed by silence, or the slight opening of a shutter, or a light movement of a curtain."[104] This description of Sartre uncannily resembles what we get in this scene from *Baran*, all the elements are there, the sound of rustling of branches via the wind, the light movement of the curtain, etc. According to Sartre, these sounds are heard at the moment he is engaged in the act of looking through a keyhole and where a feeling of shame associated with the gaze suddenly surprises the voyeur, since a gaze is what is imagined in the field of the Other. It is at this moment where the voyeur imagining himself being observed by another acquires a sense of self.[105] In this sense, as Joan Copjec states, in Sartre, the gaze acts "as an 'indispensable mediator' between the voyeur and himself, the condition necessary for precipitating him out as subject from the act of looking in which he has until this point been totally absorbed."[106] Here the voyeur emerges as a subject, without which there would only be a peering through the keyhole. Sartre's description of the voyeur peeping through a keyhole and the rustling of wind that surprises him can be precisely mapped within the coordinates of the above scene where Latif as a voyeur is peeping through the curtain, and all of a sudden at the end becomes aware of himself as subject through the intervention of some noise (wind, birds flying, footsteps, etc.) that startles him. In other words, the entire scene functions as a way to jolt Latif into self-awareness as a subject; but here Latif is less a Sartrean subject that becomes aware of himself through the gaze imagined in the field of the Other but is rather a Lacanian subject, namely, a subject of desire.[107] Thus, in foregrounding Latif as the subject of desire, we traverse from the Sartrean gaze (apropos shame) to the Lacanian gaze (apropos desire).

The (Lacanian) gaze in the scene is therefore not located in Latif's voyeuristic looking, which is where *Screen* theory would have located the gaze, but on the contrary, it is located in the inter-space that acts like a crack in reality itself, from where Latif opens the curtain to look. It is as though Baran is out there, in common existing reality, while Latif is peering at her from some in-between space, a *barazakh*, from some mysterious liminal world. As Žižek states, "This is the location of the imagined, fantasised gaze. Gaze is that obscure point, the blind spot, from which the object looked upon returns the gaze."[108] There is an intense inter-filmic dialogue at work between this scene and a similar one in Hitchcock's *Vertigo*, where we see Scottie in a position of the voyeur observing Madeleine from behind the crack of a door. This seeming crack in reality or "inter-space" from which Scottie observes Madeleine and Latif observes Baran is precisely the location of the fantasized gaze.

The key question to be asked here is: why did Latif get drawn to the kitchen in the first place to spy like a peeping Tom on Rahmat/Baran? Therein resides the key to the whole scene which stages the Lacanian notion of the gaze. In his *Seminar I* (1953–1954), Lacan states, "I can feel myself under the gaze of someone whose eyes I do not see, not even discern. All that is necessary is for something to signify to me that there may be others there. This window, if it gets a bit dark, and if I have reasons for thinking that there is someone behind it, is straight-away a gaze."[109] This is precisely what happens to Latif as he is drawn to the kitchen curtain that is being blown lightly by the wind, the window is a little dark, and he has reasons to think there is someone behind it, and this straight-away is the gaze.

The gaze than is not where we usually expect it, it is not on the side of the looking subject but located in the blurred, opaque window, which manifests the subject's (Latif's and the spectators) desire and distorts the visual field. The gaze is not on the side of the subject looking (Latif), but encountered by the spectator in the object, in the window-frame. This opacity of the window blots the visual field and distorts everything that Latif sees, as well as what the spectator's sees, since the window as blot or stain represents Latif's as well as the spectator's desire. This is why Lacan states, "And if I am anything in the picture, it is always in the form of the screen, which I earlier called the stain, the spot."[110] The gaze thereby triggers the spectator's desire in the visual field and becomes the object-cause of desire. This play of light and opacity of the window is the screen, the stain, or the spot where Latif's desire and our desire becomes manifest. It also stands for the cinematic screen itself, where our desires appear to us at such moments. Once the spectator encounters the opacity of the window as a stain or blot, suddenly the whole scene is de-naturalized, since we recognize that our desire has been accounted for by what we are looking at. In this way, Latif's desire and our desire is inscribed as a blot on the window screen and the cinematic image, and our libidinal investment in what we see is brought to the fore. This is the traumatic dimension in encountering the gaze, it forces the spectator to confront their own desire. Desire acts as a distortion of reality and de-naturalizes the world by rendering it non-neutral.

This opacity of the window is also the window or frame of fantasy that enframes reality, just as we saw above how Lacan illuminated the fantasmatic structure of the window apropos the painting *Las Meninas*. Once Latif glimpses the silhouette of Baran behind the window (whom he had originally thought to be a boy), it is at that moment that she enters his fantasy frame and the coordinates of his desire. Without this fantasmatic window enframing reality, Latif's desire would not have been aroused since it is the window or frame of fantasy that provides "the *mise en scène* of desire." Paradoxically, this is where the logic of the modesty system (*hejab*) and the Lacanian gaze become co-incident, since the opaque window is placed there by Majidi so that Latif and the spectator will not be able to directly look at Baran combing her long tresses (since women's hair is *'awra* or nakedness). In this technique of veiling Baran behind the opacity of the window while the backlighting illuminates the contours of her silhouette, the object-gaze becomes manifest.

A theoretical question imposes itself here apropos the figure of the peeping Tom or voyeur: why is it that in *Baran* (a so-called religio-mystical film) the male protagonist, Latif, assumes the position of the voyeur observing the figure of Baran? Is this an anomaly in *Baran* or does the same logic operate in other so-called "religious" or "mystic" films of the reformist era. Indeed, the same strange logic is operative in other so-called "mystic" films produced during this period in Iran. One such film is *Khoda nazdik ast* (*God is Near*, 2006) directed by Ali Vazirian, where the central character, Mohammad Esfahani, falls in love with a beautiful teacher named Leila[111] (Elnaz Shakerdoost) and assumes the position of the peeping Tom, gazing at her from outside the window of her class. It is as if the secret message in the libidinal economy of these films is the following: the only way for the religious male subject to look at a woman is to assume the position of a voyeur or peeping Tom. Besides Majidi's own commitment to Shi'ism, Hitchcock's Catholicism may be recalled here, since instances of the figure of the "peeping Tom" reverberate in his films as well, especially in *Rear Window, Vertigo*, and *Psycho*.

Baran is effectively about the sublimation of male (sexual) desire into spiritual or mystical love; which is why at the end of the film, Baran is no longer needed as she had to be overcome for Latif to become a mystic-lover (*'arif-e 'asheq*)—realizing that the true beloved (*ma'shuq-e haqiqi*) is God. From this perspective, the woman (Baran) simply functions as a vanishing mediator, once she has served her purpose, she disappears. This is precisely the obscene lesson of the Austrian Christian philosopher Otto Weininger, where he effectively claims that "woman doesn't exist," and that "*woman is the sin of man.*"[112] In this way, such films as *Baran* are often profoundly reactionary and misogynistic, since woman as the object of desire stands for lust or carnal desire (*shahwat*), which the so-called mystic-lover (Latif) must traverse in order to reach the true invisible object of desire, the divine Beloved (i.e., God). This is effectively what Majidi states, "In a way, he [Latif] renounces Baran. He leaves his cap behind, which is an indication that he goes beyond material things and becomes a spirit."[113] This is the hidden libidinal economy of the film.

Kiarostami's *Shirin* and Majidi's *Baran* are two filmic examples from the New Iranian Cinema that manifest the Lacanian *l'objet regard* or the object-gaze. The object-gaze is constitutive of the New Iranian Cinema, which renders this cinema among the few exemplars of the *cinema of desire*, along with Italian Neorealism and the French New Wave since what is often invisible or unseen in the visual field structures both the formal and narrative logic of these films. One of the consequences of the restrictions imposed on filmmakers in Iran on the visual and aural sensorium, paradoxically, rendered the New Iranian Cinema, one of the exemplary sites of the Lacanian gaze due to its uncanny correlation between the Islamic theory of the averted gaze. In Kiarostami's cinematic universe, and *Shirin* in particular, the gaze often manifests itself through absences in the visual field, which solicits the spectator's desire to see what is invisible beyond the screen image. This logic of the "unseen" or play with off-screen space structures Kiarostami's cinema and renders it *a cinema of desire*, since the gaze (and the voice) is constitutive of his cinematic world. In Kiarostami's cinema, *Shirin* function as the apotheosis of the Lacanian gaze, since in this film, the cinema screen itself returns the gaze. The famous peeping Tom scene in *Baran* contains another exemplary instance of the fantasized or imagined gaze, as it traverses from the Sartrean gaze to the Lacanian gaze. Contrary to where *Screen* theory would have located the gaze, namely in Latif's voyeuristic act of looking at Baran through the curtain and in the identification of the camera with the male gaze, the Lacanian gaze is located in the inter-space that acts as a crack in reality itself, from where

Latif opens the curtain to observe Baran. This is the site of the fantasized or imagined gaze. In the final analysis, *Shirin* and *Baran* form two filmic examples within the New Iranian Cinema that are emblematic sites of the Lacanian gaze rather than the locus of feminist gaze theory or *Screen* theory. The New Iranian Cinema may be regarded as one of the film movements in the world that is not only one of a few instances of the cinema of desire in world cinema but also an exemplary instance of the magic art of cinema itself: the dialectical tension between the gaze and the voice.

Notes

1 Jean-Louis Baudry, "Ideological Effects of the Basic Cinematographic Apparatus," in *Narrative, Apparatus, Ideology: A Film Theory Reader*, ed. Philip Rosen (New York: Columbia University Press, 1986), 286–98; cf. Jean-Louis Baudry, "The Apparatus: Metapsychological Approaches to the Impression of Reality in Cinema" [1975], in *Narrative, Apparatus, Ideology*, ed. Philip Rosen (New York: Columbia University Press, 1986), 299–318.

2 Figures such as Stephen Heath and Daniel Dayan also directly critiqued the ideological process of the cinematic apparatus in this period from a psychoanalytic perspective. See Stephen Heath, *Questions of Cinema* (Bloomington: Indiana University Press, 1981) and Daniel Dayan, "The Tutor-Code of Classical Cinema," in *Movies and Methods*, Vol. 1, ed. Bill Nichols (Berkeley: University of California Press, 1976), 438–50.

3 Jean-Pierre Oudart, "Cinema and Suture," transl. Kari Hanet, *Screen* 18, no. 4 (Winter 1977–1978): 35–47.

4 Christian Metz, *Psychoanalysis and Cinema: The Imaginary Signifier* (London: Macmillan Press, 1982).

5 Laura Mulvey, "Visual Pleasure and Narrative Cinema," in *Film Theory and Criticism: Introductory Readings*, 7th ed. Leo Braudy and Michael Cohen (New York: Oxford University Press, 2009), 715.

6 Mulvey, "Visual Pleasure and Narrative Cinema," 714.

7 Todd McGowan, *Psychoanalytic Film Theory and the Rules of the Game*, 60–1.

8 Lacan, *Four Fundamental Concepts of Psychoanalysis*, 73.

9 Copjec, *Read my Desire*, 15–6. The notion of the screen in Lacan must be understood in light of his discussion of the gaze in his seminar XI, where he states, "Only the subject— the human subject, the subject of the desire that is the essence of man—is not, unlike the animal, entirely caught up in this imaginary capture. He maps himself in it. How? In so far as he isolates the function of the screen and plays with it. Man, in effect, knows how to play with the mask as that beyond which there is the gaze. The screen is here the locus of mediation." Lacan, *The Four Fundamental Concepts of Psycho-Analysis*, 107. In other words, the screen acts as the point of mediation between the gaze and the I in the field of the visible. Once the gaze becomes manifest, the visual field takes on an uncanny dimension of alterity. It no longer seems to belong to the subject, to the enunciative I, and straightaway takes on the form of a screen. See Copjec, *Read My Desire*, 35.

10 Mottahedeh, *Displaced Allegories*, 2.

11 For a rapprochement between *Screen* theory and the Lacanian theory of the gaze, see Henry Krips, "The Politics of the Gaze: Foucault, Lacan and Žižek," *Culture Unbound* 2 (2010): 91–102.

12 This Sartrean logic of the gaze is evident in an article written by one of the early exponents of gaze theory Peter Wollen, a longtime collaborator with Laura Mulvey and the author of *Signs and Meaning* (1969). See Peter Wollen, "On Gaze Theory," *New Left Review* 44 (March–April 2007): 91–106.

13 Jean-Paul Sartre, *Being and Nothingness: An Essay on Phenomenological Ontology*, trans. Hazel E. Barnes (London: Methuen, 1958 [1943]), 256.

14 Lacan, *The Four Fundamental Concepts of Psychoanalysis*, 105.

15 Todd McGowan, *The Real Gaze*, 5–6.

16 Slavoj Žižek, *Looking Awry: An Introduction to Jacques Lacan through Popular Culture* (Cambridge, MA: MIT Press, 1992), 12.

17 Lacan, *The Four Fundamental Concepts of Psychoanalysis*, 72.

18 In a talk on Hitchcock's *Vertigo* (1957), while discussing the object-gaze, Žižek refers to this French phrase via a French joke about the famed idiot Martin, "In English I think you can say 'to cast an eye over something' but in France you can say '*jeter l'oeil*' which means literally 'to throw an eye'. There is a wonderful French fairy tale about Martin, the legendary idiot, who being an ugly boy cannot find a girlfriend, so his mother tells him 'why don't you go to a church on Saturday' and '*jeter l'oeil*' throw an eye around. So he goes first to a butcher, buys some pig eyes and throws them around and comes back and says: 'look, mother, it didn't work, no girl loved me for doing that.'" Slavoj Žižek, "Organs Without Bodies," YouTube, Thursday 6 November 2003, 17 min., 40 sec., https://www.youtube.com/watch?v=G9ddxATc_G4

19 Lacan, *The Four Fundamental Concepts of Psychoanalysis*, 96.

20 Jacques Lacan, *Les non-dupes errent*, lesson 11 (April 9, 1974), 185. (Unpublished). http://staferla.free.fr/S21/S21%20NON-DUPES....pdf

21 Todd McGowan, *The Real Gaze*, 6.

22 Lacan states, "It is here that I propose that the interest the subject takes in his own split is bound up with that which determines it—namely, a privileged object, which has emerged from some primal separation, from some self-mutilation induced by the very approach of the real, whose name, in our algebra, is the *objet a*." Lacan, *The Four Fundamental Concepts*, 83.

23 Lacan states, "The eye and the gaze—this is for us the split in which the drive is manifested at the level of the scopic field." Lacan, *The Four Fundamental Concepts*, 72.

24 McGowan, *The Real Gaze*, 7.

25 Ibid, 7.

26 McGowan, *The Real Gaze*, 69.

27 Ibid, 70.

28 Ibid, 70.

29 McGowan, *The Real Gaze*, 71.

30 Abbas Kiarostami, *Lessons with Kiarostami*, ed, Paul Cronin (New York: Sticking Place Books, 2015), 139.

31 Hamid Naficy, "The Islamization of Film Culture in Iran," in *The New Iranian Cinema: Politics, Representation and Identity*, ed. Richard Tapper (London/New York: I.B. Tauris, 2006).

32 Mottahedeh, *Displaced Allegories*, 8–9.

33 Negar Mottahedeh, "'Life Is Color!' Toward a Transnational Feminist Analysis of Mohsen Makhmalbaf's *Gabbeh*," *Signs*, no. 30 (2004): 1403–28.

34 Shahla Haeri, "Sacred Canopy: Love and Sex under the Veil," *Iranian Studies* 42 (2009):117. For sources on the proscription of the gaze or *ahkam-e negah* as it relates to the cinema in Shi'i Islamic jurisprudence, see Ayatollah Ali Moraweji, *Sinama dar ayine-ye fiqh* (Cinema in the Mirror of Jurisprudence), ed. Mohammad Reza Jabbaran (Tehran: Pazhuhishgah-e farhang va honar-e Islami, 1999).

35 On the voice, see the next chapter.

36 Cited in Haeri, "Sacred Canopy," 118.

37 Abdelwahab Bouhdiba, *Sexuality in Islam*, trans. Alan Sheridan (London: Saqi Books, 2012), 39. Originally published as *La sexualité en Islam* (Paris, Presses Universitaires France, 1975).

38 Bouhdiba states, "... the traditional corpus ... has formed a veritable super-ego presiding over all Islamic cultural development." Bouhdiba, *Sexuality in Islam*, 5.

39 Haeri, "Sacred Canopy," 117; Bouhdiba, *Sexuality in Islam*, 39; for a discussion of debates surrounding the authenticity of these traditions (*ahadith*), see Moraweji, *Sinama dar ayine-ye fiqh*, 50, 56, 74.

40 Fatema Mernissi, *Beyond the Veil: Male-Female Dynamics in the Modern Muslim Society* (rev. ed.), trans. Mary Jo Lakeland (Bloomington: Indiana University Press, 1987), 141.

41 Bouhdiba, *Sexuality in Islam*, 39.

42 Apropos the concept of *na-mahram* Haeri states, "*Namahram* may be roughly translated as 'forbidden,' as in the prohibition of association between adult women and men who are not related to each other within a certain degree of consanguinity or affinity, e.g. cousins, or strangers. Here, women must religiously observe veiling. Mahram, also roughly translated as 'permitted,' is the opposite of *namahram*, meaning that in relationships created as a result of consanguinity and affinity, e.g. nieces and paternal and maternal uncles, or father-in-law, women need not maintain veiling: in these categories men and women are considered mahram to each other." See Haeri, "Sacred Canopy," 118.

43 Haeri, "Sacred Canopy," 117.

44 Bouhdiba, *Sexuality in Islam*, 38.

45 Ibid, 38.

46 Haeri, "Sacred Canopy," 118.

47 Ibid, 118.

48 Khoe'i cited Haeri, "Sacred Canopy," 118; cf. Moraweji, *Sinama dar ayine-ye fiqh*, 53.

49 Khomeini cited in Haeri, "Sacred Canopy," 118; cf. Moraweji, *Sinama dar ayine-ye fiqh*, 53.

50 Cited in Naficy, "Veiled Visions/Powerful Presences," 132.

51 Žižek takes the locution "looking awry" from Shakespeare's play Richard II, and in his characteristic fashion states, "Richard II proves beyond any doubt that Shakespeare had read Lacan..." Slavoj Žižek, *Looking Awry: An Introduction to Jacques Lacan through Popular Culture* (Massachusetts: MIT Press, 1992), 9.

52 Hamid Naficy, *A Social History of Iranian Cinema, 4 Volumes* (Durham: Duke University Press, 2012), 107; cf. Hamid Naficy, "The Averted Gaze in Iranian Postrevolutionary Cinema," *Public Culture* 3.2 (1991): 29–40.

53 Mottahedeh, *Displaced Allegories*, 157.

54 Žižek, *Looking Awry*, 11.

55 Lacan, *The Four Fundamental Concepts*, 89; cf. McGowan, *The Real Gaze*, 7.

56 Ibid, 89.

57 This is also acknowledged by Naficy, "Veiling and the system of looking which has developed to deal with it hide aspects of women (and to some extent men).... [and] tend to turn the object of the look into an erotic object. Veiled women thus may become highly charged with sexuality, which ironically subverts the purpose of the religious principles of veiling..." Naficy, "Veiled Visions/Powerful Presences," 141.

58 See Jean Laplanche and J. B. Pontalis, "Fantasy and the Origins of Sexuality," *International Journal of Psychoanalysis* 49, no. 1 (1968): 1–18.

59 Slavoj Žižek, *How to Read Lacan* (London: Granta Books, 2006), 68.

60 Bouhdiba, *Sexuality in Islam*, 37; cf. Sartre, *Being and Nothingness*, 268.

61 Ibid, 38.

62 Quoted in Mottahedeh, *Displaced Allegories*, 90.

63 Laura Mulvey, "Kiarostami's Uncertainty Principle," *Sight and Sound* 6 (June 1998): 24–7.

64 See Godfrey Cheshire, "Abbas Kiarostami: A Cinema of Questions," *Film Comment* 8, no. 6 (July/August 1996): 3–36, 41–3.

65 Mehrnaz Saeed-Vafa and Jonathan Rosenbaum, *Abbas Kiarostami* (Urbana-Champaign: University of Illinois Press, 2003).

66 Mostafa Mokhtabad, "Kiarostami's Unfinished Cinema and Its Postmodern Reflections," *International Journal of the Humanities* 17, no. 2 (2010): 23–37.

67 Joan Copjec, "Cinema as Thought Experiment: On Movement and Movements," *differences* 27, no. 1 (2016): 143–75.

68 Shohini Chaudhuri and Howard Finn, "The Open Image: Poetic Realism and the New Iranian Cinema," *Screen* 44, no. 1 (Spring 2003): 38–57.

69 Babak Tabarraee, "Abbas Kiarostami: A Cinema of Silence," *Soundtrack* 5, no. 1 (June 2012), 5–13; cf. "Silence Studies in the Cinema and the Case of Abbas Kiarostami" (Unpublished Master's thesis, University of British Columbia, 2013).

70 On the voice in, see Farshid Kazemi, "The Acousmatic Voice in the Cinema of Abbas Kiarostmai," *The Cinematic Voice—The Cinematologists*, Ep98—March 17, 2020, 126 min., 59 sec., https://cinematologists.podbean.com/e/ep98-the-cinematic-voice/. Michel Langford has read *Shirin* through Chion's concept of "acousmatic listening," see Michel Langford, "Seeking Love in the Interstices: Acousmatic Listening as Counter-Memory in Abbas Kiarostami's *Shirin* (2008)," in *Counter-Memories in Iranian Cinema*, ed. Matthias Wittmann and Ute Holl (Edinburgh: University of Edinburgh Press, 2021), 146–66.

71 Gohar Houmayounpour, *Doing Psychoanalysis in Tehran* (Cambridge Massachusetts: MIT Press, 2012), ix.

72 For the deployment of feminist gaze theory or *Screen* theory in reading post-revolutionary Iranian cinema and the films of Kiarostami, see Negar Mottahedeh, *Displaced Allegories: Post-Revolutionary Iranian Cinema* (Durham: Duke University Press, 2009). Also see Sara Saljoughi, "Seeing, Iranian Style: Women and Collective Vision in Abbas Kiarostami's *Shirin*," *Iranian Studies* 45, no. 4 (2012): 519–35. Saljoughi argues that in *Shirin* Kiarostami "challenges the post-revolutionary modesty laws and their emphasis on not looking at women and at avoiding a spectator–image relationship based on the fulfillment of the desiring male gaze."

73 Sara Saljoughi, "Seeing, Iranian Style: Women and Collective Vision in Abbas Kiarostami's Shirin," *Iranian Studies* 45, no. 4 (2012): 519–35.

74 Mary Ann Doane, *Bigger than Life: The Close-Up and Scale in the Cinema* (Durham: Duke University Press, 2021), 140.

75 Ibid., 149.

76 Jean-Luc Nancy, *L'Évidence du film. Abbas Kiarostami.* [The Evidence of Film: Abbas Kiarostami.] (Bruxelles: Yves Gevaert Éditeur, 2001),16.

77 For the use of the Lacanian gaze, see Joan Copjec, "The Object-Gaze, Hijab, Cinema," *Filozofski Vestnik* XXVII, no. 2 (2006): 161–83; also, Farhang Erfani, *Iranian Cinema and Philosophy: Shooting Truth* (Palgrave Macmillan, 2011). Contrary to Copjec and Erfani who discuss the gaze only in relation to one of Kiarostami's films—Copjec analyzing the Lacanian gaze in *The Wind Will Cary Us* (1999), and Erfani's analysis of the gaze in *Close-Up* (1990)—I argue that the object-gaze is ubiquitous in Kiarostami's entire cinematic oeuvre. Since a full analysis of the gaze in Kiarostami's cinema is beyond the scope of this chapter, I can only briefly gesture to several other films where the logic of the object-gaze is operative. For example, in *Zendegi va digar hich* (*Life and Nothing More…*, 1992), the gaze appears at the end of the film when we are unsure if the father/director will be able to find the boy in the next village. This exemption of narrative closure is what engenders the gaze since our desire has been accounted for in the cinematic image. Similarly, in the final closing-scene of *Zir-e derakhtan-e zayton* (*Through the Olive Trees*, 1994), the two figures are staged amidst olive trees in an extreme long shot where we are unable to hear the response to the wedding proposal that would provide us with narrative closure—by being denied this closure we are left desiring as spectators, and it is at this moment that the gaze appears, since the spectator's desire has been implicated in the formal and narrative structure of the film. Lastly, in Kiarostami's *Dah* (*10*, 2002), we are denied from viewing the female driver

for about 17 minutes and only hear her voice (a voice that is acousmatic and only later becomes de-acousmatized—see next chapter on the acousmatic voice) while the camera is focused on the son. It is here that the object-gaze appears in the film (among other instances) since the subject's desire is implicated through its desire to see the invisible or absent presence in the image.

78 Geoff Andrew, "Kiarostami and the Art of the Invisible." DVD booklet for *Shirin* (London: British Film Institute, 2008), 1.

79 See Nezami Ganjavi, *Khosrow and Shirin*, trans. Dick Davis (Mage Publishers, 2023).

80 A similar memorable image of light from the cinema screen that is reflected on the face of a female character appears in the Taiwanese film *Goodbye, Dragon Inn* (2003) directed by Tsai Ming-liang—a film that is intertextually gesturing to King Hu's wuxia masterpiece *Dragon Inn* (1967).

81 For the unpublished seminar, see Jacques Lacan, *l'Objet de la Psychanalyse*, Seminar XIII (1965–66), available online: http://www.valas.fr/Jacques-Lacan-l-objet-de-la-psychana lyse,258; for a provisional translation of this seminar, see Jacques Lacan, Seminar XIII (1965–66) *The Object of Psychoanalysis*, trans. Cormac Gallagher, http://www.lacaninire land.com/web/wp-content/uploads/2010/06/13-The-Object-of-Psychoanalysis1.pdf

82 Michel Foucault, *The Order of Things* (London: Routledge, 2001), chapter 1.

83 Aaron Schuster, "The Lacan-Foucault Relation: *Las Meninas*, Sexuality, and the Unconscious," 8. Transcript of a lecture delivered at the "Lacan Contra Foucault" conference, American University of Beirut, December 4, 2015. (Unpublished). Lacan states, "the picture is a trap for the look, that it is a matter of trapping the one who is there in front…" Lacan, *The Object of Psychoanalysis*, 226. In his Seminar XI, while talking about Hans Holbein's painting *The Ambassadors*, Lacan similarly states, "This picture is simply what any picture is, a trap for the gaze. In any picture, it is precisely in seeking the gaze in each of its points that you will see it disappear." See Lacan, *The Four Fundamental Concepts*, 89.

84 Schuster, "The Lacan-Foucault Relation," 8.

85 Ibid, 8; cf. Lacan states, "believing that nothing is happening to us when we are in front of a picture, we are caught like a fly in glue"; Gallagher trans. Lacan, *The Object of Psychoanalysis*, 226.

86 Schuster, "The Lacan-Foucault Relation," 8; cf. Lacan states, "We are here to see how this picture inscribes for us the perspective of the relationships of the gaze in what is called fantasy, in so far as it is constitutive" [translation amended]. Gallagher trans. Lacan, *The Object of Psychoanalysis*, 227; cf. Lacan, *l'Objet de la Psychanalyse*, 607. The Lacanian *matheme* for fantasy is "$<>a": The $ is the symbol of the barred or split subject, *a* is *objet petit a* or object-cause of desire, and losange or diamond functions as the relation between the two.

87 Ibid, 8–9; cf. Lacan states, "It is a structure different to any representation. It is in this connection that I insist on the essential difference constituted by this term of representative of the representation, *Vorstellungsrepresentanz*, borrowed from Freud." Lacan, *The Object of Psychoanalysis*, 231; cf. Lacan, *l'Objet de la Psychanalyse*, 615.

88 Schuster, "The Lacan-Foucault Relation," 9.

89 Ibid, 9.

90 *24 Frames*, directed by Abbas Kiarostami (Iran: CG Cinema and Kiarostami Foundation, 2017), Film.

91 Schuster, "The Lacan-Foucault Relation," 9.

92 On film(s) within film, see Christian Metz, *Impersonal Enunciation, or the Place of Film* (New York: Columbia University Press, 2016). In Chapter 8.

93 Khatereh Khodaei, "Shirin as Described by Kiarostami," Volume 13, Issue 1/January 2009. http://offscreen.com/view/shirin_kiarostami

94 Schuster, "The Lacan-Foucault Relation," 9.

95 Nancy, *L'Évidence du film*, 27.
96 Slavoj Žižek, *The Fright of Real Tears: Krzysztof Kieślowski between Theory and Post-Theory*.
97 Khodaei, "Shirin as Described by Kiarostami."
98 David Bordwell, "The Movie Looks Back at Us," Wednesday | April 1, 2009, accessed 20 May, 2018. http://www.davidbordwell.net/blog/2009/04/01/the-movie-looks-back-at-us/
99 Shiva Rahbaran, *Iranian Cinema Uncensored: Contemporary Film-Makers since the Islamic Revolution* (London: I.B. Tauris, 2015), 151.
100 Blake Atwood, *Reform Cinema in Iran: Film and Political Change in the Islamic Republic* (New York: Columbia University Press, 2016), 23.
101 See Nacim Pak-Shiraz, *Shi'i Islam in Iranian Cinema: Religion and Spirituality in Film* (London and New York: I.B. Tauris, 2011), 93–122; Michael Pittman, "Majid Majidi and Baran: Iranian Cinematic Poetics and the Spiritual Poverty of Rumi," *Journal of Religion & Film* 15, no. 2, Article 4 (2012); and Cyrus Ali Zargar, "Allegory and Ambiguity in the Films of Majid Majidi: A Theodicy of Meaning," *Journal of Religion & Film* 20, no. 1, Article 3 (2016).
102 Henry Corbin, *L'Iran et la philosophie (L'Espace intérieur)* (Paris: Fayard, 1990), 157.
103 Michelle Langford, "Negotiating the sacred body in Iranian cinema(s): National, physical and cinematic embodiment in Majid Majidi's *Baran* (2002)," in *Negotiating the Sacred II: Blasphemy and Sacrilege in the Arts*, ed. E. Burns-Coleman and S. Fernandes-Dias (Canberra: The Australian National University Press, 2008), 167–68.
104 Sartre, *Being and Nothingness*, 257.
105 Ibid, 369.
106 Copjec, "The Object-Gaze," 177.
107 After a critical summary of Sartre's notion of the gaze, Lacan distinguishes it from his own concept and brings to the fore what for him is the crucial relation of the gaze to the subject of desire, he states, "But does this mean that originally it is in the relation of subject to subject, in the function of the existence of others as looking at me, that we apprehend what the gaze really is? Is it not clear that the gaze intervenes here only in as much as it is not the annihilating subject, correlative of the world of objectivity, who feels himself surprised, but the subject sustaining himself in a function of desire? Is it not precisely because desire is established here in the domain of seeing that we can make it vanish?" Lacan, *Four Fundamental Concepts*, 84–5.
108 Slavoj Žižek, *Pervert's Guide to Cinema*, directed by Sophie Fiennes, (2006). Film.
109 Jacques Lacan, *The Seminar, Book I: Freud's Papers on Technique* (New York: Norton, 1988), 215.
110 Lacan, *The Four Fundamental Concepts*, 97.
111 The name Leila itself gestures to the famed story of Leili and Majnun, who often appears in Persian mystical poetry as the figure of the beloved and represents one of the most famous works of the classical Persian poet Nizami Ganjavi composed in the 12th century. See Nezami Ganjavi, *Layli and Majnun*, trans. Dick Davis (London: Penguin Classics, 2021).
112 Otto Weininger cited in Žižek, *Metastasis of Enjoyment*, 141.
113 "Refugees in Love and Life Interview with Majid Majidi by Gonul Donmez-Colin (Film Critic)" [Reprint from *Asian Cinema Studies* 13, no. 1 (Spring/Summer 2002).], accessed September 19, 2017, http://www.cinemajidi.com/

Chapter 2

The Voice as Love Object

The Acousmatic Voice in *Gabbeh* and *The May Lady*[1]

Slavoj Žižek states that the proper tension—that is "the principal axis"—in the cinema is the one between *gaze and voice*.[2] This axis is of special significance in post-revolutionary Iranian cinema, as it revolves around the staging of the female body. For female bodies to be represented on screen, legitimate use of the voice and gaze had to be discovered within Islamic jurisprudence (*fiqh*). As Hamid Naficy states, "Theologians mined Islamic doctrines to develop further guidelines about women's representation, their on-screen relations with men, and the permissible uses of *voice and gaze* – theirs as well as those of men"[3] [my emphasis]. Fascinatingly, the New Iranian Cinema is born out of the problem of representing the female body between the voice and gaze.

Though the gaze has been discussed to some extent in the scholarly literature on Iranian cinema, and more extensively within film theory, the voice has not received the theoretical attention that it rightly merits.[4] In this chapter, I theorize the deployment of the voice in post-revolutionary Iranian cinema, especially through what the French film theorist Michel Chion calls *acousmêtre*, or the acousmatic voice. The acousmatic voice is a voice without a body or disembodied voice: a character's voice emanates from an offscreen space as if detached from a particular body. The acousmatic voice often operates within post-revolutionary Iranian cinema as a way to circumvent the restrictions on staging bodies (both male and female) in intimate or erotic configurations. This phantom-like voice without a body haunts the entire landscape of post-revolutionary Iranian cinema like a spectral presence.

I will look at two instances in which the acousmatic voice is deployed as a way to subvert the logic of veiling the female voice through the acousmatization of the male voice, focusing on Rakhshan Banietemad's *Banoo-ye ordibehesht* (*The May Lady*, Iran, 1997) and Mohsen Makhmalbaf's *Gabbeh* (Iran/France, 1996). Voice in these films represents a feminist move and a counter-ideological gesture, since it is the male voice, rather than the female voice, that is rendered acousmatic. This male acousmatic voice acts to subvert the logic of veiling the female voice, since representing the male voice without a body critiques the foregrounding of the male subject as the privileged site of subjectivity in the Islamic Republic. In this way, the acousmatic voice foregrounds female (rather than male) desire, drawing out the erotic potential of the male voice—a dimension only ascribed to the female voice

DOI: 10.4324/9781003531029-4

in Islamic jurisprudence. Relating Chion's concept of acousmêtre to Lacan's notion of the voice as *objet petit a*—alongside the concept of "voice-off" in feminist film theory of Mary Ann Doane and Kaja Silverman—this chapter argues that the voice acts as a signifier of desire and becomes a love object in place of the forbidden erotic configurations of bodies on the screen. In New Iranian Cinema, the acousmatic voice fills in the erotic void created by the censors.

2.1   Chion, Lacan, and the Voice in Feminist Psychoanalytic Film Theory

One of the foremost theorists of the voice in cinema is the French composer and film theorist, Michel Chion. In *The Voice in Cinema*, Chion refers to a voice whose source or origin is obscured from the visual field as acousmêtre or the acousmatic voice. He states, "For the spectator… the filmic *acousmêtre* is 'offscreen,' outside the image, and at the same time in the image…It's as if the voice were wandering along the surface, at once inside and outside, seeking a place to settle. Especially when a film hasn't shown what body this voice normally inhabits."[5] Though Chion borrowed the term acousmêtre from his teacher, Pierre Schaeffer (whom in turn borrowed it from Pythagoras and the Greeks), it is to Chion that we owe its full articulation in relation to the cinema. The acousmatic voice, therefore, is a voice that is heard in the film's diegesis but not specifically attached to a body. It is a disembodied voice—a freely floating spectral voice. For Chion, different forms of the *acousmêtre*—such as the complete or partial *acousmêtre*, commentator, radio, telephone, and already visualized—are operative in cinema.[6] According to Chion, once the acousmatic voice is finally anchored in a specific face or body, the voice becomes de-acousmatized. Therefore, for Chion, the acousmatic voice becomes a cinematic object no less powerful than the images that pervade the cinematic screen.

In referring to this illusive object-voice in cinema, Chion makes a subtle but important connection to Jacques Lacan's theory of the voice as object. Chion considers Lacan to have provided "a serious theoretical elaboration of the voice as an object."[7] Indeed, Lacan added two more objects, the voice and gaze, to the list of the Freudian partial objects.[8] As Chion notes, "Lacan… placed the voice – along with the gaze, the penis, the feces, and nothingness- in the ranks of '*objet (a)*', these part objects which may be fetishized or employed to 'thingify difference.'"[9] For Lacan, *objet petit a* acts as a partial object, an element that is imagined as separable from the rest of the body, such as the voice. There is a crucial distinction to be made between what you desire, the loved one, and what *causes* you to desire. The Lacanian *objet petit a* is not the object of desire (the beloved, etc.), but rather the object-cause of desire, that ever elusive feature which causes one to desire, the surplus that produces or evokes desire.[10] As Žižek puts it, "*Objet petit a,* the object-cause of desire [is]: an object that is, in a way, posited by desire itself. The paradox of desire is that it posits retroactively its own cause, i.e., the object *a* is an object that can be perceived only by a gaze 'distorted' by desire…."[11] In a similar way, the voice as *objet petit a* is an object that can be heard in the aural field only by an ear that is 'distorted' by desire. The voice as *objet petit a* is a distortion of the aural field through the subject's desire.[12] This is how the acousmatic voice can become a love object, not in the sense that one would fall in love with a voice, but in the sense that it is a medium, "a catalyst that sets off love."[13] The voice as object-cause of desire is intimately connected with the acousmatic voice.

Lacan's notion of the voice as *objet petit a* provides an important supplement to Chion's acousmatic voice, since Lacan foregrounds the dimension of desire in the voice and its ability to function as a love object. The logic of desire that inheres in the voice operates in the invocatory drive: "At the scopic level, we are no longer at the level of demand, but of desire, of the desire of the Other. It is the same at the level of the invocatory drive, which is the closest to the experience of the uncon-scious."[13] It is here that the voice as object-cause of desire and the dimension of desire in the female voice in post-revolutionary Iranian cinema coincide.[14]

One of the first sustained applications of psychoanalytic film theory to the voice in cinema, Kaja Silverman's *The Acoustic Mirror* foregrounds the female voice in its analysis of classic cinema in the same way that 1970s feminist gaze theory or *Screen* theory (particularly Laura Mulvey) foregrounded the male gaze. Silverman critiques Chion's analysis of the voice in the cinema on the grounds that he does not address the question of gender and sexuality of the voice in classic Hollywood cin-ema. She writes, "unfortunately, Chion's sorties into the domain of sexual differ-ence seem motivated primarily by the search for poetic props, and so remain for the most part both uncritical and devoid of self-consciousness."[15] Silverman goes on to say that Chion's discussion of the voice remains "within existing gender demar-cations" and "assumes much of the symptomatic value of a Hollywood film…"[16] Her foregrounding of the gender of the voice in classic Hollywood cinema, and the female voice in particular, is especially relevant to post-revolutionary Iranian cin-ema. Indeed, for Silverman Chion's analysis occludes the fact that the acousmatic or disembodied voice is often male, while the female voice is generally confined to the spectacle of her body. Although Silverman's critique of Chion is generally apt, she may be overstating the case, since Chion seems to be aware of the gender of the acousmatic voice, as he states, "most *acousmêtres* are masculine."[17] According to Silverman, classic Hollywood cinema, "holds the female voice and body insist-ently to the interior of the diegesis, while relegating the male subject to a position of apparent discursive exteriority by identifying him with mastering speech, vision, or hearing."[18] Authority and power are located in the disembodied voice that is either a voiceover or voice-off, which speaks while remaining invisible. This voice is almost always male. Conversely, the female voice is often confined to her body, which means that she cannot assume the role of narrator or enunciator. From this perspective, she is disempowered, as she cannot control the story or speak from a theological position outside the diegesis.[19]

In *Gabbeh* and *The May Lady*, the voice operates according to a different logic. Because of modesty laws, to have the female voice manifested by a character that one can see grants her apparent discursive powers. Conversely, to have the male voice as a disembodied voice with a voice-over, remaining unseen while speaking, does not give power to that voice but renders it impotent since space or spatial relations are gendered in the visual economy of New Iranian Cinema: what is visible or public is considered male space, and what is invisible, private, or should remain hidden is female space—hence the logic of the veil.[20] By rendering invisible the male body from the screen image, the male voice is feminized formally through its acousmatization.

The auditory regime of the New Iranian Cinema therefore operates under a different logic than that of classic Hollywood cinema owing to the logic of the veil, in which the female voice is often asynchronous with bodies, emanating from beyond the frame. For Silverman, the synchronization of sound and image is "the sound analogue of the shot/reverse shot formation"; in classic Hollywood cinema, synchronization and the shot/reverse-shot pattern both function to suture the spectator into the diegesis.[21] Significantly, the standard shot/reverse-shot pattern is largely absent in the New Iranian Cinema, especially when the scene presents an unrelated man and woman. This shift away from the rule of synchronization affects the auditory register of the film and exposes the illusion of the unity of voice and body mediated by the cinematic apparatus and the film's site of enunciation. In this way, the female voice in post-revolutionary Iranian cinema often functions as an acousmatic voice, with her body remaining invisible from the visual field within the screen. This shift away from the rule of synchronization exposes the illusion of the unity of voice and body mediated by the cinematic apparatus and the film's site of enunciation. Post-revolutionary Iranian cinema actively desutures the spectator from the diegesis. Paradoxically, then, the New Iranian Cinema is the realization of the ideals of feminist voice theory espoused by theorists such as Doane and Silverman. Negar Mottahedeh notes something similar at the level of the gaze, when she claims, somewhat hyperbolically that "Iranian cinema is the apotheosis of 1970s feminist gaze theory."[22]

Upon closer scrutiny, however, such claims are not entirely correct. Post-revolutionary Iranian cinema cannot be considered an "apotheosis" of feminist voice theory (or gaze theory for that matter); it only appears so on the surface. The sound regime of Iranian cinema hinges on Shi'ite laws that veil the female voice because of its erotic power over the heterosexual male subject both within and without the diegesis. Though Iranian cinema paradoxically achieves, at the level of form, some of the goals of feminist voice theory (asynchronous, not confined to women's bodies, emanating from offscreen spaces, etc.), an emancipatory feminist logic does not necessarily follow.

There is a theoretical correspondence or homology between Chion's acousmatic voice and voice-off (voix-off in French at once denotes both voiceover and voice-off)[23] in feminist film theory. Few theorists have explored the connection between the acousmatic voice and voice-off. The voice-off is a voice that is present in the diegesis but emanates from an offscreen space, detached from the body. Doane describes voice-off in her foundational article, "The Voice in the Cinema: The Articulation of Body and Space": "Voice-off refers to instances in which we hear the voice of a character who is not visible within the frame. Yet the film establishes, by means of previous shots or other contextual determinants, the character's 'presence' in the space of the scene, in the diegesis. He/she is 'just over there,' 'just beyond the frameline,' in a space which 'exists' but which the camera does not choose to show."[24] This description of the voice-off is virtually identical to the way that Chion has characterized the acousmatic voice. Chion states that the complete *acousmêtre* is "the one who is not-yet-seen, but who remains liable to appear in the visual field at any moment."[25] For Silverman, however, the voice-off is gendered and "sexually differentiated in much the same way that a synchronized voice is" which means that the male voice is the privileged site of voice-off.[26] In contrast to this, Shi'ite laws of veiling render the female voice a voice-off or acousmatic in post-revolutionary Iranian cinema. To illustrate the operation of the acousmatic voice in cinema, Chion provides examples such as the mother's voice in Alfred Hitchcock's *Psycho* (1960), Dr. Mabuse's voice in Fritz Lang's *The Testament of Dr Mabuse* (*Das Testament des Dr Mabuse* (1933)), and the director's voice in Orson Welles' *The Magnificent Ambersons* (1942).[27] Like Žižek and Dolar, he draws attention to the uncanny and haunting effects of the acousmatic voice, whereby the voice through its acousmatization acquires the terrifying dimension of becoming all-pervasive, all-knowing, and all-seeing.[28] Doane also highlights the uncanny effects of the voice-off and how it reveals itself as a signifier by detaching from the body.[29] In their examples, the acousmatic voice and voice-off are theoretically homologous; their uncanny effect on the spectator is due to the decoupling of the voice from its source.

However, the New Iranian Cinema is less concerned with the uncanny dimension of the acousmatic voice than with its capacity to become a love object: the voice as *objet petit a* or object-cause of desire. The acousmatic voice possesses a different libidinal economy in this cinema. Before turning to this aspect of the acousmatic voice in *Gabbeh* and *The May Lady*, especially through the complete and partial *acousmêtre*, I provide some contextual background for an Islamic theory of the female voice that informs the auditory sensorium of post-revolutionary Iranian cinema.

2.2   Veiling and Aurality: An Islamic Theory of the Female Voice

Besides the censorship on visuality, discussed in the previous chapter on the gaze, another important guideline of the system of modesty was the proscriptive veiling of the auditory sensorium. This was to ensure that the female voice would not be represented on screen in a way that would evoke male desire, since in the libidinal economy of the Islamic Republic heterosexual desire is desire par excellence. According to the logic of the veil (*hejab*), the female voice must be veiled or concealed from men's aurality, since it may cause them to become sexually aroused. In an Islamic jurisprudential theory of the voice, the voice of women is considered part of her *'awra*; it is deemed a "shameful" private part of her body (*pudenda*) that should be covered or concealed before unrelated men (*na-mahram*).[30] As Abdelwahab Bouhdiba states, "the voice of a Muslim woman is also *'aura* [*'awra*]. Not only because of the sweet words coming from her mouth must be heard only by her husband and master, but because the voice may create a disturbance and set in train the cycle of zina [unlawful sexual relations or adultery]."[31] Though there is no direct reference to the proscription of the female voice in the Qur'an, some scholars who argue for the female voice as *'awra*, refer to verse 24:30–31. But the concept of the veil or *hejab* (literally meaning a curtain) has both a visual and aural dimension as is evident in this Qur'anic verse: "And when you ask of [the wives of the prophet] anything, ask it of them from behind a curtain. That is purer for you and their hearts" (33:53).

Similar injunctions on the female voice are found in Judaism and Christianity.[32] Perhaps the precise homologue to the Islamic concept is provided in the Babylonian Talmud, a Jewish Rabbinic text that states, "a women's voice is nakedness."[33] Many Shi'i traditions (*hadith*) indicate that only the husband or a relative can, or should, hear the voice of a woman. For instance, there is a *hadith* attributed to Imam 'Ali prohibiting women from speaking more than five words with anyone other than her husband or a relative (*mahram*).[34] Similar *hadith* exist in Sunni sources: "Women is a 'shameful thing' [*'awra*]. If she goes out, Satan attempts to control her."[35] According to some Sunni jurists, the female voice is considered *'awra* that must be veiled before men.[36] This logic of the female voice is also operative within Sufism (Islamic mysticism), which is often thought to value music and the aesthetics of the voice, especially through the practice of *sama* (spiritual audition). For instance, a Sufi hagiography relates that a certain 'Umar Murshidi, sojourning through the desert, heard a beautiful voice that gave him great pleasure. He was overcome with a powerful desire to see the person to whom the voice belonged and could not cast out the idea from his mind even after he had returned to his Sufi lodge. As Bashir relates it:

> Then, when he was reading the Qur'an, he suddenly heard a voice commanding, "Look!" When he did this, he said, "I saw a woman, naked from head to foot, sitting and showing me her vagina, unhesitatingly and boldly, uncovering herself in a way that no wife would ever do in front of her husband." The voice then said, "This is the woman whose voice you had heard and taken pleasure from." *Your hearing of her voice is the same as seeing her vagina* [my emphasis].[37]

In this way, even within Sufi discourse the ideology of Islamic legal theory mediates the social relations among the sexes, whereby hearing the voice of women indexes the possibility of unlawful or adulterous sexual relations.[38]

Regarding the question of the female voice, Shi'ite cleric and leader of the new Islamic Republic Ayatollah Ruhollah Khomeini stated that, "the conversation of a women with a man in a provocative manner, the mellowing down of her expression, the softening of her talk, and the prettifying of her voice so that a heart-sick person is enticed is *Haram* [forbidden]."[39] Unrelated men must make themselves known by their voice before entering a home, so that women in the house will have a chance to arrange the mise-en-scène before the male gaze. As Naficy explains, "A woman must not only veil her body from unrelated men but also her voice. The veiling of the voice involves using formal language with unrelated males (and females), a decorous tone of voice, and the avoidance of emotional expressions such as singing or boisterous laughter, although grief or anger are allowed."[40]

Traditionally, women veiled their voices in Iran by distorting them. For instance, when an unrelated man would knock at the door of the house (in many old traditional houses in Iran there were two separate doors with separate gate handles for women and men), a woman would answer by distorting her voice by placing her index finger in the side of her mouth and pulling it while speaking. The Babi and feminist Sadigheh Dawlatabadi (1882–1961)[41] describes this practice, "For instance, previously it was said if a virtuous woman was obliged to talk to a man, she should curl her tongue like a nut, so her voice would not sound alluring or attractive and be the cause of corruption. This is foolish."[42]

This veiling mandate often operates in Iranian cinema through the distortion of the female singing voice. This changing of the female singing voice is rendered palpable in Ali Hatami's film, *Delshodegan* (*The Love-Stricken*, Iran, 1992), in which a group of Persian classical musicians in the Qajar era go abroad to make a recording of their music on a gramophone. The composer Hossein Alizadeh (b. 1951), who composed the score for the film, "used the wordless voice of Sudabeh Salem (b. 1954), a pre-revolution soprano singer, to create a powerful nostalgic effect."[43] In this precise way, Salem's voice was distorted through a heteroglossia of voices in a wordless song of inarticulate speech. Interestingly in *Del shodegan*, Leila (Leila Hatami), a blind Turkish princess, falls in love with the acousmatic voice of Taher (Amin Tarokh), the lead singer of the group. Taher's singing voice is performed by the famous maestro of Persian classical music, Mohammad-Reza Shajarian (1940–2020). The scene in which Leila hears and follows the voice of Taher is one of the masterpieces of post-revolutionary Iranian cinema.

The female voice can also be veiled with the literal veil (*chador*) itself, lifted before the face as a protective screen while speaking to unrelated men. This image is exemplified in the iconic freeze-frame that ends Mohsen Makhmalbaf's film, *Nun va goldun* (*A Moment of Innocence*, 1996), when the young girl (Maryam Mohamadamini) lifts her veil (*chador*) like a screen or curtain while asking the young policeman the time. This freeze-frame gestures to other iconic freeze frames in cinema history such as the one at the end of François Truffaut's *The 400 Blows* (1959). In post-revolutionary Iranian cinema, the gender of the voice is significant. Since the female voice is conceived as part of a woman's private body parts, it must be veiled or concealed from unrelated men, but the male voice does not have the same prohibitions attached to it.

Apropos the singing female voice, Bahman Ghobadi's mesmerizing *Niwemang* (*Half Moon*, Austria/France/Iran/Iraq, 2006) is a resounding critique of the proscription on female singing in and outside the cinematic screen. The film was banned in Iran and has never been allowed screening in the country. The film critiques the restriction imposed by the Islamic Republic on solo female singing, through directly staging a female character named Hesho (Hedieh Tehrani), who is said to have a "celestial voice," to sing in the film. An elderly Kurdish musician, Mamo (Ismail Ghaffari), who has been invited to Iraqi Kurdistan to give a concert, is intent upon bringing the female singer Hesho for the concert, where she has been exiled to a village along with 1,334 women singers who were consigned there as punishment for their public singing in the past. In a remarkable scene, Hesho is seen off by many of the women, who all gather around her and line up on rooftops singing (although the female voices are extra-diegetic) and playing the *daf* (a sacred hand drum for the Kurds), while she leaves with Mamo. Then comes the scene which is one of the most beautiful moments of the liberation of the female singing voice in post-revolutionary Iranian cinema, where Hesho sings a solo piece in a practice session, and the verse of the Kurdish love-song that she sings signifies all too well the plight of these women: "the heart of the world is full of joy/but only my heart is filled with sorrow." In the end, the problem is how to conceal Hesho from the Iranian authorities at the border, but they discover her in the bus and take her back to the village.

Through a short-circuiting reading, one of the paradoxes that comes to light is that the Lacanian theory of the female voice has certain correspondences with the Islamic theory of the female voice, in which at least for some men, the female voice may act as the cause of their desire. As Bruce Fink notes, "In the case of certain men it is a woman's voice that is of primary importance; it is not so much what she says as the way in which she says it, the tone and timber of her voice, that arouses their desire."[44] The difference between the psychoanalytic theory of the female voice vs. an Islamic theory is that in the Islamic context the erotics of the female voice is universalized to all men, whereas in psychoanalytic theory it is rather confined to certain (heterosexual) men who eroticize the female voice and are thereby aroused by it. In her discussion of sexuality within a Muslim framework, Fatima Mernissi has argued that the eye "is undoubtedly an erogenous zone."[45] Indeed, in Islamic jurisprudence the ear is an erogenous zone as well. According to some compendia of Islamic jurisprudence, "'aural adultery' (*zina al-udhuni*) was considered a constant danger even where the veil impeded 'visual adultery' (*zina al-'ayni*)."[46] For Lacan the ear also functions as an erogenous zone, which forms part of the invocatory drive that is related to sexual desire. (Lacan identifies four partial drives, the oral, anal, scopic, and invocatory). According to the logic of an Islamic theory of the voice, therefore, there is always an erotic surplus in the female voice that must be veiled or contained through various means, so that the full disclosure of the voice in all its erotic dimensions may be veiled from the male character on screen, or the male spectator in the cinema. In this sense, the soft and sonorous timber associated with the female voice acts as an exposed private bodily part that is thought to be the cause of men's desire.

In order to delimit the eros of the gaze in Iranian cinema, the voice is often foregrounded. But according to the above theory, the voice itself is filled with eros, and since the female voice is eroticized in the Islamic theory of the female voice: the attempt to contain it backfires, and the voice retains its erotic surplus. This is one of the central concerns of post-revolutionary Iranian cinema: how to de-eroticize the female voice. But of course, such a procedure of censoring, veiling, or containing the voice (and gaze) is impossible, as there is always an *indivisible remainder* (to borrow a phrase from Žižek that he takes from Schelling), a surplus in the voice that resists de-eroticization. This is the voice as *objet petit a* or object-cause of desire. The more you focus on the erotic potentiality of the female voice (and the gaze), by trying to erase it or to efface all traces of eroticism in it, the more it escapes your grasp, remaining ever elusive and uncontainable—the over avoidance itself thus draws more attention to the voice and foregrounds it as the object-cause of desire.

The proper theoretical question to be asked here then is: what then is the appropriate mode of aurality in an Islamic theory of the female voice? The paradox is that the ideal mode of hearing the female voice in Islamic voice-theory would be the acousmatic voice: to hear the voice without the source of its origin, namely the female body, and to have the body properly veiled from the visual field of the male spectator. In this precise sense, the female voice would be rendered acousmatic and hence religiously acceptable. But the problem is that the acousmatic voice, this voice without a body, can still function as a love object and hence become the object-cause of desire. Moreover, according to Silverman and Doane, the voice whose source is invisible is more powerful than the embodied voice: it seeps into the extra-diegetic register, where it is free to roam in the enunciative space of the text. Male voices in classic Hollywood cinema thus tend to be given greater liberty: they are permitted to narrate, to be detached from the body, to emanate from off-screen spaces. By contrast, female voices tend to be synched up and confined to the bodies from whence they emanate. However, in certain examples of Iranian cinema, this paradigm is reversed: the mandate to veil the female body results in her voice occupying an acousmatic, offscreen space normally reserved for male characters. As the two examples illustrate below, the acousmatic voice subverts and destabilizes the modesty system's injunction to veil the female voice by rendering acousmatic the male voice and by turning the voice into an object, a love object that provokes desire.

2.3   The Acousmatic Voice in *Gabbeh*

Among the best-known art-house films produced after the revolution in Iran, Mohsen Makhmalbaf's *Gabbeh* epitomizes the colorful visual poetics and aesthetics associated with post-revolutionary Iranian cinema. Occupying the middle period of Makhmalbaf's career, *Gabbeh* was the last film he made in Iran before becoming a diasporic and exilic director. At first, he had intended to make a documentary about Iran's Qashqa'i nomads, and their colorful *gabbeh* rugs, but he settled on a fiction film.

Gabbeh is ostensibly about a young Qashqa'i girl in Iran who is in love with a young man on horseback, whom her possessive father prevents her from seeing.

The frame narrative begins with an elderly couple bickering about which one of them will wash the gabbeh carpet woven by the Qashqa'i tribe's women, and which contains the story of the couple's love. A girl called Gabbeh (Shaghayegh Djodat) magically materializes from the rug. She begins to tell her family history to the elderly couple, including how she came to love the stranger on horseback despite her father and uncle's other plans. As her story unfolds, we slowly realize that Gabbeh is in fact the elderly woman, and the elderly man is her lover on horseback. The narrative temporalities of the film are not presented in chronological order but are woven together like the warp and weft of the gabbeh rug in which past, present, and future simultaneously occur in a timeless present.

The first thing to be noted at the outset is the *gabbeh* carpet on which the figure of Gabbeh appears is the same type of Qashqa'i carpet that adorns Freud's famous couch, the couch being synonymous with psychoanalysis itself. The psychoanalytic connection between the carpet on Freud's couch and the *gabbeh* carpet is a fortuitous conjunction, as Gabbeh who magically materializes on the carpet begins to talk and narrate her story, much like psychoanalysis which was called "the talking cure" by the first female patient Anna O who went into analysis with Freud and may have reclined on that very gabbeh-adorned couch. Gabbeh narrates her troubled love story, with the figure of the father functioning as the ultimate obstacle to the erotic relationship between her and the lover on horseback. This image is not incidental as a woman appearing on the rug (or couch) also evokes the image of Shahrazad in the frame narrative of *The Thousand and One Nights*, which was based on ancient Sanskrit and Middle Persian or Pahlavi source(s) from the pre-Islamic Sasanian era called, *A Thousand Tales* (*Hezar Afsan*), that is now lost. There is a profound link between Shahrazad and the female voice in Iranian mytho-poetic textual universe, in which the figure of Shahrazad is related to the old Indo-Iranian goddess of the voice, speech, poetry and song namely Vac or Vak.[47] In her excellent essay, "Freud's Couch: A Case History," Marina Warner refers to the film *Gabbeh* and notes the psychoanalytic connection to the carpet on Freud's couch and to Shahrzad,[48] but although she evokes the figure of Shahrazad in this connection, she is unaware of the links between Shahrazad and the ancient Iranian female divinity of the voice, Vac.[49] Warner also recalls incorrectly the detail of the appearance of Gabbeh and states, "… she appears, stepping out of the stream…"[50] whereas Makhmalbaf had her appear from the *gabbeh* itself in a magic realist turn, in order to establish a connection between the two.

In an early scene, Gabbeh is centered in medium close-up, her back to the camera as she faces a gabbeh. A wolf-like howl from offscreen prompts her to turn around and face the camera. Though at first glance it looks as though she is directly gazing at the camera and hence the spectator, we come to see that her gaze is directed off-screen (which in film studies is called, a "look of outward regard"[51]) toward the source of the howl outside the frame. In the classical Hollywood cinema, such a look anticipates an eye-line match, but in the New Iranian Cinema this formal procedure is absent due to the proscription on the exchange of glances between men and women. Here, the logic of the averted gaze of the modesty system is operative within the frame, and therefore her gaze does not visually address the spectators sitting in the theater. In this sense, the close-up shot does not allow the direct gaze or the taking pleasure of looking, or the activation of scopophilia in the spectator – that is, the spectator is not implicated as the subject of Gabbeh's gaze. This forecloses the possibility of the direct relay of looks between Gabbeh and the offscreen lover as well as between Gabbeh and the spectator. The scene's formal structure ensures that the spectator is not sutured into the diegesis. Gabbeh's desiring gaze is directed elsewhere—toward the offscreen body of her lover as well as to the voice.

This voice without a body is what Chion calls "acousmêtre," what Doane calls voice-off, and what Silverman calls "the disembodied voice." Such a voice often operates within Iranian cinema to circumvent the representation of bodies, especially female bodies, in erotic configurations. This phantom-like voice is exemplified by the howling voice of the youthful lover in Gabbeh. The lover's voice, however, is partially de-acousmatized or embodied. Even though we see the lover's body in long and extreme long shot, we never see him speak or make the howling sound; we only see parts of his body such as his hands. He thus formally remains a partial acousmêtre. (Or to use the language of Doane and Silverman, his voice remains asynchronous with his body.) But in contrast to the power Doane and Silverman ascribe to the asynchronous male voice, his disembodied voice subverts the logic of veiling female voices and bodies on-screen, since representing the acousmatic male voice critiques the foregrounded male subject as the privileged site of subjectivity.

In *Gabbeh*, the voice also acts as an erotic signifier. It becomes a love object in place of the lover's body, which cannot be displayed erotically on-screen with Gabbeh. The lover's acousmatic voice fills the erotic void created by the censors. For Lacan, the voice, as *objet petit a*, acts as a part-object that sets off desire and thus distorts the aural field, the very way we hear the world. In *Gabbeh*, the lover's howling voice is precisely the Lacanian partial object or object-cause of Gabbeh's desire. Within the voice there is an inflection that eludes embodiment: present as an autonomous, disembodied specter, the voice becomes the object-cause of desire and eroticizes the aural field. This dimension parallels Gabbeh's gaze toward the howling voice—a gaze that sets off desire and distorts the visual field just as the howl distorts the aural field. The cinematic form uncannily suggests that it is not the lover's body or person that Gabbeh desires but rather the voice itself. She even states in an early scene, "I fell in love with a horseman, with a strange voice, with an illusion, that, like a shadow, followed our tribe to take me away." The lover's acousmatic wolflike howl is literally the love object for Gabbeh.[52]

Apropos the voice in the film, there is a structural parallel between the lover's voice and the voice of Gabbeh's uncle's betrothed. In one scene, Gabbeh's uncle—who dreamed the night before of a canary by the stream—follows a female acousmatic voice (coming from offscreen) singing a Turkish poem. The uncle follows the voice to the stream and discovers the "singing canary by the stream": the daughter of Alladad singing a poem she composed the night before. Unlike Gabbeh's lover's voice, Alladad's daughter's voice is de-acousmatized and attached to a specific body. Through her voice and poetry, Alladad's daughter becomes the canary of the uncle's dreams, and he asks for her hand in marriage. The acousmatic voice of the young lover on horseback also gestures toward a poetic secret, which Gabbeh states in an earlier scene. When the elder Gabbeh asks the younger Gabbeh why his voice sounds like the howl of a wolf, she replies, "It's a secret between him and me," and provides the meaning in the coded message of the voice, which (in a more complete translation from the Persian) states: "I've gone mad from love's desire/I've become restless, why don't you come?" The youthful lover's acousmatic voice, typified by the howling voice that often acts as the partial acousmêtre, is literally the love object for Gabbeh, as her desiring gaze is directed always to this haunting wolf-howl.

It is not incidental that the lover's voice is technically not a male voice, but the voice of a wolf stripped of its human dimension and hence of its erotically charged potential. The same is true for Alladad's daughter, whose voice is symbolically substituted with the voice of a canary. This is why the singing voice of Alladad's daughter is heard offscreen. Her singing voice remains acousmatic; her face and mouth are never shown as she sings. Both voices are deprived of their human dimension by assuming an animal form and are thereby denied the capacity to signify erotically. Such a transformation is an attempt to contain the voice in all its erotic ambiguity.

The end of the film narratively foregrounds the voice, in all its radical ambiguity, as the site of libidinal investment and the love object par excellence. Gabbeh's closing voice-over narration states, "My father had not killed us, but it was rumored everywhere that he had. So that from now on, my sisters may not lose their heart and religion by *the voice* of a howling wolf. That is why, since forty years on, no one has heard, from any spring, the song of a canary." Here the two voices—the lover's wolflike howl and Alladad's daughter's canarylike song—are intimately linked. Both narrative and formal structure enunciate these voices as the object of erotic desire, as love object.

2.4 The *Acousmêtre* in *The May Lady*

Since starting her career as a documentary filmmaker in the mid-1980s, Rakhshan Banietemad has been perhaps one of Iran's most celebrated female directors (along with Samira Makhmalbaf and Tahmineh Milani). Banietemad's *The May Lady* tells the story of female documentary filmmaker Forough Kia (Minoo Farshchi)—whose name gestures toward the modernist female poet Forugh Farrokhzad[53]—a divorced single mother in her early 40s who lives with her rebellious teenage son Mani (Mani Kasraian). While working on a television documentary about the lives of bereaved mothers who lost their husbands and sons to the Iran-Iraq War, she has a romantic relationship with a man named Dr. Rahbar, to whom she is not married, and whom her son dislikes. Through both the diegetic documentary and the narrative fiction, *The May Lady* self-reflexively ruminates on societal expectations for mothers in Iran. Single mothers like Forough are denied love and intimacy by the superego-like injunctions of Iranian society, where to be a "good" mother is to remain interminably single after being widowed or divorced.[54]

Such a story must contend with the censorship codes imposed on directors in post-revolutionary Iran, especially when it comes to staging on-screen sexual intimacy. How, then, does *The May Lady* represent Forough's liaison? In a word: through the *voice*. Banietemad turns the lover into a complete acousmêtre who is rendered present in the diegesis only through the voice. As Chion states, "When an acousmatic presence consists of a voice—and above all when that voice has not been visualized, and one cannot therefore yet put a face to it—one is dealing with a being of a particular sort, a kind of talking, acting shadow, which I have named acousmêtre—that is, an acousmatic being."[55] By rendering the lover's voice acousmatic through the apparatus of the telephone, Banietemad circumvents the censors and ultimately critiques Iranian cinema's veiling of the female voice. Naficy notes the unique uses of the voice in *The May Lady*: "One of the narrative innovations is the way the male lover is simultaneously both effaced and inscribed in the film by means of a complex game of veiling and unveiling as well as voicing and unvoicing. He is visually absent from the entire film, but he is simultaneously present throughout by the epistolary means of telephone, letters, and voice-over poetry."[56] Although Naficy does not explicitly state it, this is the acousmatic voice. In Laura Mulvey's reading of *The May Lady*, what is foregrounded is women's silence rather than the voice, the film "address[es] the cultural oppression of women's silence alongside urgent social issues." For Mulvely, the film also gestures to the filmmaking process itself, "since as a film about film, with a protagonist who is a documentary filmmaker, *The May Lady* cannot help but lead to reflection on cinema as such."[57]

Throughout the film, the male lover's body remains offscreen, absent from the spectator's visual field but ever present through his acousmatic voice heard only through the telephone, the answering machine, and the apartment intercom. Cinema has often relied on apparatuses such as the telephone to convey the acousmatic voice, as in *When a Stranger Calls* (dir. Fred Walton, US, 1979).[58] But cinema typically foregrounds the uncanny dimension of the acousmatic voice, whereas with *The May Lady*, it is not so much the uncanny aspect of the acousmatic voice that is staged (though this does occur) but the voice's ability to become the love object: the voice as objet petit a. In this instance, the telephone as "technology is a catalizer [sic], it enlarges and enhances something which is already here"—the voice as partial object.[59] Indeed, *The May Lady* deploys the telephone to foreground the male lover's voice as an erotic signifier. The lover's voice as acousmêtre becomes a love object for Forough—since the lovers' bodies cannot be displayed on-screen, Dr. Rahbar's acousmatic voice and Forough's conversations with him fill the erotic void created by the censors.

One scene involving Forough and Dr. Rahbar conversing over the phone subtly overlays her voice onto his acousmatic voice. As he reads one of his love letters, their voices become superimposed. It is as though the merging and fusion of their voices simulate the act of lovemaking; since their bodies cannot be displayed in an erotic embrace, their voices merge and unite in lieu of their bodies. As Naficy explains, "These interweaving male and female voices symbolically substitute for the desired but dreaded—because outlawed—physical contact between unmarried couples. By means of the verbal epistolary communications, [Forough and Dr. Rahbar] are able to express their mutual love for one another and by means of voice fusion, they are able to become one vocally."[60] Indeed, when asked why she chose to have the lover remain invisible throughout the film and represented only as a voice, Bani-Etemad explains, "The limitations we have in Iran in regard to showing realistic relations between opposite sexes determined my choice of the technique of the letter and the voice to display a much more natural relationship of love between a man and a woman."[61]

There is an intimate connection between the evocation of the telephonic voice in *The May Lady* and a poem by Forough Farrokhzad called, *All That Remains is the Voice (Tanha seda-st keh mi-manad)*.[62] Michael C. Hillmann in his book on her life and poetry renders the title of the poem as "It is Only Sound that Remains,"[63] but the problem with this rendering is that it occludes the sense in which the word "*seda*," means both voice and sound, and in the context of the poem it is intended by Farrokhzad as the voice, the voice that reads her poems, the voice of poetry, her voice. We still have recordings of Farrokhzad's recitation of her own poetry that she made for the radio, as well as her voice-over in her poetic documentary *The House is Black (Khaneh siah ast*, 1962). Indeed, others have also noted the allusion to Farrokhzad's poem in relation to the voice in *The May Lady*,[64] but what is missing in such passing references is precisely the acousmatic dimension of the voice that is evoked here by Farrokhzad, since the voice that remains is an acousmatic voice, a disembodied and spectral voice, gesturing to her vocal recitations of her poetry and film that will remain in recordings on cassette tapes, and on the film's soundtrack; a technology which foregrounds the haunting and spectral dimension of the voice, the voice as a partial object that insists beyond life and death.

Forough and Dr. Rahbar's intimate telephone conversations strangely recall phone erotica. Before the advent of "sexting," the phone served the purpose of indulging sexual fantasies. The acousmatic voice on the other side of the telephone line enabled listeners to enact their fantasies. As Chion explains, "A person you talk to on the phone, whom you've never seen, is an *acousmêtre*."[65] The industry of phone erotica was based on the logic of the acousmatic voice, according to which the acousmatic voice can offset desire and function as the fantasmatic support for erotic fantasies. In the absence of the body, the voice occupies the fantasmatic void, entering the fantasy frame as a partial object and becoming the object-cause of desire (or objet petit a). In this sense, the acousmatic voice functions in *The May Lady* as a fantasmatic support for both Forough's and the spectator's desire.

This is precisely why the acousmatic voice that is never de-acousmatized holds a certain power of fascination and takes on an uncanny dimension. The acousmatic voice of the male lover, Dr. Rahbar, holds this power of fascination for the viewer, and causes the viewer's desire; the spectator desires to see the source of the voice, which forever remains obscured and haunts the surface of the screen. This is the voice as the *objet petit a*. Detached from its origin, it becomes a partial object, and thereby the love object. In this way, the viewer's desire is implicated, since the viewer also fantasizes about the absent source of the acousmêtre.

There is an Oedipal imbroglio between the mother and the son in the film that is operative at the level of the mother's voice—the maternal voice. Since one of the central motifs of the film is the role of the mother, there is a fascinating correlation between the mother's voice and the libidinal economy of the son, since the primordial acousmatic voice is precisely the maternal voice. As Dolar states, "'the mother of all acousmatic voices' is precisely the mother's voice, by definition the acousmatic voice, the voice whose source the infant cannot see—his tie with the world, his umbilical cord, his prison, his light."[66] The threat that Dr. Rahbar poses to Mani therefore is the loss of the maternal object signified through the mother's voice, the maternal object-voice to which he is libidinally attached. It is as if the son's (Mani) jealousy of the lover (Dr. Rahbar) is located at the level of the mother's voice as the object-cause of desire (*objet petit a*), since through the telephonic apparatus, it is the lover who has access to the mother's acousmatic voice, which acts not only as an object-cause of desire for Dr. Rabar but more primordially for the son, since in the matrix of the womb it is the mother's voice that was the first sonorous envelope that enfolded him and provided him with auditory pleasure. Therefore, the libidinal threat that Dr. Rahabar poses to Mani is in possessing the maternal voice, or more precisely the mother's acousmatic voice.

In one scene, the son's libidinal attachment to the maternal voice is clearly indicated. While Forough is having dinner with her son, she reprimands him for falling asleep in school and for staying up and watching films late into the night stating, "now go ahead again and watch films every night. I should take your hand by force at 8 pm every night, as I used to do when you were a child, and recount to you so many stories until you would fall asleep." At this moment, in a reverse-shot to Mani, while looking at her Mani says, "you had several phone calls," alluding to Dr. Rahbar's phone message. It is precisely at the moment of the significance of the voice, in her narrating stories to him before falling sleep as a child that he looks at her with a sense of longing and despondency indicating that someone else is now the recipient of the auditory pleasure of her voice, the mother's lover. In an interview Banietemad was asked about the relationship between the mother and son in the film and its almost sensual dimension, which the interviewer describes as "very Oedipal..."[67] Banietemad effectively confirms her sentiment and states, "Naturally, the relationship between the lone boy and the mother has a specific form as well as a broader definition. Apart from all these definitions, such relationships endure specific qualifications of our society. For instance, [Iranian] men are very sensitive in issues regarding their women, wives or mothers. The boy has such feelings. *We can also name it Oedipus complex as a psychological issue*" [emphasis added].[68] Here Banietemad herself endorses an Oedipal scenario in the relationship between the mother and son.

Finally, not only does Dr. Rahbar's voice remain acousmatic for the viewer but, throughout the film, Forough's voice is acousmatic for Dr. Rahbar. Since what we see is that he only hears the voice of Forough but never sees her (regardless of the implication that they have meetings that are not staged for the viewer), her voice remains acousmatic for him, though it is de-acousmatized for the spectator. The important point is that since Dr. Rahbar is consistently offscreen as an acousmatic voice, the film obeys the formal requirements of the Islamic theory of the voice: the female voice should be heard through a veil, a screen, or an obstacle. *The May Lady* accomplishes this through the apparatus of the telephone, which acts as a veil that covers Forough's voice and thereby renders her voice acousmatic for her lover.

Gabbeh and *The May Lady* provide two examples within the New Iranian Cinema in which the acousmatic voice works to bypass the censorship restrictions imposed on filmmakers attempting to represent heterosexual desire. The acousmatic voice in Iranian cinema has a political and counter ideological dimension— filmmakers can mobilize the acousmêtre to resist or subvert the injunction to veil the female voice. By rendering the male body invisible, the acousmatic voice critiques the privileging of the male voice over the female voice, male desire over female desire, and, ultimately, masculinity over femininity. To render the male voice acousmatic, or to distort one into a wolf's howl, is to stage what is often done to the female voice in Iranian cinema and society at large. Both films indicate that an unveiled or de-acousmatized voice is the only proper way for a woman's voice to be heard. But to deploy the acousmatic voice in this manner stages another dimension of the voice: its potential as the Lacanian *objet petit a* or the object-cause of desire. Just as Islamic theories of the voice grant the female voice an erotic surplus, *Gabbeh* and *The May Lady* demonstrate that the male voice can also possess an erotic dimension that can act as the object-cause of desire. By rendering the male voice acousmatic, these films foreground the female voice's ability to incite desire (ironically, the very aspect the rules of modesty seek to minimize). Disembodied, the male lovers' voices act as love objects. Ultimately, in the formal texture of the films, Forough and Gabbeh seem to be in love with "a voice and nothing more."[69]

Notes

1 An earlier version of this chapter was submitted to *Camera Obscura* and accepted for publication on September 28, 2016, but due to the journal's long queue it was published on May 2018. See Farshid Kazemi, "The Object-Voice: The Acousmatic Voice in the New Iranian Cinema," *Camera Obscura: Feminism, Culture, and Media Studies*, 33, no. 2 (2018): 57–81.

2 Slavoj Žižek, *Reflections of Media, of Politics and Cinema*. Interview with Geert Lovink, *InterCommunication* 14, February 27, 1995, http://www.lacan.com/zizek-reflections.htm. Žižek formulation apropos gaze and voice evokes the work of the French filmmaker and theorist Pascal Bonitzer, see Pascal Bonitzer, *Le regard et la voix: Essais sur le cinéma* (Paris: Union Générale d'Éditions, 1976).

3 Hamid Naficy, *A Social History of Iranian Cinema*, Vol. 4. (Durham, NC: Duke University Press, 2012), 111.

4 At present there is only one study that addresses aspects of the female voice in Iranian cinema, see Rosa Holman, *Iranian Women's Cinema: Recovering Voice, Reclaiming Authority* (Unpublished Ph.D. Thesis, UNSW, Australia, 2014). The vast majority of film scholarship has focused on visuality or the gaze, with only a handful of studies devoted to the female voice in Hollywood or classic cinema. Besides Mary Ann Doane and Kaja Silverman, see Amy Lawrence, *Echo and Narcissus: Women's Voices in Classical Hollywood Cinema* (Berkeley: University of California Press, 1991); Sarah Kozloff, *Invisible Storytellers: Voice-Over Narration in American Fiction Film* (Berkeley: University of California Press, 1988); Britta Sjogren, *Into the Vortex: Female Voice and Paradox in Film* (Urbana and Chicago, IL: University of Illinois Press 2005).

5 Michel Chion, *The Voice in Cinema,* trans. Claudia Gorbman (New York: Columbia University Press, 1999), 23.

6 Chion, *The Voice in Cinema,* 19.

7 Ibid., 1.

8 In *The Four Fundamental Concepts of Psychoanalysis* Lacan states, "These are the *objets a* –the breasts, the faeces, the gaze, the voice. It is in this new term that resides the point that introduces the dialectic of the subject qua subject of the unconscious." See Jacques Lacan, *The Four Fundamental Concepts of Psychoanalysis*, trans. Alan Sheridan (New York: W. W. Norton & Co., 1978), 242.

9 Chion, *The Voice in Cinema,* 1.

10 For a full discussion of the gaze as *objet petit a*, see Chapter 1. Cf. Jacques Lacan "Of the Gaze as *Objet Petit a*," in *The Four Fundamental Concepts of Psychoanalysis*, 67–119.

11 Žižek, *Looking Awry*, 12.

12 Todd McGowan states, "Though Chion doesn't explicitly identify himself with psychoanalytic theory, the *acousmêtre* is a conception of the voice as *objet a*. When the spectator hears the *acousmêtre*, she or he encounters the voice as a detached object. The voice as *objet a* manifests the subject's desire because it is what can be heard beyond the regime of sense." See McGowan, *Psychoanalytic Theory*, 77. But as I have indicated, Chion does refer to Lacan at the beginning of his book, and therefore implicitly makes a connection between the voice as *objet petit a* and the *acousmêtre*.

13 Slavoj Žižek and Renata Salecl ed., *Gaze and Voice as Love Objects* (Durham: Duke University Press, 1996), 3.

14 Lacan, *The Four Fundamental Concepts*, 104.

15 Kaja Silverman, *The Acoustic Mirror: The Female Voice in Psychoanalysis and* Cinema (Bloomington: Indiana University Press, 1988), 49.

16 Silverman, *The Acoustic Mirror*, 49.

17 Chion, *The Voice in Cinema*, 55.

18 Silverman, *The Acoustic Mirror,* ix.

19 McGowan, *Psychoanalytic Theory*, 76.

20 This feature of a gendered space was even part of the architectural structure of traditional homes in Iran, which contained what is called a *biruni*, an outer public space, reserved for men, and the *andaruni* or inner private space, reserved for the women of the household to which men had no access. This gendered architecture was not unknown in the Europe of the 18th and 19th centuries as well, where the *parlor* (from the French, "to speak") in the house was a women's room vs. the *gentlemen's room* was reserved for men.

21 Silverman, *The Acoustic Mirror*, 45.

22 Mottahedeh writes, "In the attempt to cleanse its technologies, the post-Revolutionary Iranian film industry came to produce a cinema that I will argue is the apotheosis of 1970s feminist gaze theory." Mottahedeh, *Displaced Allegories*, 2.

23 Regarding the voice-off Chion writes, "The French term for the word 'voiceover' is 'voix-off' (as if any voice could be 'off') and it designates any acousmatic or bodiless voices in a film that tell stories, provide commentary, or evoke the past. Bodiless can

mean placed outside a body temporarily. Detached from a body that is no longer seen and set into orbit in the peripheral acousmatic field." Chion, *The Voice in Cinema*, 49.

24 Mary Ann Doane, "The Voice in the Cinema: The Articulation of Body and Space," *Yale French Studies*, no. 60, Cinema/Sound (1980): 37.

25 Chion, *The Voice in Cinema*, 22.

26 Silverman, *The Acoustic Mirror*, 48.

27 Chion, *The Voice in Cinema*, 18–19.

28 Ibid, 25.

29 Doane, "The Voice in the Cinema," 40.

30 Ayatollah Ali Moraweji, *Sinama dar ayine-ye fiqh* [Cinema in the mirror of jurisprudence], ed. Mohammad Reza Jabbaran (Tehran: Pazhuhishgah-e farhang va honar-e Islami, 1999). On the question whether the female voice is '*awra*, see 36–47. Also see, Shahla Haeri, "Sacred Canopy: Love and Sex under the Veil," *Iranian Studies*, 42 (2009): 116, 119, 124–25.

31 Bouhdiba, *Sexuality in Islam*, 39.

32 For the interdiction against the female voice in the New Testament, see Corinthians 14:34–5, and 1 Timothy 2:11.

33 Efrat Tseëlon, "On Women And Clothes And Carnival Fools," in *Masquerade and Identities: Essays on Gender, Sexuality and Marginality*, ed. Efrat Tseëlon (London/New York: Routledge, 2001), 155.

34 Abu Ja'far Muhammad b. 'Ali b. al-Husayn b. Babuya al Qummi al-Shaykh al-Saduq, *Man la yahduruhu al-faqih*. Vol. 4, accessed December 15, 2015, http://www.alhassanain.org/arabic/?com=book&id=216

35 L. Clark, '*Hijab* According to the *Hadith*: Text and Interpretation', in *The Muslim Veil in North America*, ed. S.S. Alavi, H. Hoodfar, & S. McDonough, pp. 214–86 (Toronto: Women's Press, 2003) 218.

36 A. El Fadl, *Speaking in God's Name: Islamic Law, Authority and Women* (Oxford: Oneworld, 2001) 185.

37 Shahzad Bashir, *Sufi Bodies* (Columbia: Columbia University Press, 2011), 148. It is important to note that both the female voice and the voice that the Sufi hears later while reciting the Qur'an are each acousmatic voices.

38 Ibid, 149.

39 Ayatollah Ruhollah Khomeini, *Resaleh-ye novin* [New treatise], trans. 'Abdul Karim Baizar-e Shirazi (Tehran: Ketab, 1982), 69. For a discussion of the proscription on the female voice, see Farzaneh Milani, *Veils and Words: The Emerging Voices of Iranian Women Writers* (Syracuse, NY: Syracuse University Press, 1992), 48–52.

40 Naficy, *A Social History of Iranian Cinema Vol. 4*, 104.

41 See Farzin Vejdani, *Making History in Iran: Education, Nationalism, and Print Culture* (Stanford California: Stanford University Press, 2014), 104. In this connection, Vejdani states, "opponents of the women's movement accused many feminists of being irreligious, atheistic, or Babi. The specter of being labeled *Babi*—a term made synonymous with heresy—haunted pioneering women journalists and editors of the late 1910s and 1920s."

42 Lloyd Ridgeon, *Religion and Politics in Modern Iran: A Reader* (London/New York: I.B. Tauris, 2005) 82.

43 Parmis Mozafari, "Carving a Space for Female Solo Singing in Post-revolution Iran," in *Resistance in Contemporary Middle Eastern Cultures: Literature, Cinema and Music* ed. by Karima Laachir, Saeed Talajooy (New York/London: Routledge, 2013), 265. Mozafari notes that since there is a ban on female solo singing in Iran to this day, there are five ways in which female singing is staged in post-revolutionary Iran: (1) singing in choruses, (2) singing along with a second or third voice, (3) singing in a changed voice, (4) singing in private gatherings inside houses, (5) singing in female-only performances in music halls.

44   Bruce Fink, *The Lacanian Subject* (Princeton: Princeton University Press, 1995), 92.

45   Mernissi, *Beyond the* Veil, 141.

46   Bouhdiba, *Sexuality in Islam*, 39; also see H. E. Chehabi, "Voices Unveiled: Women Singers in Iran," in *Iran and Beyond,* ed. Rudi Matthee and Beth Baron (Costa Mesa, California: Mazda Publishers, 2000) 151.

47   Shahrazad who speaks at night and tells stories to her husband King Shahriyar in the frame narrative of *The Thousand and One Nights,* with her sister Dinazad or Dinarzad are in fact the two sisters mentioned in ancient Iranian sources, namely Sanghavak and Arenavak. The two sisters appear in Ferdowsi's *Shahnameh* as Shahrnaz and Arnavaz in the mythic section of the story of Zahak, but they are derived from the much older Zoroastrian Avesta in relation to the myth of Yima (Jamshid) and Azhi Dahaka (Zahak), where they are called: Sanghavak and Arenavak. Note both names end with Vak the female divinity of the voice. See Beyzaie, Bahram Beyzaie, *Hezar Afsan Kojast*? [Where is A Thousand Tales?] (Tehran: Roshangaran va motale'at-e zanan, 2011), 211–34; Also see Farshid Kazemi, "The Speaking Tree: The Mytho-poetics of the Female Voice in Bahram Beyzaie's Cinema," in *The I.B.Tauris Handbook of Iranian Cinema* (London/New York: I.B. Tauris, 2024).

48   Marina Warner, "Freud's Couch: A Case History," *Raritan,* 31, no. 2 (2011): 146–63. See also, Nathan Kravis, *On the Couch: A Repressed History of the Analytic Couch from Plato to Freud* (Cambridge, Massachusetts, MIT Press, 2017). In Kravi's otherwise fine book, the Iranian mytho-history related to the carpet and the couch and its connection to the female voice remains "repressed." For the complex history of the entanglement of Persian carpets as a national commodity in the transnational circuitry see, Minoo Moallem, *Persian Carpets: The Nation as a Transnational Commodity* (London/New York: Routledge, 2018).

49   Warner is fascinated by the frame story of Shahrazad in *The Thousand and One Nights,* and its relation to the female voice and storytelling and has dedicated an entire book in exploring it, but since she does not read Persian, she has not been able to uncover the genealogy of Shahrazad back to the *Shahnameh* and ancient Zoroastrian sources, that I have briefly gestured to. See Marina Warner, *Stranger Magic: Charmed States and the Arabian Nights* (Boston: The Belknap Press/Harvard University Press, 2012).

50   Warner, "Freud's Couch," 154.

51   Roy Huss and Norman Silverstein, *The Film Experience: Elements of Motion Picture Art* (New York: Dell, 1968), 20.

52   For another reading of *Gabbeh* largely from feminist gaze theory of the 70s, see Negar Mottahedeh "'Life Is Color!' Toward a Transnational Feminist Analysis of Mohsen Makhmalbaf's *Gabbeh,*" *Signs,* no. 30 (2004): 1403–28; cf. Mottahedeh, *Displaced Allegories,* 157–68.

53   See Hamid Naficy, *A Social History of Iranian Cinema, 4 Volumes* (Durham: Duke University Press, 2012), 161; also Gönül Dönmez-Colin, *Cinemas of the Other: A Personal Journey with Film-Makers from the Middle East and Central Asia* (Bristol: Intellect, 2006) 20.

54   On Banietemad's cinema see *ReFocus: The Films of Rakhshan Banietemad,* ed. Maryam Ghorbankarimi (Edinburgh: Edinburgh University Press, 2021).

55   Michel Chion, "The Impossible Embodiment," in *Everything You Always Wanted to Know About Lacan, but Were Afraid to Ask Hitchcock,* ed. Slavoj Žižek (London/New York: Verso, 1992), n1 206.

56   Hamid Naficy, "Veiled Voice and Vision in Iranian Cinema: The Evolution of Rakhshan Banietemad's Films," *SOCIAL RESEARCH,* Vol. 67, No. 2 (Summer 2000), 572; cf. Naficy, *A Social History of Iranian Cinema, Volume 4,* 160.

57   Laura Mulvey, *Afterimages: On Cinema, Women and Changing Times* (London: Reaktion Books, 2019), 126.

58   Dolar, *A Voice and Nothing More,* 66.

59 Mladen Dolar, "Telephone and Psychoanalysis," *Filozofski Vestnik*, 29, no. 1 (2008): 12, quoted in Slavoj Žižek, *Less Than Nothing: Hegel and the Shadow of Dialectical Materialism* (London: Verso, 2012), 674.

60 Naficy, "Veiled Voice," 572.

61 Dönmez-Colin, *Cinemas of the Other*, 23.

62 Forough Farrokhzad, *Iman biavarim be aghaz-e faşl-e sard* [Let Us Believe in the Cold Season] (Tehran: Morvarid, 1963), 74–81.

63 See Michael C. Hillman, *A Lonely Woman: Forugh Farrokhzad and Her Poetry* (Washington, DC: Mage, 1987), 160–62.

64 Sheila Whitaker writes, "Safari refers to the use of the telephone as having '… echoes of a well-known poem by Farrokhzad, *All That Remains is the Voice*'." Sheila Whitaker, "Rakhshan Bani-Etemad," in Rose Issa and Sheila Whitaker, *Life and Art: The New Iranian Cinema* (London: British Film Institute, 1999), 72.

65 Chion, *The Voice in Cinema*, 21.

66 Dolar, *A Voice and Nothing More*, 65–66.

67 Gönül Dönmez-Colin, *Cinemas of the Other*, 24.

68 Ibid, 24.

69 The title of Dolar's book on the voice is drawn from a saying reported by Plutarch, "A man plucked a nightingale and, finding but little to eat, said: 'You are just a voice and nothing more.'" Plutarch, Moralia: Sayings of Spartans [Apophthegmata Laconica]. Quoted in Dolar, *A Voice and Nothing More*, 3.

Part II

The Fright of Real Desires

Chapter 3

From Femininity to Masculinity and Back

The Feminine "No!" in *Daughters of the Sun*

In her groundbreaking book, *Professing Selves: Transsexuality and same-sex desire in contemporary Iran*, Afsaneh Najmabadi provides perhaps the most incisive analysis on transsexuality and same-sex desire in modern Iran.[1] Deploying an anthropological methodology as well as theories of gender and sexuality, Najmabadi problematizes the either/or logic that considers Iran either "as a transsexual paradise,"[2] or as the place where "sex reassignment surgery…[is]… performed coercively on Iranian homosexuals."[3] In her analysis Najmabadi notes that Khomeini was the first cleric to have issued a *fatwa* (legal opinion) on transsexuality and thereby inaugurated the whole complex of "legal, Islamic jurisprudential (*fighi*), and biomedical/psycho-sexological discourses"[4] of the State that categorize and partially subsidize sex reassignment surgery. Najmabadi's analysis covers the historical changing relationship with transsexuality, the religio-cultural categories of femininity and masculinity, the emergence of gay, lesbian, and feminist discourses of the 1970s, the advent of the Iranian Revolution and its impact on, medical, political, and religious disputes. She also discusses the autobiographical lived lives of transsexuals narrating their own self-narratives, trans activism, and aspects of popular culture and media coverage. Najmabadi, however, does not take up the task of analyzing Iranian cinema or Iranian documentaries on the subject, and notes, "The international effect of these television and video documentaries [on transsexuality] obviously deserves more than one line noting their quantity, but this is not a task I take up in this book."[5] Indeed, there is an immense lacuna in the scholarship on the subject of transgender and same-sex desire in Iranian cinema.[6] Therein resides the theoretical need for a sustained analysis of the filmic texts that bear on these motifs in post-revolutionary Iranian cinema.

In this chapter, I read Mariam Shahriar's film *Daughters of the Sun* (*Dokhtaran-e Khorshid*, 2000), through the prism of the logic of the feminine "No" and feminine jouissance in Lacanian theory. In the film, the female protagonist Amangol's gender is re-signified from feminine to masculine by her father through the act of shaving her hair and cross-dressing her as a boy in order to send her to a carpet-weaving shop to earn money for the family. This re-signification of her femininity into masculinity stages several motifs that run throughout the film such as transgender, gender and sexual ambiguity, same-sex desire or homoeroticism, and cross-dressing

DOI: 10.4324/9781003531029-6

or transvestism, all of which function as a subversive gesture that problematizes concepts of gender, sexuality and desire in the Iranian cultural imaginary. I focus on several different registers in the representation of Amangol's embodiment of masculinity in both the filmic form (e.g., *mise-en-scène*, cinematography) and content (narrative), in particular how the re-signification of Amangol's body functions as the site of erotic desire, especially the feminine body as the locus where socio-political-religious tensions are staged. Indeed, the technique of shaving Amangol's hair and unveiling her, as well as gender masquerading and passing (as male), enables Shahriar to deploy such strategies of unveiling to problematize and critique not only the imposition of the veil on women in the Islamic Republic, but also the loss of feminine identity, enacted through the repressive measures of the patriarchal symbolic order exemplified in the Iranian State. In the end, Amangol enacts the Lacanian ethics of the authentic act, namely the logic of the feminine "No," where she stands up to the patriarchal symbolic order, through a radical act that entails a suicidal gesture of burning down the carpet-weaving sweat shop and thereby sacrificing the masculinity she had thus far embodied. In this way, she traverses from femininity to masculinity and back, and exemplifies what Lacan calls the feminine "No," through the reassertion of her feminine self-identity by standing up to the figures of paternal authority embodied in the State and religion.

3.1   Daughters of the Sun (*Dokhtaran-e Khorshid*)

Daughters of the Sun (*Dokhtaran-e Khorshid*, 2000) by the first-time director Maryam Shariar, is perhaps one of the underrated art-house films of the post-revolutionary Iranian cinema or New Iranian Cinema. Upon its release the film won several international awards, such as the best fiction film at the Montreal World Film Festival in 2000, and circulated widely in gay and lesbian film festivals and was marketed as "the Iranian *Boys Don't Cry* [1999] – a shocking drama of forbidden love,"[7] and has been called "Iran's first lesbian film."[8] As a diasporic filmmaker Maryam Shahriar returned to Iran after 10 years in Italy during the time of the presidency of Mohammad Khatami (1997–2000), in which some of the regular censorship restrictions imposed on filmmakers by the Ministry of Culture and Islamic Guidance (MCIG) were thought to have loosened due to Khatami's liberal tendencies and his predilection toward the arts. Shahriar returned to shoot *Daughters of the Sun* and initially got an approval for the script by MCIG, but as she finished and submitted the final cut, the censors asked her to cut out the first and final scenes of the film, to which she bravely replied, "over my dead body!" However, she eventually complied with the objections raised by the MCIG and in one night cut out all the "touching" scenes in order to show the film at the annual Fajr International Film Festival in Tehran. The censors never allowed her to screen the film at the festival and after Shahriar convinced one of the representative censors that there "was nothing political" in the film, they finally granted her permission to screen it in theaters outside the festival at 11 p.m. The censors objected that the film was "too bitter" in its portrayal of Iranian society and had questions as to why she had dedicated the film to the late poet Ahmad Shamloo (1925–2000), who was persecuted by both the Shah's regime and the Islamic Republic, and whose belief in the separation of state and religion were well known.[9] The film was never again allowed official screening in Iran.

The film's narrative story centers on the life of a young rural girl, Amangol (Altinay Ghelich Taghani), whose head is shaved by her father and sent out as a "boy" named Aman, to another village to work as a carpet weaver to help support the family. S/he is then locked within a weaving shop, effectively a sweatshop, with three girls (one girl is blind and remains nameless, and the other two are named Bibigol and Belqis), and a domineering and harsh master overseer who punishes them regularly. While there s/he develops an erotic love relationship with one of the girls named Belqis, whose uncle wants her to marry an elderly man, but she wants Aman to marry her and to leave together for her home village Tiva. A wandering darvish (a dervish, or Sufi), who has come to the village, often plays music outside her room and also falls for Aman, and eventually proposes her to run away with him, but s/he refuses to leave with him. Aman eventually refuses Belqis' proposal as well and while returning to the shop after being beaten by the master overseer, finds that Belqis has hanged herself. In the end, as retaliation for their harsh treatment and their slave-like work conditions, Aman sets fire to the weaving sweatshop. There is perhaps a deliberate ambiguity in the ending of the film, as we are unsure if Aman committed suicide by setting the sweatshop on fire while remaining in it. The final scene may be a shot of the real Amangol on the road to her village, or a spectral apparition of Amangol freed from the toils and burdens of the sweatshop.

Since *Daughters of the Sun* (*Dohkhtaran-e Khorshid*), represents one of the few films in the New Iranian Cinema where the logic of cross-dressing opens up the possibility of a transgender or gender passing reading, other scholars have also noted the significance of these elements within the film. In his discussion of the film, Naficy refers to the deployment of these motifs as a way of circumventing the imposition of the veil on women, "Transgender masquerade and passing were among the strategies of critiquing the imposed rules of veiling, while they introduced their own narratives of mistaken gender identity and political complications."[10] As Naficy has pointed out, by removing the veil and shaving the hair, films such as *Daughters of the Sun* render, "faces sufficiently androgynous and ambiguous in their beauty and sexuality to be read as both male and female, creating doubt about both the sexual orientation and the gender of the characters, a most disturbing and counterhegemonic move under a regime founded on the clear demarcation of sexes and their complete separation."[11] Minoo Moallem also reads the film as staging the theme of "passing," as well as containing non-normative modes of erotic desire and sexuality. Moallem states apropos *Daughters of the Sun* that, "the transgendered hero(ine) [Amangol]… by staging antinormative erotic desire, permits fantasizing about and promotion of alternative sexualities. Through silence, eye contact, gestures, and dress codes, an erotically ambivalent situation is set up that allows a display of sexual deviance."[12] Moallem provides a queer reading of the gender ambiguity operative in *Daughters of the Sun* and states, "The queering of the gendered citizens of the Islamic republic and the cinematic display of bodies that are ambiguous with respect to gender mean that... *Daughters of the Sun* transgress the boundaries of citizenship and subvert veiling as a disciplinary tool."[13] Roshanak Kheshti grounds her reading of the film on "cross-dressing" and "passing" as well. She reads the film as a "transgender move" that creates "a temporary space of political and agential potential that many spectators—both domestic and diasporic—seek in the post 1990s New Iranian cinema."[14] Kheshti also sees films such as *Daughters of the Sun* as a way to "help construct sites of gender and sexual transgression that resonate beyond the screen, creating spaces of queer and transgender potential within the Iranian mediascape."[15] Similarly, Vanzan in her brief analysis of *Daughters of the Sun*, sees the film as staging "the queerness of gender" and considers that the motifs of "cross-dressing" in the film, "implies issues of gender identity and ... challenges the heteronormative [film] canon."[16]

Though these scholars consider the deployment of these motifs in such films to be subversive of the Islamic Republic's "essentialization" of gender norms and valorization of heterosexuality as normative, Naficy does not seem to consider these elements to be a truly subversive or transgressive gesture in such films as the *Daughters of the Sun*. Naficy writes, "However transgressive, subversive, or modern these strategies of gender masquerade and passing may seem, in reality they were not, ... [as] there is a rich tradition both in *taziyeh* performances and in the history of modern theater, dance, and cinema in Iran of men playing women's parts."[17] However, Naficy seems to forget that that is precisely the point, since in these older traditions of *ta'ziyeh* it was men who played women's roles or gender masqueraded as women, but in these new films it is women who are playing men's roles, thus the gender role playing are reversed.[18] In fact, the *ta'ziyeh*—the dramatic passion play that represents the martyrdom of Imam Hosayn in Karbala, the third Shi'i Imam—was also performed among women, who cross-dressed for male roles, but all of these Qajar performances of the *ta'ziyeh* was confined to a private female only audience, and not for the general male public.[19]

It should be recalled that motifs such as transgendered bodies, gender passing or masquerading, same-sex desire or homoeroticism, gender/sexual ambiguity, cross-dressing and transvestism are mobilized within several post-revolutionary Iranian films that effectively subvert, transgress, and critique the discourses on gender, sexuality, and desire operative in Iran. Aside from *Daughters of the Sun,* this constellation of motifs is operative within several post-revolutionary Iranian fiction films that include *Adam Barfi* (1995), *Baran* (2001), *Women's Prison* (*Zendan-e zanan*, 2002), and *Offside* (2006), with *Facing Mirrors* (*Aynehaye Rooberoo*, 2011) as the only film that directly addresses the issue of trans lives in Iran.[20] The filmic representation of these motifs is often staged through female characters (excepting *Adam Barfi*, a comedy in which a man cross-dresses as a woman in order to escape Iran) that are gender masquerading or gender passing as male, often with their heads shaved and unveiled, which enables the directors to deploy such techniques of unveiling to problematize and critique the imposition of the veil. Indeed, these motifs are deployed not only as a critique of the veil but can be seen as strategies to critique the oppressive measures on non-normative genders and sexualities in Iranian socio-political imaginary.

This gender masquerading reversal in which women are gender passing as men through the technique of cross-dressing in post-revolutionary Iranian cinema exemplified by *Daughters of the Sun*, is part of the transgressive dimension of these films, but as I argue the subversive core of the film lies elsewhere, in Aman's ethical act of the feminine "No!" enacted at the film's end as the reassertion of her feminine identity which was put under erasure. However, none of the scholars mentioned above theorize the transgender field in Iranian cinema through the prism of psychoanalytic theory. The only single study solely dedicated to the representations of transgender in cinema is the book by John Phillips called *Transgender on Screen*. Indeed, Phillips in his book also deploys Freudian and Lacanian psychoanalytic film theory as a theoretical lens for reading the transgender subject in the filmic texts that he analyses, as he states, "…my approach presupposes an unconscious sub-text which is accessible to psychological and psychoanalytical investigation. Hence, the application of Freudian and Lacanian theory – essential tools in the exploration of a powerful textual unconscious."[21] Therefore, my own deployment of psychoanalytic theory will fill the gap in the scholarly literature on theorizing transgender representation and female homoerotic desire in Iranian cinema, and in cinema more broadly, in light of Lacanian film theory.[22]

Before I proceed directly into the analysis of the film, it is important at the outset to clarify some terms that I deploy throughout this chapter. The term "transgender," is often deployed as an umbrella term that designates bodies that have been re-signified male or female. Therefore, by transgender I mean broadly the act of passing or traversing from one gender to another (from male-to-female or female-to-male), which may or may not involve medical treatments (hormone treatments, etc.) or sexual reassignment surgery (which in Amangol's case it clearly does not). This can include the symbolic re-signification of the subject's body as either "female," even when biologically "male" (male sexual organ) or as "male," even when biologically "female" (female sexual organ) (which is what is at work in Amangol's case). My engagement with the transgender field operative in this film is a contribution to a broader rapprochement between Lacanian theory and transgender studies, as well as to gender and queer theory.[23]

I also use the terms cross-dressing and transvestism synonymously as an act of dressing, behaving, or appearing in ways that are normatively associated with the opposite sex, regardless of sexuality. In this respect Marjorie Garber's definition of transvestism is relevant here, as she states, "transvestism is a space of possibility structuring and confounding culture: the disruptive element that intervenes, not just a category crisis of male and female, but the crisis of category itself."[24] In this reading, trasvestism or cross-dressing stages the crisis of the category of male/female, heterosexual/homosexual, but I would go even further and suggest from a Freudo-Lacanian perspective, the crisis of category itself is constitutive of sexuality as such.

In another instance Garber relying significantly on Lacan's notion of the symbolic order states that, "there can be no culture without the transvestite, because the transvestite marks the entrance into the Symbolic."[25] In other words, at the very threshold of entrance into the symbolic order stands the figure of the transvestite, signaling that the symbolic functions to categorize and stabilize through the signifier concepts of gender and sexuality, male vs. female, heterosexual vs. homosexual. However, I would argue that when we are dealing with sex and the subject, since in psychoanalytic theory the subject is always a sexed subject, the subject is not reducible to the signifier, but is its ultimate misfire. There is no way of having any knowledge of a sexed subject (him or her), as Copjec says, "*Sex serves no other function than to limit reason, to remove the subject from the realm of possible experience or pure understanding* [emphasis in the original]."[26] This is why sexuality is always co-incident with subjectivity in psychoanalytic theory, which is unknowable and unfathomable to sense and reason. As Copjec states, "sex... for psychoanalysis, [is] never simply a natural fact, it is also never reducible to any discursive construction, to sense, finally."[27]

Therefore, what the cross-dressing figure stages is the radical undecidability of sexuality itself; in other word, cross-dressing foregrounds the logic of ambiguity at the abyss of human sexuality, and what psychoanalysis teaches us is "not [to] confuse the fact of bisexuality -that is, the fact that male and female signifiers cannot be distinguished absolutely with a denial of sexual difference."[28] To put it in Lacanian terms: sexual difference is real, rather than symbolic[29]; that is to say, sexual difference resists symbolization absolutely.[30] This is the antinomy at the heart of human sexuality, which throws reason into contradiction at every turn in its efforts to understand it, as Lacan states, "Everything implied by the analytic engagement with human behavior indicates not that meaning reflects the sexual, but that it makes up for it."[31] In other words, the sexual makes up for our inability to make sense of it, not that it reflects meaning or sense.

3.2 Symbolic Castration and the Name-of-the-Father

In the opening scene of the film Amangol is framed in the foreground looking offscreen with a large portion of her hair partially revealed (a clear violation of the system of modesty), and three female figures (her sisters) are framed in the background mise-en-scène. Then in the next shot the camera shows in a medium close-up the ground and pieces of her long hair falling to the ground at the center of the frame. The loss of her hair is symbolic of her feminine identity—her gendered signifier as a woman has been shorn off. Through the act of cutting her hair she is re-signified from femininity to masculinity. Then in a long shot Amangol is shown sitting while her father continues to shave off her hair and the camera through a close-up of her face shows her melancholy face and downcast glance. She is clothed in a dress in this scene, which acts as another signifier of her female gender and feminine identity. Amanghol's father, who is cutting her hair, is blurred or out of focus in the background, as she slowly raises her head and gazes off-screen into the distance, foreclosing the possibility of the direct gaze into the camera as part of the system of modesty in Iranian cinema. Naficy in his brief analysis of this scene in *Daughters of the Sun* states, "shorn of her hair and androgenized, the girl may also reveal the other forbidden feature of a woman: her direct gaze in close-up, which masculinizes her, since this counters the demure and averted look required of women."[32] However, the problem is that there is no direct gaze into the camera by Aman, as the gaze is toward an invisible point off screen. In this precise way, the logic of the averted gaze in the Islamic system of modesty is maintained.

In the film the cutting of Amangol's hair has an important symbolic and metaphorical function. Indeed, for Maryam Shahriar the shaving of Aman's head, "became a great metaphor for the loss of identity."[33] The image of shaving Amangol's hair has historical reverberations with the penal shaving of women's hair in 19th- and early 20th-century Iran, where "the penal shaving of women's hair, [was] almost always done in cases involving illicit sex, whether adultery, prostitution, or procurement. Shaving women's hair was a way of removing a core element of their sexuality."[34] Not to mention femininity. The emphasis on the forced cutting of women's hair was on public "humiliation and shame," where these women would usually be paraded on a pack animal backward through the town or city.[35] Although there is no explicit reference to the history of shaving women's hair as a penal punishment, the image of shaving Amangol's hair by her father unconsciously excavates this past, sedimented as it were in Amangol's sorrow laden countenance.

Hamid Naficy reads the shaving of Amangol's hair as a strategy for unveiling or showing the female hair without a veil, "She [Shahriar] shows the protagonist's long hair at the film's beginning, violating the modesty rules, however, only when it is detached from her, and in extreme close-ups as the locks fall to the ground after being cut. With this strategy, Shahriar pointedly noted that the only permissible way to show women's actual hair is in its disembodied form."[36] Although the shaving of her hair is a clear strategy of unveiling, however, beyond this formal technique of unveiling there is another significance to the shaving of Aman's hair in the narrative structure of the film. To put it in psychoanalytic terms: the cutting of Amangol's hair represents *castration* and the *loss of the mother*. In Jeffry Anderson's psychoanalytic interpretation of the fable of Rapunzel (1980), there are three symbolic meanings or functions to the cutting of hair, namely "castration, loss of the mother, and reparation."[37] Indeed, as we shall see, excluding reparation, the other two symbolic registers of castration and the loss of the mother are operative in the cutting of Amangol's hair.

There is a structural parallel between the shaving of Amangol's hair, and the cutting of her name from Amangol to Aman. The motif of gender passing is gestured in the name of Amangol being transformed to Aman, as the name itself is at once a "castrated" name. Here the "name" stands as the signifier for the resignification of gender identity. The excising of the feminine element of the name from the masculine inscribes within itself the gender passing process. The name Aman is a male name meaning "protection" (literally s/he is the "protection/ Aman" of the family from poverty) and the word *gol* means "flower" in Persian. In this way *gol*, which is cut off from the first part of the name Aman, like her hair, is the feminine aspect that must be cut in order for her to be re-signified as masculine. In this sense, she is "castrated" from her feminine identity, from her flower or *gol*, symbolizing her vagina, which incidentally many Iranian mothers often call their baby daughter's vagina *gol*, or playfully redoubled *gol-gol*, which is an instance of what Lacan would have called *lalangue*,[38] and with the further connotation of sexual de-flowering, which will have reverberations within the later part of the filmic narrative. Here, the cut or castration of *gol* from Aman, which stands as the signifier of feminine identity, is the Lacanian symbolic castration. In Žižek's formulation of Lacan, symbolic castration occurs when the subject, in this instance Aman, experiences the "gap between my direct psychological identity and my symbolic identity, (the symbolic mask or title I wear, defining what I am for and in the big Other)..."[39] As Žižek states elsewhere, "I am what I am through signifiers that represent me, signifiers constitute my symbolic order"[40] Thus, Aman is represented through the signifiers of her shaved head and new name, and thereby (re)inscribed into the symbolic order as a masculine subject through these signifiers.

This symbolic castration is re-doubled cinematically in the next shot. As Aman is shown leaving the village with her/his hair completely shaven, s/he is foregrounded while her/his family is out of focus in the background, s/he then glances back at the family and the father blocks her mother with his hand, so as to obstruct their reunion. The key feature to be noted here is the gesture of obstructing the mother by the father, in other words to prohibit access to the mother. This is the enactment of Lacanian symbolic castration signified by the term, "The-Name-of-the-Father" *(le nom-du-père)* the paternal symbolic authority. According to Lacan, The-Name-of-the-Father (not the real father as such) is associated with the symbolic order, also called the big Other: the network of pre-existing social reality, such as language, laws, and customs (which is why in Lacan's ternary register of the imaginary, symbolic, and real – The-Name-of-the-Father is one of the operations of the symbolic order), into which the child is born. As Lacan states, "It is in the *name of the father* that we must recognize the support of the symbolic function which, from the dawn of history, has identified his person with the figure of the law."[41] Lacan often played with the homophony "of *le nom du père* (the name of the father) and *le 'non' du père* (the 'no' of the father)," as an emphasis of the "legislative and prohibitive function of the symbolic father."[42] In Lacan's earlier seminars the Name-of-the-Father is related to Freud's notion of castration, as the process that severs the child's attachment to the mother. For Lacan, "[This] relationship to the phallus ... is established without regard to the anatomical difference of the sexes."[43] Therefore since the phallus is symbolic in its signification, both girls and boys go through the castrating experience through the operation of the Name-of-the-Father.[44] Thus, the father in this scene stands as the Lacanian Name-of-the-Father, who castrates Aman's attachment to the mother by denying access to the (m)other, and thereby (re)inscribing her/him into the symbolic order as masculine.

The exemplary case of the deployment of the motifs of gender ambiguity and cross-dressing in the figure of Aman(gol), is brought to bear at the very beginning of *Daughters of the Sun*. In the same scene before leaving the village, s/he is shown in a medium close-up with her clothes as yet unrevealed, but as the camera is positioned behind her and shows her walking on the road, we see that she is dressed as a boy, head shaved and no longer in a dress. The re-signifying of her body, or trans gendering her identity is staged through two markers: hair and dress. Here the motif of cross-dressing or transvestism comes to the fore in the figure of Aman. The cross-dressing motif also gestures toward the performance of gender by Aman, but *not* the "performativity" of gender as theorized by Judith Butler where she states, "There is no gender identity behind the expressions of gender; … identity is performatively constituted by the very 'expressions' that are said to be its results."[45] Aman's performance of masculinity is gestured to in another scene in the film, where Aman arrives at the village where s/he is to work as a weaver. Aman is shown in a long shot walking on the road, with her gait mimicking a "man," or the way she imagines a man would walk, performing and enacting masculinity with her feet striding wide apart from each other.

3.3   The Depressive Position and Melancholic Identification

One of the consistent scenes throughout the *Daughters of the Sun* is the anguish and melancholia that is palpable on the face of Aman(gol). The close-ups of Aman(gol)'s shaved head and face recalls another similarly shaved head and anguished face in the history of cinema, namely the close-up of the face of Joan of Arc (Renée Jeanne Falconetti) in Carl Theodor Dreyer's masterpiece, *The Passion of Joan of Arc* (1928). How to read the melancholy writ large on Aman(gol)'s face. In Kristeva's deployment of Klein's concept of the child's normal psychic development, the child accepts the depressive position in the process of "normalization"; following this formulation, Aman seems unable to accept the depressive position due to her hair being shaved (the signifier of her femininity) and seems to persist in it. On the other hand, Aman's melancholy throughout the film may recall Butler's interpretation of melancholic identification (reinterpreted from Freud) with the lost object or the mother, and her desire for the reconstitution of gender identity or feminine self-identity. What must be problematized apropos Amangol's re-signification into a masculine identity is that she is forced into the masculine transgender subject position. The new transgender identity is forced or imposed upon her from outside by paternal authority, the figure of the father, perhaps with the logic that by becoming re-signified as a masculine subject, she may be less harassed in her new work environment (which of course does nothing to save her from the abuses and beatings of the master overseer). This is significant, since she has not chosen to go through the "gender reassignment right,"[46] as Kheshti calls it, of her own accord. There is no agency here, but rather a forced choice. Unlike the standard categories of transgender identity in the West, in which trans subjects themselves choose to go through the transitioning process, either from male-to-female or female-to-male, Aman has had no choice but to go through the "transitioning" process as it were. This precisely stages the depressive dimension and melancholia writ large on the face of Aman as she leaves her village, and through-out the film. Deleuze and Guattari's statement that "the face is a veritable mega-phone,"[47] applies perfectly to the face of Amangol, bespeaking the silent scream of her sorrow. Since Aman experiences symbolic castration through the Name-of-the-Father (*le nom du père*, a phrase in French with its homophony, the "No" of the father, which Lacan often plays with) by severing her attachment to the mother and denying her access to the object of desire, the father thereby inscribes Aman into the world of language and culture: in other words, into the symbolic order through this violent inscription, which is why she persists in the depressive position and internal-izes the lost object (mother) via melancholic identification.

Julia Kristeva in her discussion of "depression" deploys the psychoanalyst Mela-nie Klein's notion of the "depressive position" at the origin of the subject's entrance into the symbolic order.[48] According to Kristeva, within the subject's normative psy-chic development, "the ego takes shape by way of a depressive working through."[49] In this view of the child's standard psychic development, as Elaine Miller notes, depression "is caused by the child's gradual and necessary separation, as it grows older, from its 'mother,' or primary provider, and its subsequent assumption of a subjective identity in the 'father's' realm of language and social interaction."[50] In this perspective, the subject must be installed into the world of language, law, and culture or the symbolic order, and cannot go back to the earlier stage of being fused with the mother, though the child can, and often does attempt to recover the mother, "along with other objects, in imagination and, later, in words."[51] Therefore, the de-pressive position, as Klein calls this transitionary phase, is effectively a necessary stage in the process of the child's normative development. Miller then rhetorically asks why Kristeva would deploy the image of "decapitation and recapitation as a figure for this process?" She then states, "Decapitation has long been associated with castration in the literature of psychoanalysis."[52] Indeed, if we replace the "cut-ting of hair" rather than "decapitation" as the figure for this process, as Anderson's psychoanalytic discussion of the cutting of hair as a symbol of castration demon-strates (see above), then we can see how Aman has gone through this process and persists in the *depressive position*. Hence, the trans or transsexual subject in Iran may be said to persist in the "depressive position," unable to accept it as the normal course of psychic development, since normative Iranian society's stigma on trans subjects (in this instance not the Law (*sharia*) but social customs) does not allow for an easy traversal of the depressive position by the transgender subject.

A related question apropos Aman's character is that of melancholia. Why does Amangol seem to persist in melancholia throughout the film? It is possible that she persists in her attachment to the lost object, namely the mother. Given the gender and sexual undecidability operative in the very texture of the film related to Aman, the question is if her attachment to the mother is related to the Freudian incest taboo, or to a prohibition of homosexual desire for the (m)other? In one reading, this melancholic identification with the lost object may be constitutive of her gender identity and sexuality, since for Judith Butler gender is at least partly acquired "through the repudiation of homosexual attachments; the girl becomes a girl through being subject to a prohibition which bars the mother as an object of desire and installs that barred object as a part of the ego, indeed, as a *melancholic identification* (my emphasis)."[53] Hence, for Butler gender identity is formed partially as the result of rejecting homosexual attachment (i.e., a girl's attachment for the mother as the object of desire), and thus the identification contains both the "loss and the desire" which forms the melancholic identification.

According to Butler heterosexuality is produced through the prohibition of homosexuality even prior to the prohibition of incest, as Butler states, "This heterosexuality is produced not only through implementing the prohibition on incest but, prior to that, by enforcing the prohibition on homosexuality."[54] For Butler then, the homosexual attachment has a more originary or primordial prohibition then incest taboo, since the first object of libidinal attachment for the child is the same-sex parent, while the price for becoming a "normal" heterosexual subject is to identify with the lost object, in order to become a "normal" subject. A girl identifies with maternal femininity, a boy identifies with the paternal masculinity, and in this way, you accept the loss and symbolize it, since you identify with the lost object and become a normalized subject. In Butler's reading, since homosexuals remain true to their love for the lost object (e.g., mother or father), and are unable to symbolize the loss, they internalize and incorporate the lost object within their psychic economy and in this way, they persist with *melancholic identification*. But this line of argument by Butler seems to contradict her theory of gender as "performatively produced."[55] Butler provides a succinct definition of performativity: "In the first instance, performativity must be understood not as a singular or deliberate 'act,' but, rather, as the reiterative and citational practice by which discourse produces the effects that it names."[56] If this is true, then how can the child identify with the same-sex parent prior to performative identification? It is as it were, the girl or boy experiences sexual difference (father or mother) prior to any performative constructions through discourse in society and seems to indicate an essentialization of homosexual identity before any performative enacting or construction of gender. This is one of the theoretical problematics inherent in Butler's gender theory of performativity.

Now, the properly theoretical question to be asked here is: why does Aman persist in her melancholic identification as it were? This question is answered within the formal texture of the film, especially at the film's end, since Amangol's melancholy is due to the loss of feminine identity, and the forced choice of embodying masculinity, rather than to the loss of the "homosexual attachment" à la Butler. In this way, the film may also represent a subversive gesture to the possibility of enforced sexual reassignments in the Islamic Republic, as Naficy notes, "Significantly, this use of transsexual passing in fictional films was happening at the same time that transgender surgery as a social practice was on the rise among young men and women and dealt with in documentary films."[57] Indeed, due to the prohibition on homosexual desire in Islamic Law (*sharia*) in the Islamic Republic, some men or women who are homosexuals have been persuaded to go through the transitioning process.

Apropos the motif of cross-dressing, in one scene the blind girl is shown putting pieces of black wool threads as a mustache on Bibigol. Here the masculine gender masquerading has a comedic effect, and the two girls start to laugh. The mustache of course stands for virility, masculinity, and the phallus.[58] It is as if there is something inherently comical about the masculine subject. There is always a minimum of comedic effect with masculinity, with this imagined "thing" (the male member) protruding outward – the penis – from the male figure. It is as if there is inherently a dimension of "imposture" to the male subject,[59] to masculinity as such, and the female subject or femininity is the real subject.[60]

This is precisely what Lacan himself states apropos the female subject, "By and large, woman is much more real and much truer than man…"[61] What Lacan means here by "more real" is that the female subject or the feminine position is closer to the real, that is, femininity is at the inherent limit of signification; hence women are closer to the void at the heart of human subjectivity. Now the laughter of the girls draws the attention of the master overseer, who directs his threatening gaze toward them to see why they are laughing and enjoying themselves. The master figure represents the Iranian state apparatus at its purest—the figure of paternal authority always denying or controlling access to enjoyment, or jouissance. This figure of the master with all its patriarchal trappings, acts as the Lacanian Name-of-the-Father, namely the whole symbolic network of language, laws, and customs (in this instance laws based on Islamic jurisprudence or *fiqh*) with its super-ego injunctions and prohibitions and its controlling machinery. The scene could also gesture to another ambiguity, the possibility of the girls' knowledge of the gender masquerading of Amangol, her cross-dressing: that is they may already know that "he" is really a "she," and find the whole masquerade somewhat comical.

In one of the most cinematically beautiful scenes in *Daughters of the Sun*, Aman is shown behind the weaving apparatus or loom, which thinly veils her like a curtain or screen. S/he begins to silently read a letter and one of the girls (Belqis) asks her if it's a letter from her parents. Then in one of the most formally beautiful shots in the film the profile of the face of Belqis is foregrounded, while in the background the figure of Aman is framed with her shaved head, behind the screen of the carpet tapestry. The mise-en-scène separates the two of them with the weaving apparatus as we view Aman through the threads of the loom, while Belqis stands on the other side of the loom in the foreground. The screen not only gestures to the prison like reality of the weaving shop in which they live but symbolizes the patriarchal and masculinist order of the Islamic Republic in Iran. At the narrative level, this division of Belqis and Aman via the screen of the loom, already formally gestures through the mise-en-scène that the love between the two is doomed at the outset, even before we learn of their erotic interlude later in the narrative.

3.4 Female Homoeroticism and *Objet petit a*

In an important scene, the beginning of the homoerotic relation between Belqis with Aman is staged while sitting alone in the room weaving on the loom. Belqis glances at Aman and says to him/her "come" (*bia*—both the English and the Persian word here have obvious sexual connotations), and Aman goes and sits beside her. The whole scene is shot from behind the loom, it is as if the loom acts as a protecting screen from the overflowing of erotic tension as they turn and glance at each other silently and longingly and we get a scene cut. The loom as screen or veil also functions formally at the level of censorship imposed on visuality by the Islamic Republic on Iranian cinema and foregrounds the tension that the only way to show the possibilities of an erotic relay of glances on screen is when both characters are literally female. Then there is a scene cut to black. This scene cut may be interpreted as the moment in which the two will have an erotic intimacy, which for obvious reasons could not have been represented on screen due to the Islamic system of modesty (*hejab*). In this scene, same sex or lesbian desire is staged through the gender ambiguity or cross-dressing of Aman.

Gender passing as a boy Aman(gol) finds herself the object of Belqis' desire. It is through this gender passing or masquerading that a full configuration of female homoerotic desire is staged between Aman(gol) and Belqis. Therein resides Lacan's lesson of *objet petit a,* or the object cause of desire. Here, gender ambiguity acts as a signifier for the arbitrariness of the signified, in which desire acts as its own cause, namely as the object-cause of desire, where who one desires (regardless of which gender, sex, etc.) is of little or no consequence—for the motif of misrecognition itself stages the ambiguity inherent in or constitutive of desire. This is the Lacanian *objet petit a,* at its most elementary. As Slavoj Žižek states the object-cause of desire is: "an object that is, in a way, posited by desire itself. The paradox of desire is that it posits retroactively its own cause, i.e., the object *a* is an object that can be perceived only by a gaze 'distorted' by desire [like the distorted gaze of Belqis for Aman], an object that does not exist for an 'objective' gaze."[62] In this sense, the gaze of Belqis is distorted by her desire, which is precisely why she *sees* in Aman what she desires (i.e., a man), not what Aman is in her/himself in objective reality. Therefore, though Aman is misrecognized as male and desired by Belqis, but conversely Aman seems to desire Belqis precisely as woman, even though s/he is gender masquerading as male. But, upon closer inspection things may even be more complex and ambiguous here: since Aman was first misrecognized as a boy, after the erotic encounter (with all the formal elements of the scene indicating that they were intimate) Belqis could no longer have remained innocent of Aman's true gender identity, or could she?[63] Anna Vanzan in her reading of the relation of Aman and Belqis has also noted this ambiguity operative in the film, "It is true that Bilghis does not know (or does she?) that Aman is a girl, but Aman is well aware of being a girl: or isn't s/he? Cross-dressing, in this case, opens a window onto gender ambiguity, as it allows the film to suggest that 'other' ways of love and desire are also possible."[64]

Let us imagine the erotic scene as it would have been staged had there been no censors to cut the scene and to prevent its enactment. The erotic encounter could have been structured like the scene in Freud's description of the primal trauma of fetishism, as Žižek notes apropos the inversion of this primal scene and the failed sexual encounter in Neil Jordan's *The Crying Game* (1992), "the child's gaze, sliding down the naked female body towards the sexual organ, is shocked to find nothing where one expects to see something (a penis) - in the case of *The Crying Game,* the shock is caused when the eye finds *something* where it expected *nothing.*"[65] But, in the case of the *Daughters of the Sun*, the shock would have been caused when Belqis finds *nothing* where she expected *something*. This is the inversion of the standard metaphysical question: why is there nothing, instead of something? The metaphysical question being: why is there *something*, instead of *nothing*? If we were to gender this metaphysical question, then it is clearly on the side of femininity. This is why the primal scene of the trauma of fetishism, has something of the order of a metaphysical problem to it, not simply of masculinity or femininity but of *sexuality* as such.[66]

It may be argued that the film continues with this formal ambiguity, because it allows the spectator to read Belqis' continued desire for Aman, possibly as a sign of her love beyond the discovery of her gender identity as female. It is precisely here, after the potential revelation of Aman's feminine gender that the dimension of true love emerges in Belqis since she persists in her love of Aman perhaps despite this revelation. In another scene, in a moment full of fragility, Belqis exposes herself to Aman, in all her vulnerability, and says to her, "come let us go together to Tiva." Then Belqis describes Tiva to Aman in all its ethereal beauty, as a paradisal place full of luxurious and verdant trees and fragrant groves and colorful flowers, where they can build a house together. Then in a moment of full pathos Belqis says to Aman, "marry me, I'll make you happy." Aman, welled up with tears, responds: "Okay, I will." Indeed, this is the sublime moment in which true love emerges, where the beloved one (Aman), returns the love of the loving one (Belqis), as Žižek has noted apropos the transvestite character, Dil, in *The Crying Game*: "It is only at this point that true love emerges... we witness the sublime moment when *eromenos* (the loved one) changes into *erastes* (the loving one) by stretching out her hand and 'returning love'. This moment designates the 'miracle' of love, the moment of the 'answer of the Real...'"[67] This perhaps enables us to understand what Lacan means when he considers that the subject itself has the status of an "answer of the Real."[68]

Aman's statement "Ok, I will" to Belqis' proposal, is precisely the Lacanian "answer of the Real," the moment where she stretches out her hand "returning love." Perhaps in this instance what the other, Belqis, sees in Aman, is what there is in her/him more than himself/herself, the *objet petit a* or object cause of desire; in this sense the asymmetry of the loving one (Belqis) who loves the beloved one (Aman) is that what she sees in the loved one, may be a "man," while what the loved one knows of himself/herself is that s/he is a "woman." However, it may be that Belqis loves Aman regardless of the discovery of her gender identity as "woman," and it is precisely here that true love emerges when the object of love, also becomes the subject of love, that is, when the one who is moved by this gesture of love, the beloved, also returns love. This is the "miracle of love." Lacan states, "... the lover appears here as the desiring subject [*le sujet du désir*], with all the weight that the term 'desire' has for us, and the beloved as the only one in the couple who has something."[69] This something is the *objet petit a*. One evidence in the film that gestures to the possibility that Belqis may know Aman's true female identity is gestured to when Belqis discovers the letter that Aman's parents have sent about her mother being sick. Since it is a private letter, which Belqis only accidentally discovers and reads, it is very unlikely that Amangol's parents would have still pretended that she was a boy. Thus, the letter would have been addressed to her as their daughter Amangol. As Lacan may have put it, "a letter always arrives at its destination"[70]; since although the addressee at the level of imaginary and symbolic was Amangol, but its real addressee (real in its full Lacanian sense) was Belqis.

In this formulation, love is the "answer of the Real,"[71] the real in the Lacanian sense of "the impossibility of symbolization" or that which is "beyond symbolization," which causes the loving one to see the beloved one through the distorted prism of desire. At the formal level, the gender and sexual ambiguity is maintained as we are no longer sure if Aman is being proposed as "man" or as "woman," since if an erotic interlude did occur, then it is likely that this is an instance of female homoerotic desire, especially after the revelation of the content of the letter. This formal ambiguity or formal tension is maintained due to the censors, since Aman by masquerading and cross-dressing as a "man" (or as transgender) would not be scandalous simply by displaying affection for Belqis, but rather if what is staged on screen is homoeroticism between two women, or lesbian love and desire, which in the very formal texture of the film it is precisely what is staged, since both actors are literally women.

The radical core of the *Daughters of the Sun*, is its female homoeroticism or same-sex desire, which is staged through the transgender move. Indeed, sexual reassignment in Iran which is approved and even encouraged by the state apparatus, should not be considered or thought of as radical, for this procedure signifies nothing radical for the Islamic Republic, as through surgery what is still maintained is the distinction between the two genders, female and male, masculine and feminine. What is unacceptable, however, is to have subjects (male or female) that desire the same sex: this is the radical category, which the state would not tolerate. You can transition from one sex to another, since you are still dealing with the accepted sexual difference, male vs. female, which remains within the coordinates of Shi'i legal discourse in Iran, even sanctioned by its spiritual and political leader Ayatollah Rouhallah Khomeini, but once you have same-sex desire, that is the unlawful category, since that is the disavowed kernel of the Iranian states sexual imaginary which is deemed illegal and even punishable by death.

But where is Tiva, this paradisal space for which we would look for in vain in the geographical coordinates of Iran, since no such village exists in Iran. Perhaps Tiva than is an imagined space, a utopian space beyond the Law—with all its super-ego injunctions and prohibitions—that stands for an autonomous zone of freedom, beyond the coordinates of the patriarchal symbolic order and the imposition of the *sharia*, exemplified by the authoritarian figures such as the master overseer, Amangol's father, and Belqis' uncle, all of whom may represent the oppressive and repressive aspects of the Iranian state apparatus and its patriarchal trappings.

3.5   Love beyond Law and Feminine Jouissance

On an errand outside with the master overseer in the woods, Aman hears the sound of a musical instrument located in an off screen space, the *tar* (the instrument is played by the Persian master composer Hossein Alizadeh who has composed the musical score for the film), whose sound seems to fascinate Aman and s/he follows the sound of the diegetic music while the overseer stops to relieve himself. Then when the camera pans to her point of view, we see the village in a long distant shot, whilst the diegetic music echoes from the village. In the next scene, Aman is sitting in her/his dimly lit room beside her loom, in a medium shot, the camera zooms in and moves steadily closer to her face, and we hear the sound of instrumental music again that s/he heard whilst walking outside, but this time the instrument is *setar* (also played by Alizadeh), and Aman is shown slowly rubbing her hands and her face and her shaved head. At the level of the pure texture of the filmic text, it is as if the character of Aman is relishing her freedom from the injunction of the *hejab*, and through this formal strategy of unveiling, Shahriar seems to allude to this freedom being unavailable to women in Iran. The camera begins to move to a close-up of her face—with a look of a distinct enjoyment, an ecstatic enjoyment, which in Lacanian terms is called feminine jouissance.[72] Then s/he is shown putting on a dress and begins to dance like a whirling darvish to the ecstatic undulations of the Sufi music and with her dress flowing like the garment of the Mowlavi whirling dervishes—the Sufi order of the Persian Sufi mystic and poet Jalal al-Din Rumi—she spins in ecstasy (what in Sufi discourse is termed, *hal*).[73] In fact, Lacan alludes to the Sufis in relation to the "knowledge of jouissance," and speaking of Buddhism and Islam where such knowledge may be found he states, "Need I mention the tantras, for one of these religions, and the Sufis for the other?"[74] Now, this moment may be read as an instance of what Lacan calls "Love beyond the Law" and feminine jouissance, in which there is a feminine sublimation of the drives, through the "asexual" or non-sexual "Thing" or *das Ding*, such as *music* in this instance, as an enactment of ecstatic surrender that is emancipatory. Referring to this logic of love beyond the law Žižek states that what one should bear in mind about "this direct asexual sublimation of drive, is that it is… beyond meaning: meaning can only take place within the (symbolic) Law; the moment we trespass the domain of Law, meaning changes into enjoy-meant, jouissance."[75]

Through this feminine jouissance or enjoyment expressed through her body via music and dance, Aman reaches an experience of "ecstatic surrender" and freedom. Aman seems to rise above the imperative of the Law symbolized by the oppressive master overseer and by extension the Law as symbolized by the Islamic Republic with its constant prohibitions and super-ego injunctions to obey the religious law (*sharia*), etc. However, here Žižek fails to go as far as Lacan himself, for Lacan equates this feminine jouissance with mysticism or the ecstatic experience of the mystics. This Lacanian notion of feminine jouissance is not unlike the experiences of the Sufis during *sama'*, which has a precise bodily component, in their acts of reaching ecstatic states (*vajd* or *hal*) via dance and music.[76] Lacan in the seminar *Encore* (meaning "again" which gestures toward the never ending or unsatifiability of desire or the circuit of jouissance in the derive, but also Lacan's promise to return to the questions of his Seminar VII, *the Ethics of Psychoanalysis*), specifically articulates the idea of a feminine jouissance as "a supplementary jouissance," beyond what the phallic function designates as jouissance, as he states, "There is a jouissance, a jouissance of the body that is…'beyond the phallus'."[77] This feminine jouissance "of the body" is, according to Lacan, ineffable, since men and women may experience it, but know nothing about it.[78] It is at the very limits of being and language, and therefore it is an encounter with the real. As Žižek admits in one instance, "mysticism… is the encounter with the Real."[79] Again, here there is a homology between the ineffability of the experience of the Sufi mystics (and the mystics of most religious traditions), which has been termed by Michael A. Sells as the "Mystical Languages of Unsaying."[80] Indeed, later in the same text Lacan explicitly links this feminine jouissance with the experience of the mystics, exemplified by the female Christian mystic Saint Teresa. He writes, "There are men [mystics] just as good as women. It happens. And who also feel just fine about it. Despite – I won't say their phallus – despite what encumbers them [men] that goes by that name, they get the idea or sense that there must be a jouissance that is beyond. Those are the ones we call mystics."[81] This jouissance or enjoyment that is beyond the phallus is feminine jouissance. Here, Aman's experience is at once erotic and ecstatic—it is a perfect instantiation of what Lacan calls feminine jouissance. In this way, Shahriar seems to deploy the various elements of this scene—Aman's unveiled shaved hair, dancing, and enjoyment of music; all things which are forbidden to women in public spaces according to the system of modesty laws or *hejab* in Iran—as a strategy to perform a critique of the Islamic Republic and its repressive and oppressive laws against women.

3.6 Misrecognition and Male Homoeroticism (*shahed-bazi*)

One of the central elements of the *Daughters of the Sun* is the logic of misrecognition, wherein the misrecognition of identity in the motif of gender ambiguity and cross-dressing are deployed to stage this logic. This misrecognition can be linked to Badiou's discussion of the "passion of the Real," where taking up Lacan's concept of "misrecognition" in the mirror stage, he suggests that there is a "power of misrecognition" (*puissance de la meconnaissance*) and moreover that "there is a function of misrecognition that makes it such that the abruptness of the real operates only in fictions, montages, and masks."[82] In this way, the mask concealing Aman's true gender, stages the real of illicit desire (i.e., homoeroticism) repressed in the filmic unconscious and in the Iranian cultural imaginary. Now, during Aman's dancing, at once the diegetic music abruptly comes to a halt, and the camera turns to a shot of an instrument hitting the ground, the instrument is clearly a *setar*. The shot shows a shadow across her small windowpane, and it gestures to the spectral presence of someone—the darvish who was playing the instrument has seen her/him put on a dress and dance. Does this scene stage an instance of homoeroticism (*shahed-bazi*) in which the darvish misrecognizes Aman as a male who is "effeminate," especially by putting on the dress of one of the girls? Or is this an instance of recognition that Aman while masquerading as a "boy," or gender passing as male, is in reality a "woman"? Here it seems that the masculine signifier is divided into the "feminine" in the figure of Aman whose mask of "male" or "masculine" status is compromised. It is as if Aman as a "male" subject is now cross-dressing as "female." This redoubling of the cross-dressing motif further reinforces the gender and sexual undecidability in the filmic text, as well as the logic of desire as the erotic force that is beyond gender signification. The ambiguity is important here since it redoubles the narrative tension in which Belqis also misrecognizes Aman's gender identity. In other words, just as Aman is misrecognized for being "male" by Belqis, s/he may also be misrecognized by the iterant darvish.

Another formal element in the scene is that the darvish hidden behind the window-pane is like a voyeur gazing at Aman from outside the window, we never see his voyeuristic gaze, since to show him literally looking at Aman with an erotic gaze and voyeuristic pleasure, would have been another cause for censoring the scene, therefore the only strategy to gesture to his offscreen presence and his voyeuristic gaze (other than the strategy Majidi took in *Baran*, namely by 'veiling' her behind the opaque window), is to have an abrupt break or jolt of the music ending with the shot of the instrument (*setar*) hitting the ground. This voyeuristic "looking" can be read through the prism of what is called *shahed-bazi* or homoeroticism and the logic of *nazar-bazi* (play of glances).[83] There is a long tradition of homoeroticism in Persian mystical poetry and in Sufi discourse called in Persian *shahed-bazi* or the "witness play," which was the act of contemplating divine beauty in beardless youths or pubescent boys[84] and has been interpreted as an instantiations of pre-modern "homosexuality."[85]

In his exploration of homoeroticism (*shahed-bazi*) in Iran through the prism of classical Persian poetry, Sirus Shamisa states, "Persian lyrical literature is essentially a homosexual [*hamjens garaie*] literature."[86] Similarly Janet Afary notes in her *Sexual Politics in Modern Iran*: "In nearly half of lyric poems, the love object is unquestionably an adolescent boy. In the other half, which is also often homoerotic, the distinction is lost to the reader because the same adjectives can apply to either male or female objects of desire."[87] What is of particular interest is that, as Afary states apropos Shamisa, there is a rich lexicon in Persian of homoerotic relations embedded in the language itself, as she states, "The Persian language itself is rich with allusions to homoerotic relations.[88] Indeed, throughout the film the overseer does not call Aman by name, but by the term *pesar* (boy). Aman also has no facial hair or is beardless (*bi rish*) and an *amrad*, a beardless youth.

The motif of pederastic courting and the cult of the *ephebe* has a long genealogy that reaches back to classical Greece, in such institutions as the *symposium*, and through both the literary (poetry, philosophy, drama) and visual (art, vase paint-ings) cultural production of Greece, which reached as far as the Hellenistic Middle East.[89] The motif of pederasty itself also goes back to the ancient Greeks, especially with the god of wine Bacchus and in the ways "boys" were contemplated as gods.[90] In his Seminar VIII on *Transference*, where Lacan has an extended commentary on Plato's *Symposium*, he states, "You'll have to get used to the idea that Greek love was love for young pretty boys. And… that's it."[91] However, such sexual practices in the pre-modern period should not be called homosexuality, as we understand it in the modern sense of the term, since homosexuality is related to the politics of identity, which is a modern category (Foucault already noted the construction of the category of homosexuality in the Europe of 19th century),[92] and hence a more proper term in the older Iranian context would be homoeroticism.

In the context of the emergence of Iranian modernity, Afsaneh Najmabadi has demonstrated the existence of a "pre-modern and early modern Persian homoerotic culture."[93] In the 19th and early 20th centuries, the Qajar culture was pervaded by male homoerotic practices, typified by such terms as *amradparasti* (love of young adolescent men), *ghilman* (youth or boys, slaves) and *wildan* (boys), all of whom did not yet show signs of adult masculinity or manhood, namely they were beardless, and were regarded as objects of desire by older men. Similar terms for youth or boys were deployed in Arabic with regard to homoerotic relations, such as *shabb* (youth).[94] Najmabadi contends that after Europeans were exposed to these homoerotic practices in Iran, and the subsequent scornful "European gaze" that these practices elicited, Ira-nians "began to reconfigure structures of desire by introducing a demarcation to dis-tinguish homosociality from homosexuality."[95] The encounter with the foreign gaze resulted in an identification with it and the consequent "disavowal" of the homoerotic culture in the Iranian past.[96] In this sense, it could be said that this predilection for homoeroticism in pre-modern and early modern Iranian history and literature was not only disavowed but also *repressed* in the wider cultural imaginary.

In an important scene, we get a shot of the darvish playing an instrument called the *tanbour* outside Aman's window.[97] A hand emerges from the windowpane like a partial object and Aman gives him something to drink through the window. But the master overseer sees this and goes in and begins to beat Aman again complain-ing, "I brought you here to work and to oversee the girls." After being beaten, Aman looks up at the wool strings hanging from the rope in the room and walks back and forth with her head bent backward and rubs her face into the wool strings and smells their fragrance. The scene again gestures to the activation of the Lacan-ian feminine jouissance and ecstatic freedom. Incidentally, the unnamed musician that I call a "darvish," is often standing by her window or door, which is precisely what the etymology of the term *darvish* is derived from, namely "standing by the door."[98] Indeed, there are many wandering *darvishes* or *qalandars*, itinerant Sufis who roam the Iranian countryside and villages, often playing music or telling tales. Although they are less prevalent in modern times, as Sufis are severely persecuted by the Iranian state apparatus, but it is still possible to find them wandering the remote villages in Iran.[99]

In a later scene Aman suddenly wakes up when the wind slams the door of the room open, which was almost always locked by the overseer. Aman looks around the room, and then we see that the darvish is in the room and s/he becomes frightened. He grabs a bundle from where she sleeps, which seems to be Aman's belongings. Among hides behind the weaving loom, afraid of his intentions. As he leaves, s/he looks at him with trepidation, and he turns back to look at her, and she closes the door. With this act the darvish is proposing to Aman to come with him, to go away with him from this prison-house, full of pain and suffering. This moment is filled with erotic ambiguity and possible misrecognition, does the male darvish recognize that Aman is a girl masquerading as a boy, or does he want to be with Aman as a "boy"? Thus, the question is: is his desire for Aman a heterosexual or a homoerotic desire? But Aman does not go after him and rejects his offer of love—in this instance the darvish's love remains unrequited. In the morning, Aman goes outside and brings back the sack that he took outside the house, and we get a long shot of the darvish with his back to the camera leaving the village, an image that cinematically reverberates in the last scene of the film, this time with Aman leaving the village.

3.7   The Lacanian Act and the Feminine "No!"

At the very end of *Daughters of the Sun* there is a double catch, a double ambiguity even operative at the last scene, as we see a shot of Aman(gol) leaving, singing the same melancholic Azari song that she sang at the beginning of the film with her shaved head, but now she has donned her female dress.[100] Is the final scene, then, to be read as the reassertion of her female identity and agency over patriarchal imposition?[101] Indeed, it may be argued that this is the ultimate lesson of the film. Aman's gender re-signification (or trans gendering) was not her choice, but a forced choice, a choice that was imposed on her by paternal authority. This reading of the reassertion of her feminine identity is corroborated in Shahriar's own statement regarding the film, as she states, "I never saw the shaving of the head as a physical thing…. It became a great metaphor for the loss of identity. What is your role now? How do you find out who you are? It's not a cultural thing. Unfortunately, all of us in the world have reached the same level… I wanted to say aside from our roles in society we should celebrate our femininity. No matter who you are or what you are, it's wonderful to be a woman."[102] This gesture of Aman remaining faithful to the end to her femininity/female identity is itself the ultimate subversive act and can be read as an instance of the Lacanian "authentic act" and the feminine "No!" at its purest. In Lacanian ethics, the supreme ethical act or the "authentic act" is one in which the subject does not cede with respect to his or her desire.[103] According to Lacan, the question that must be asked when speaking of the ethical act is, "Have you acted in conformity with the desire that is in you?"[104] This is contrasted to "traditional ethics" of philosophers such as Aristotle or Kant. In traditional ethical theory, ethics revolves around a conception of the "Good," where different kinds of "good" compete with the position of the "Sovereign Good."[105]

In Lacanian ethics, this ideal of the "good" is seen as an obstacle to desire; hence in performing an authentic act, "a radical repudiation of a certain ideal of the good is necessary."[106] This ideal of the "good" is often what is purveyed as the Law in society. In this formulation, Aman burns the weaving sweatshop, which represents the patriarchal core of Iranian society and the state as the lynchpin of the Law (i.e., Islamic law), by remaining faithful to the end to her feminine self-identity. This is the enactment of the Lacanian "act" at its most subversive.

This final act of Aman in which she burns the sweatshop may be read in light of Žižek's interpretation of Antigone's suicidal act via Lacan in Seminar VII, *The Ethics of Psychoanalysis*, as the feminine act, and an instantiation of Lacan's feminine jouissance. For Žižek, the feminine character of the radical act is characterized as a "mad" act, which may appear always as a "crime," or a "transgression" of the inherent limit of the community to which one belongs. In this sense, the act always entails an irreducible *risk*; it is always *negative*, an act of annihilation.[107] In this sense, the pure act has something common with the Hegalian "tarrying with the negative," as Hegel puts it, "Spirit ... [looks] the negative in the face [i.e., death] and [tarries] with it."[108]

In this perspective Aman's "No! of the pure act" is a transgressive act that stands up to all that the figure of the paternal master overseer and the prisonlike sweatshop symbolize—the Iranian State as the lynchpin of (Islamic) Law. Indeed, once the subject performs the act, s/he is no longer the same as before. This is precisely what Žižek formulates apropos Anigone's act of saying "No!" to Creon (in Sophocles' tragic play *Antigone*), "...the act is not simply something I 'accomplish' – after an act, I'm literally 'not the same as before'...The act involves a kind of temporary eclipse, *aphanisis* [annihilation], of the subject."[109] This is how Aman returns to femininity from "masculinity," through the act she passes through masculinity as it were, via the passage through the *act* of burning the sweatshop. This act of using petrol to burn the weaving sweatshop is exactly how Lacan describes jouissance in Seminar XVII, where he states that jouissance, "Begins with a tickle and ends with blaze of petrol." That's always what jouissance is.[110] Through the act, Aman's "masculine" subjectivity is "annihilated," an *aphanisis* through the fire as it were, and she is subsequently "reborn" anew in her femininity as a woman, signified through her wearing of the dress once again, the marker of the reassertion of feminine identity. Thus, like Antigone, Aman's feminine "No!" of the pure ethical act of burning the overseer's sweatshop, is the eruption of the real into the symbolic and stands as a powerful symbol of the emancipatory potential and resistance of women in Iran to the authoritarian rule and patriarchal state of the Islamic Republic. In this instance, Aman's character also represents or stands as the *alter ego* for Shahriar the director of the film herself, and her own act of defiance through the making of this film. It is little wonder then that the censors wanted the last scenes to be cut out of the film, since they were politically savvy enough to read the subversive core of the film's message at the end, but Shahriar refused saying, "Over my dead body," and we are left with one of the most memorable scenes of feminine defiance in the history of Iranian cinema.

Notes

1 See Afsaneh Najmabadi, *Professing Selves: Transsexuality and Same-Sex Desire in Contemporary Iran* (Durham and London: Duke University Press, 2013).
2 Rochelle Terman, "Trans[ition] in Iran." *World Policy Journal*, Spring 2014. http://www.worldpolicy.org/transition-iran
3 Najmabadi, *Professing Selves* 2.
4 Ibid, 15.
5 Ibid, 305.
6 Najmabadi refers in the notes to only a single essay related to the subject by Roshanak Kheshti, "Cross-Dressing and Gender (Tres)Passing: The Transgender Move as a Site of Agential Potential in the New Iranian Cinema." *Hypatia* 24, no. 3 (summer 2009): 158–77. Although this is a completely new field of study in Iranian cinema, there is, at present, more than one study and they will be discussed accordingly throughout the chapter.
7 Kheshti, "Cross-Dressing," 171.
8 Gönül Dönmez-Colin, *Women, Islam and Cinema* (London: Reaktion Books, 2004), 181. Kheshti does not refer to this study and its discussion of *Daughters of the Sun*. Apropos the appellation, "Iran's first lesbian film." It should be recalled that in the pre-revolutionary era there were a few films with lesbian themes, and perhaps the most famous example is Mohammad Reza Aslani's magnificent *Shatranj-e baad* (*Chess Game of the Wind*; 1976).
9 The following information is based on Judy Stone, "Daughters of the Sun," DVD booklet on *Daughters of the Sun* (Chicago, Illinois: Facets Video, 2004), 4–6.
10 Naficy, *Social History*, 130.
11 Ibid, 133.
12 Minoo Moallem, *Between Warrior Brother and Veiled Sister: Islamic Fundamentalism and the Politics of Patriarchy in Iran* (Berkeley: University of California Press, 2005), 149.
13 Moallem, *Between Warrior*, 149.
14 Kheshti, "Cross-Dressing," 158.
15 Ibid, 159.
16 Anna Vanzan, "The LGBTQ question in Iranian cinema: a proxy discourse?" *DEP n25* (2014): 47–48.
17 Naficy, *Social History*, 130.
18 On cross-dressing in the *ta'ziyeh* see Negar Mottahedeh, "Ta'ziyeh: Karbala Drag Kings and Queens" *The Drama Review* (1988–), 49, no. 4 (Winter, 2005).
19 For women's *ta'ziyehs* see Negar Mottahedeh, *Representing the Unpresentable: Images of Reform from the Qajars to the Islamic Republic of Iran* (Syracuse University Press, Syracuse, 2008), 83–85.
20 The scholarly examination of non-normative genders, trans and queer sexualities in Iranian cinema is in its infancy, but more scholarly works have emerged in recent years. See Shima Houshyar, "Queer and Trans Subjects in Iranian Cinema: Between Representation, Agency, and Orientalist Fantasies," *Ajam Media Collective*, 2013. https://ajammc.com/2013/05/11/queer-and-trans-subjects-in-iranian-cinema-between-representation-agency-and-orientalist-fantasies/; Kaveh Bassiri, "Transgender Identity in Iranian Cinema," in *Global Encyclopedia of Lesbian, Gay, Bisexual, Transgender, and Queer (LGBTQ) History, Volume 1*, ed. By Howard Chiang (Charles Scribner & Sons, 2019), 1623–27.
21 John Phillips, *Transgender on Screen* (Basingstoke, UK: Palgrave Macmillan, 2006) 5.
22 More recently another monograph dedicated to transgender cinema has appeared, see Rebecca Bell-Metereau, *Transgender Cinema* (New Brunswick: Rutgers University Press, 2019).
23 For select studies on Lacanian psychoanalytic theory and trans studies, see all the essays in *TSQ: Transgender Studies Quarterly*, 4, no. 3–4 (November 2017); also Patricia Gherovici, *Please Select Your Gender: From the Invention of Hysteria to the Democratizing of Transgenderism* (London: Routledge, 2010); cf. *Transgender Psychoanalysis: A Lacanian Perspective on Sexual Difference* (New York: Routledge, 2017); Oren Gozlan,

Transsexuality and the Art of Transitioning: A Lacanian Approach (New York: Routledge, 2015); Shanna T. Carlson, "Transgender Subjectivity and the Logic of Sexual Difference." *differences* 21, no. 2 (2010): 46–72.

24 Marjorie Garber, *Vested Interests: Cross-dressing and Cultural Anxiety* (New York, NY and London: Routledge, 1992), 17.

25 Ibid, 34.

26 Copjec, *Read My Desire*, 207; also see Alenka Zupančič, *What Is Sex?* (Cambridge Massachusetts, MIT Press, 2017).

27 Ibid, 204.

28 Ibid, 216.

29 Slavoj Žižek, "The Real of Sexual Difference." In *Reading Seminar XX: Lacan's Major Work on Love, Knowledge, and Feminine Sexuality*, ed. Suzanne Barnard and Bruce Fink (Albany, NY: SUNY Press, 2002), 57–76.

30 Copjec, *Read My Desire*, 207.

31 From Lacan's unpublished Seminar XXI cited by Jacqueline Rose in "Introduction II," in *Feminine Sexuality: Jacques Lacan and the ecole freudienne*, ed. Juliet Mitchell and Jacqueline Rose (New York and London: W. W. Norton, 1982), 47.

32 Naficy, *A Social History of Iranian Cinema*, 131.

33 Stone, DVD booklet, 4.

34 Farzin Vejdani, "Hair and Hat Ritual Shaming Punishments in Nineteenth-Century Iran," *Iranian Studies* 56, no. 4 (October 2023): 2. https://doi.org/10.1017/irn.2023.40.

35 Ibid., 8.

36 Naficy, *A Social History of the Iranian Cinema*, 131.

37 Jeffry J. Anderson, "Rapunzel: The Symbolism Of The Cutting Of Hair." *Journal of the American Psychoanalytic Association*, 28 (1980):69–88, Cited in Alessandra Lemma, *Minding the Body: The Body in Psychoanalysis and Beyond* (New York: Routledge, 2015) 139.

38 On Lacan's notion of *lalangue* Bruce Fink writes, "The French… *lalangue*, is a term Lacan creates simply by putting together the feminine article la with the noun langue (language, but specifically spoken language as in tongue). Lacan discusses what he means by *lalangue* in the course of this seminar… very roughly speaking, it has to do with the acoustic level of language, the level at which polysemy is possible due to the existence of homonyms (like those Lacan plays on throughout this seminar). It is the level at which an infant (or songwriter) may repeat the one syllable of a word (for example, 'la la la'), the level at which language may 'stutter…'" See *The Seminar of Jacques Lacan, Book XX: On Feminine Sexuality, the Limits of Love & Knowledge 1972–73: Encore*, ed. Jaques-Alain Miller, trans. Bruce Fink (London: W.W. Norton, 1998), 44

39 Žižek, *How to Read Lacan*, 34.

40 Žižek, *How to Read Lacan* note 15, 122. Lacan borrowed the term "signifier" from the semiotic theories of Ferdinand de Saussure (1857–1913), but used the term in a novel way, as Žižek states in the same note, as "a feature, a mark, which represents the subject."

41 Lacan, *Écrits,* 67.

42 Evans, *Dictionary*, 122.

43 Jacques Lacan, *Écrits: A Selection*, trans. Alan Sheridan (London: Tavistock Publications, 1977), 282.

44 As Miller states, "Lacan argues that all speaking subjects, masculine and feminine, are 'castrated' by their entrance into the symbolic order." Elaine P. Miller, *Head Cases: Julia Kristeva on Philosophy and Art in Depressed Times* (New York: Columbia University Press, 2014), 192.

45 Judith Butler, *Gender Trouble* (London: Routledge, 2011), 25. Ever since the publication of this book, Butler has been at pains to distinguish her notion of "performativity" from "performance." For a critical appraisal of Butler's notion of gender performativity see below.

46 Kheshti, "Cross-Dressing," 170. This critical dimension is not referred to by Kheshti, in whose reading the "gender reassignment right" is read as a subjective choice of Aman, which is clearly not the case.

47 Gilles Deleuze and Félix Guattari, *A Thousand Plateaus: Capitalism and Schizophrenia*, trans. Brian Massumi. (Minneapolis: University of Minnesota Press, 2003) 179.

48 Miller, *Head* Cases, 26–7.

49 Julia Kristeva, *Melanie Klein*, trans. Ross Guberman (New York: Columbia University Press, 2001), 89.

50 Miller, *Head Cases*, 27.

51 Ibid, 27.

52 Ibid, 28.

53 Judith Butler, *The Psychic life of Power: Theories of Subjection* (New York: Columbia University, 1997), 136.

54 Butler, *Psychic life of Power*, 135.

55 Butler, *Gender Trouble*, 24.

56 Judith Butler, *Bodies that Matter* (New York: Routledge, 1993), 2.

57 Naficy, *A Social History of Iranian Cinema Volume 4*, 132. Naficy refers to Sharareh Attari's documentary *It Happens Sometimes* (2006). Another documentary is written and directed by Tanaz Eshaghian called *Be Like Others* (2008) (aka *Transsexual in Iran*).

58 See Hassan Daoud, "Those Two Heavy Wings of Manhood: On Moustaches," in *Imagined Masculinities: Male Identity and Culture in the Middle East*, ed. Mai Ghoussoub and Emma Sinclair-Webb (London: Saqi, 2000), 273–80.

59 Lacan states, "...I will say that in man's realm there is always the presence of some imposture..." Lacan, *Anxiety*, 191.

60 This is how Žižek formulates it in his analysis of Hitchcock's *Vertigo* (1957): "A subject is a partial something, a face, something we see. Behind it, there is a void, a nothingness. And of course, we spontaneously tend to fill in that nothingness with our fantasies about the wealth of human personality... To see what is lacking in reality, to see it as that, there you see subjectivity. To confront subjectivity means to confront femininity. Woman is the subject. Masculinity is a fake." *Pervert's Guide to Cinema* (2006), directed by Sophie Fiennes.

61 Lacan, *Anxiety*, 191.

62 Žižek, *Looking Awry*, 12.

63 According to Judy Stone, "To comply with those objections [by the censors], she cut all the 'touching' scenes in one night, which wreaked havoc with the editing to get it ready for the annual Fajr International Film Festival in Tehran." DVD booklet, 5.

64 Anna Vanzan, "The LGBTQ question in Iranian cinema," 48.

65 Žižek, *Metastasis of Enjoyment*, 103.

66 Žižek puts this metaphysical conundrum at the heart of human sexuality in this way, "Freud focuses on sexuality because, for him, the most elementary break with animal life, the passage to a meta-physical dimension, happens here, in the emergence of a sexual passion detached from the biological needs of animal coupling." Slavoj Žižek, *Disparities* (London: Bloomsbury Academic, 2016), 17.

67 Žižek, *Metastasis of Enjoyment*, 103. Žižek's formulation here is derived from Lacan's seminar on *Transference*.

68 Ibid., 103.

69 Jacques Lacan, *Transference, The Seminar of Jacques Lacan Book VIII*, ed. Jacques-Alain Miller, trans. Bruce Fink (Cambridge: Polity Press, 2015), 34.

70 Jacques Lacan, "Seminar on 'The Purloined Letter,' (1966)," in *Écrits*, trans. Bruce Fink (New York: WW Norton, 2006), 30.

71 Lacan, *Transference*, 103.

72 The French term jouissance, means both "orgasm," as well as "enjoyment." In Lacan's writings, this ambiguity of the term must always be retained, which is why it is often left untranslated.

73 See, Jean During, "Hal." In *Encyclopaedia Iranica*, vol. 8., ed. Ehsan Yarshater (New York: Encyclopaedia Iranica Foundation, 2003), 580. Kheshti reads this moment in these terms, "Aman relishes in the joys of flowing fabric, billowing around legs that

twirl like a little girl or a meditating Sufi, whirling around in a trance-like state to the sounds of mystical music" (172). For a Lacanian reading of Rumi's mystical poetics, see Mahdi Tourage, *Rumi and the Hermeneutics of Eroticism* (Leiden: Brill, 2007).

74 Jacques Lacan, *...or Worse: The Seminar of Jacques Lacan Book XIX*, trans. A. R. Price (Cambridge: Polity Press, 2018), 148.

75 Slavoj Žižek, "*Love Beyond Law,*" accessed March 20, 2015, http://www.lacan.com/zizlola.htm

76 See Shahzad Bashir, *Sufi Bodies: Religion and Society in Medieval Islam* (New York: Columbia University Press, 2011), 74–77. For general discussions of *sama'* in Sufi praxis see Fritz Meier, "The Dervish Dance: An Attempt at an Overview," in *Essays in Islamic Mysticism and Piety* (Leiden: Brill, 1999), 23–48; Leonard Lewisohn, "The Sacred Music of Islam: Samā' in the Persian Sufi Tradition," *British Journal of Ethnomusicology*, 6 (1997): 1–33.

77 Lacan, *Encore*, 74.

78 In *Encore* Lacan states that some women may experience feminine jouissance, but not all, though all mystics do experience it. See Lacan, *Encore*, 74, 76. See also Lacan, *Anxiety*, 183–84.

79 Žižek, *Metastasis of Enjoyment*, 117.

80 Michael A. Sells and James Webb, "Lacan and Bion: Psychoanalysis and the Mystical Language of Unsaying." *Theory and Psychology* 5.2 (1995): 195–215; cf. Michael A. Sells, *Mystical Languages of Unsaying* (Chicago and London: University of Chicago Press, 1994).

81 Jacques Lacan, *Seminar XX: Encore*. Trans. Bruce Fink. Ed. Jacques-Alain Miller. (New York: W.W. Norton & Co., 1999) 76. Speaking of mystical texts, Lacan incredibly calls his own book *Écrits* a mystical text, "These mystical jaculations are neither idle chatter nor empty verbiage; they provide, all in all, some of the best reading one can find – at the bottom of the page, drop a footnote, 'Add to that list Jacques Lacan's *Écrits*,' because it's of the same order." Lacan, *Seminar XX: Encore*, 76.

82 Alain Badiou quoted in Adrian Johnson, *Žižek's Ontology: A Transcendental Materialist Theory of Subjectivity* (Evanston, Illinois: Northwestern University, 2008), 183.

83 For *nazar-bazi* in Iranian cinema see Shahla Haeri, "Sacred Canopy: Love and Sex under the Veil," *Iranian Studies*, 42 (2009): 113–26.

84 Shahzad Bashir writes apropos *shahed-bazi*, "The practice of contemplating young boys as beautiful forms that represent divine beauty is usually known through the term *shahidbazi* and has a controversial history in Sufi texts... while it is difficult to substantiate *shahidbazi* as a widespread practice, such 'looking' is a common feature of Persian poetic rhetoric." Bashir, *Sufi Bodies* 146.

85 See Sirus Shamisa, *Shahedbazi dar Adabiyat-e Farsi* (Tehran: Ferdows Press, 2002); for a valuable discussion of homoeroticism and homosexuality in Iran, see Janet Afary, *Sexual Politics in Modern Iran* (Cambridge: University of Cambridge Press, 2009). For homoeroticism in pre-modern Islamic sources, see Khaled El-Rouayheb, *Before Homosexuality in the Arab-Islamic World, 1500–1800* (Chicago: University of Chicago, 2005), especially Chapter One: Pederasts and Pathics 13–52; Walter G. Andrews and Mehmet Kalpaklı, *The Age of Beloveds: Love and the Beloved in Early-modern Ottoman and European Culture and Society* (Durham and London: Duke University Press, 2005), 32–84. On homosexuality in Islamic law see, E. K. Rowson, "HOMOSEXUALITY ii. IN ISLAMIC LAW," *Encyclopædia Iranica*, XII/4, pp. 441–45.

86 Shamisa, *Shahedbazi* 10, quoted in Afary, *Sexual Politics*, 88.

87 Afary *Sexual Politics*, 87–88.

88 Shamisa, *Shahedbazi* 10, quoted in Afary *Sexual Politics*, 88.

89 For the literary evidence, see Andrew Lear and Eva Cantarella, *Images of Pederasty: Boys Were Their Gods* (London and New York, 2008).

90 When they asked the poet Anacreon why he wrote hymns to boys instead of the gods, he replied, "because boys are our gods." "Footnote to an ancient edition of Pindar's second Isthmian Ode (iii 213 Drachmann)." Quoted in Andrew Lear and Eva Cantarella, *Images of Ancient Greek Pederasty*, 8.

91 Lacan, *Transference*, 30.

92 See Michel Foucault, *The History of Sexuality, Volume 1: An Introduction* (New York, Vintage Books, 1990), 43.

93 Afsaneh Najmabadi, *Women with Mustaches and Men Without Beards* (California: University of California, 2005), 15. Also see, Willem Floor, *A Social History of Sexual Relations in Iran* (Washington, DC: Mage Publishers, 2008), especially Chapter Four.

94 As Khaled El-Rouayheb notes, "Homosexual relations in the early Ottoman Arab East were almost always conceived as involving an adult man (who stereotypically would be the 'male' partner) and an adolescent boy (the 'female'). The latter—referred to in the texts as *amrad* (beardless boy); *ghulam* or *shabbi* (boy); or *fata, shabb*, or *hadath* (male youth)—though biologically male, was not completely a 'man' in the social and cultural sense; and his intermediate status was symbolized by the lack of the most visible of male sex characteristics: a beard." El-Rouayheb, *Before Homosexuality* 26.

95 Najmabadi, *Women with Mustaches*, 38.

96 Ibid, 38. Interestingly Najmabadi often uses the psychoanalytic term "disavowal" to characterize the denial of this past.

97 The *tanbour* is an instrument that is considered sacred by the Sufis, especially among the Kurdish Sufis in Iran called *Ahl-e Haqq* (the People of Truth), who make ablutions before playing it; hence the instrument has a liturgical and ceremonial function in relation to the practices of *zekr* (remembrance), *sama* (audition), and mystical states of ecstasy (*hal*).

98 Carl W. Ernst, *Sufism: An Introduction to the Mystical Tradition of Islam* (Boulder, Colorado: Shambhala Publications, 2011), 3.

99 For wandering *darvishes* and *qalandars* in Iranian history and thought see, Muhammad Reza Shafi'i-yi Kadkani, *Qalandariyah dar Tarikh: Digarandisi-ha-yi yek Ide'olozhi* (Tehran: Sokhan, 1386/2007); de Bruijn, J. T. P. "The Qalandariyyat in Persian Mystical Poetry from Sand'i Onwards" in *The Legacy of Mediæval Persian Sufism*, ed. Leonard Lewisohn (Oxford: Oneworld Publications, 1992), 61–75; Ahmet T. Karamustafa, *God's Unruly Friends: Dervish Groups in the Islamic Later Middle Period. 1200–1550* (Salt Lake City: University of Utah Press, 1994).

100 According to Judy Stone, the sensors "wanted her [Shahriar] to cut the first and final scenes, but she adamantly refused. Her reaction was: 'Over my dead body.'" See "Daughters of the Sun," DVD booklet, 5.

101 Moallem also reads the end of the film as Aman's return to femininity. See Moallem, *Between Warrior*, 145.

102 Maryam Shahriar cited in Judy Stone, DVD booklet, 4–5.

103 Frances L. Restuccia, *The Taming of the Real: Zizek's Missed Encounter with Kieslowski's Insight*," accessed April 01, 2015. http://www.lacan.com/white.htm

104 Evans, Dylan. *An Introductory Dictionary of Lacanian Psychoanalysis*. (New York: Routledge, 1996), 57.

105 Dylan, *An Introductory Dictionary*, 57.

106 Ibid, 57.

107 Slavoj Žižek, *Enjoy Your Symptom!* (New York: Routledge, 2001), 44.

108 G. W. F. Hegel, *Phenomenology of Spirit*, trans. A. V. Miller (Oxford: Oxford University Press, 1977), 19; see also, Slavoj Žižek, *Tarrying with the Negative: Kant, Hegel and the Critique of Ideology* (Durham, NC: Duke UP, 1993).

109 Žižek, *Enjoy Your Symptom!*, 44.

110 Jacques Lacan, *The Seminar of Jacques Lacan: The Other Side of Psychoanalysis Book XVII*, ed. Jacques-Alain Miller, trans. Russell Grigg (New York/London: W.W. Norton & Company, 2007), 72.

Chapter 4

Dreaming of a Nightmare in Tehran

The Fright of Real Desires in *Atomic Heart*

Before the eve of the 1979 Iranian Revolution, Michel Foucault, who was intensely engrossed with the events in Tehran, wrote a series of articles on the revolutionary events, in one of which he posed an uncharacteristically psychoanalytic inflected question: "What are the Iranians dreaming about?"[1] After the events of the 2009 presidential election and the subsequent protest movement, which functions as the backdrop for *Atomic Heart*, we may ask the question again today: what are the Iranians Dreaming of in Tehran? The cinematic answer provided by *Atomic Heart* at least seems to be, they are dreaming of a nightmare in Tehran. The nightmare in the film is not only related to the fears and anxieties of a possible nuclear destruction of Tehran, but more precisely to the totalitarian nightmare of the Islamic Republic, personified in the monstrous dictatorial figure of Toofan.

In this chapter, I focus on the double or two-part structure in Ali Ahmadzadeh's "surrealist" road film *Atomic Heart* (*Qalb-e atomi*, 2015), in which the first part is considered as the realist and the second part as the surrealist half of the film. I argue that the two parts of the film represent the world of fantasy in the first and the world of desire in the second that are staged horizontally as it were.[2] This formal double-structure is advanced by the director's own reading of the film, as he states in a post-screening of the film at the Berlin Film Festival, "The most important aspect of the film for me is that the first part and second part are differentiated. The first part is reality and the second part, when the character of Mohammad Reza Golzar [Toofan] appears, is the surreal part. The film is a contrast between realism and surrealism."[3] However, this standard reading has to be turned around, as I suggest that the first part of the film is the fantasy half, and the second part of the film is the reality half. By "reality" here, I intend a very precise psychoanalytic notion of reality, that is: when reality is deprived of its fantasmatic supplement, reality itself turns into a kind of nightmarish surreality. When reality is stripped of its frame of fantasy, we do not just get reality as such, but what we get is "an 'irreal' nightmarish universe," too traumatic to be approached directly, which is why we must fictionalize it. As Kant knew very well, we can never know the real kernel of reality *in-itself*. Kant made a distinction between phenomenal reality as appearance, to which we have access, and the noumenon as the *thing in-itself*, which we cannot access with our categories of reason; this is precisely where our reason falls

DOI: 10.4324/9781003531029-7

into antinomies or contradictions; in this sense, reality always already requires a transcendental schema in order to be constituted as reality.[4] The psychoanalytic name for the Kantian transcendental scheme is fantasy.[5] As Žižek states apropos the notion of fantasy in Lacan, "when the phantasmic frame disintegrates, the subject undergoes a '*loss* of reality' and starts to perceive reality as an 'irreal' nightmarish universe with no firm ontological foundation;" But as Žižek is quick to point out, "this nightmarish universe is not 'pure fantasy' but, on the contrary, *that which remains of reality after reality is deprived of its support in fantasy.*"[6]

Although on the surface it appears that the first part of the film is reality, shot in a realist style, where there is the normal run of things and the second part swerves to surreality; what I argue instead is that the first part is the fantasy narrative or the fantasmatic scenario, and the second part is reality deprived of its fantasmatic support. It is precisely when reality is deprived of its support in fantasy that we encounter the traumatic real, the real in the precise Lacanian sense, that which appears in reality more than reality itself and distorts it, twists it, renders it surreal or uncanny. In the film, this real appears as the real of desire, which acts as a distortion of reality, since the way "desire inscribes itself into reality, [is] by distorting it. Desire is a wound of reality."[7] In this sense, desire acts as a distortion of reality in the second half of the film and what we get is a kind of nightmarish reality or surreality, since the fantasy support that sustained the coordinates of reality has collapsed. Therefore, I argue that *Atomic Heart* is comprised of three ontological registers: fantasy, reality, and the real.[8] The first part represents the world of fantasy and the second part the world of desire. It is in the world of desire in the second part of the film that the real in all its traumatic horror appears through the character of Toofan, and where Arineh and Nobahar are confronted not only with the fright of the real of their own forbidden desire—forbidden because it is a homoerotic desire, but also with the enigma of the Other's desire (Toofan as symbolic of the State) in all its uncanny dimension. In another formulation, the entire film is structured like a dream where the first half is the dream as fantasy or the dream as wish fulfillment (in Freudian terms), and the second half of the film is where the dream sequence turns into a nightmare where we are confronted with the (traumatic) real of desire.

4.1   *Atomic Heart* between the Weird and the Eerie

I have argued elsewhere that there is a noticeable shift that is discernable in the new types of films that are emerging from Iran in recent years that evoke and critique "the menacing environment of post-2009 Iran."[9] Indeed, Ali Ahmadzadeh's "surrealist" road film *Atomic Heart* (*Qalb-e atomi*, 2015) also called *Atomic Heart Mother* (*Madar-e qalb atomi*), must be included in this band of new Iranian films where a visible shift can be detected between the New Iranian Cinema of the mid 1990s and 2000s, with its unique style and recognizable conventions (i.e., the blurring of documentary and narrative fiction, the use of non-professional actors, rural landscapes, etc.), and these emerging art and genre bending films. Despite some minor continuities between this film and the older generation of Iranian films, such as the well-known motif of an entire film centering on characters driving and talking in a car, it is in its discontinuities that we may discern the shift away from the earlier New Iranian Cinema.[10] Specifically, I situate Ahmadzadeh's film among the films that are part of a new filmic movement that I have termed: *Unheimlich between the Weird and the Eerie*. Deploying Mark Fisher's theorization of the two modes of "The Weird and the Eerie," I consider *Atomic Heart* to exemplify the logic of the weird and eerie, but especially the weird or the strange, and its relation to Freud's theory of the uncanny (*Unheimlich*).[11]

In *The Weird and the Eerie* (2016), Fisher considers that although the weird and the eerie are two distinct modes, there is a common logic that structures them both, namely the logic of "the strange," and the "outside," as he states, "What the weird and the eerie have in common is a preoccupation with the strange.[12] According to Fisher the weird concerns what does not belong, as he states, "*the weird is that which does not belong*," which makes us question the very sense of the world we inhabit, while the eerie[13] "is constituted by a failure of absence or by a failure of presence,"[14] which engender questions about agency and the mysterious or invisible forces that seem to act on the world beyond our understanding.[15] For Fisher, the experience of the weird has something to do with "a particular kind of perturbation. It involves a sensation of *wrongness*: a weird entity or object is so strange that it makes us feel that it should not exist, or at least it should not exist here."[16] According to Fisher, what the weird stages is that the sense of wrongness is not with the weird thing as such, but what it renders palpable is the very inadequacy of our conceptions and categories to account for it.[17]

Fisher is at pains to distinguish the weird and eerie from Freud's concept of the uncanny (*unheimlich*) ("unhomely" in the original German and rendered as the "uncanny" by James Starchey). He notes that, "The *unheimlich* is often equated with the weird and the eerie," and that "Freud's own essay treats the terms as interchangeable."[18] Indeed, Fisher does consider that the weird and the eerie do have something in common with the *unheimlich* since "They are all affects, but they are also modes: modes of film and fiction, modes of perception, ultimately, you might even say, modes of being."[19] Despite this, Fisher considers the uncanny to be a secular retreat from the *outside*, which is one of the central characteristics of the weird. Although this may be the case, the retreat is not inherent to the concept of the uncanny itself, but perhaps to Freud's own discomfort with the "outside" (Freud's analysis of the uncanny emerges from his reading of E.T.A. Hoffman's tale "The Sandman," which certainly does evoke the outside). However, what the uncanny and the weird do have in common is the logic of *Verfremdung* or rendering strange or estrangement, that is inherent in the concept of the uncanny. In this sense, the weird and *Verfremdung* may be correlated to another concept called *ostrannenie* "making it strange" (coined by the "Russian Formalist" Viktor Shklovsky in 1917).[20] It is this palpable sense of weird(ness) or *Verfremdung* that one feels when watching the second half of *Atomic Heart*.

The director that Fisher considers to be the master practitioner of the weird mode in cinema is David Lynch, especially the way curtains, doorways, or gateways appear in his films. As we see, the Lynchian universe is a point of reference for Ahmadzadeh's film in many respects. Indeed, it is more the elements of the weird rather than the eerie that appear to structure the second half of *Atomic Heart*. Although aspects of the "weird and eerie" guide the reading of the film in this chapter, it is the Freudo-Lacanian theoretical apparatus that will take center stage. Though it should be noted that in a brilliant turn, Fisher foregrounds Lacan's early relation to the surrealists and therefore considers him to be the exponent of "a *weird psychoanalysis*, in which the death drive, dreams and the unconscious become untethered from any naturalization or sense of homeliness."[21] Indeed, Lacan was close to the surrealist circles and drew inspiration from the surrealist movement early on, yet it should be recalled that Freudian psychoanalysis was already weird enough from the beginning.[22] The weirdness of psychoanalysis itself (especially its discovery of the unconscious and the significance of dreams in the psychical life of subjects) is the reason that the surrealists were attracted to psychoanalysis in the first place.

In a recent book, *Crisis Cinema in the Middle East: Creativity and Constraint in Iran and the Arab World,* Shohini Chaudhuri has expanded on my reading of *Atomic Heart* apropos the logic of "weird and eerie" forms of estrangement, and my linking of *Atomic Heart* to the strangeness of the Lynchian cinematic universe, as well as my categorization of the film as an instance of a new band of Iranian films that evoke the menacing atmosphere of post-2009 Iranian society.[23] Chaudhuri deploys the modes of the weird and eerie "more broadly to point to science-fictional strategies that have emerged in the economic, political and social downturn of this period."[24] In Chaudhuri's reading, the film's environment "produces Lynchian strangeness," that is "enhanced by science-fiction tropes," with the first part of the film exemplifying "utopian moments," while "the second is its dystopian transfiguration."[25]

What distinguishes and characterizes the films of this new film movement that I have related to the modes of the "the weird and the eerie" is their evocation of the menacing environment of post-2009 Iran, and a number of thematics that they commonly share. For example, among the various components shared by this movement are such motifs as political and ideological critique through the deployment of supernatural elements or occult phenomenon (devil/satan, vampires, *jinn, Aal* and *zaar*, etc.).[26] They also touch on such taboo subjects as (female and male) sex/sexuality, homosexuality, or queerness in Iran. They are often pervaded by doubles or Doppelgängers, dreamlike worlds, nightmarish landscapes, paranoid and menacing atmospheres, invisible threatening forces, and a sense of pervading fear and terror or impending doom. Some of these thematics appear in the film form or style which share certain formal features with the universe of German expressionism and *film noir* that includes such techniques as contrasts of light, dark, and shadows; evoking a sense of mystery, dread, existential angst, moral corruption and crime; these are evident especially in their use of color, light and darkness (low-key lighting, or chiaroscuro lighting), the mise-en-scène, setting, objects and spaces; and camera techniques such as strange unbalanced (tilted) off angle shots (Dutch angle) or oblique angle shots, long takes, extreme long takes, and even the entire film as a single take. This is precisely why I consider such films to constitute a new movement, since beyond embodying the two modes of the weird and the eerie, they share a common set of motifs that evoke the menacing and suffocating atmosphere of post-2009 Iranian society.

Ahmadzadeh's film seems to be inspired and influenced not only by Iranian cinema and literature, but also by transnational cinema and literature. Among some of the literary works that seem to have an uncanny relation to the film is Mikhail Bulgakov's novel *The Master and Margarita* as the lead character of that novel is the devil, and the novel deploys the supernatural as an allegory of the totalitarian structure of the Soviet State with the devil as Stalin. Another possible influence may be George Orwell's book *1984*, in which the figures of Big Brother or Ministry of Truth function as important points of reference. The works of Kafka such as *The Trial* may also have exerted an influence, as well as Dostoevsky's *The Double*, especially the logic of the double or Doppelgänger operative in it since it is one of the instances of the Freudian *unheimlich*. However, it is perhaps to the cinema of David Lynch, the emblematic cinema of the weird, that Ahmadzadeh's film has the most striking resemblance. In its formal structure *Atomic Heart*, more than any other Iranian film, has an uncanny resemblance to the two-part structure of the two masterpieces of the Lynchian universe, namely *Lost Highway* (1997) and *Mulholland Drive* (2001), but especially to the latter.

4.2   Reality Structured by Fantasy or Fantasy as an Ideological Category

On the surface the first part of *Atomic Heart* has a straightforward narrative realism that does not require any explication. The first part of the film's narrative story can be summed up briefly. After a night of partying in one of the underground house parties in Tehran, two upper-middle class girls in their 20s Arineh (Taraneh Alidoosti) and Nobahar (Pegah Ahangarani) leave, half drunk, in their car after midnight. Once they are on the road, they run into their friend Kami (Mehrdad Sedighiyan) (the absent character of Alizadeh's previous film, *Kami's Party* (2013)) who is walking home at night wearing a pair of sunglasses. After a short ride the three of them stop by the side of the road overlooking Tehran, with the implication that they have just smoked a joint. They start conversing about subjects ranging from the history of the structure of Western toilets (see below) to the nuclear issue; from ridiculous male pickup lines to Kami's nightmare about the nuclear destruction of Tehran (which incidentally was not called Tehran in the dream, but *Atomic Heart Mother*, after the title song of the same name by the British rock'n'roll band Pink Floyd). After this they cruise the highway in Tehran, like other bored Iranian youth, and start to sing together the song by Michel Jackson, "We are the World," after which they get into an accident (as I discuss later, this is not incidental, since the accident functions as the abrupt jolt that concludes the film's fantasy half and inaugurates the second part of the film, where we are confronted with reality devoid of fantasy; the appearance of the real in all its monstrosity).

After the accident which inaugurates the second half of the film, they meet a mysterious stranger named Toofan, who pays for the damages to the owner of the other car and does not accept to be reimbursed but asks for a ride. It is here that the story turns into the weird and the eerie, since Toofan is not what he seems. Soon after, while driving through Tehran at night, Arineh and Nobahar are introduced to a nightmarish world of dead dictators and parallel worlds and cannot seem to escape the hold of Toofan who becomes ever more menacing, and who seems to bend time and space and reappear at will. I come to an analysis of the second part of the film later.

The narrative story of the first part of the film has a clear and straightforward realism, which is why Alizadeh himself considers it to be the realist half of the film. After leaving the party and looking for where they may have parked their car (since they are drunk and can't remember where they parked the car), one of the girls says, "I will now divide the street into two parts, before the revolution, and after the revolution." And the other girl says, "I'll go to before the revolution." Beside an allusion to the two-part structure of the film again, this is one of the narrative clues as to the formal logic of the film, where the first part represents in a way pre-revolution Iran, or the Pahlavi era, but again a fantasmatic pre-revolutionary Iran where the middle and upper class youth imagine or fantasize it to be a time of unfettered freedom, enjoyment and pleasures, and the second half as post-revolutionary Iran, a kind of nightmarish universe in which the two girls are terrorized by Toofan who is the embodiment of the State (or as we see a figure that simultaneously embodies diabolical evil or the devil, the figure of a dictator and Mahmud Ahmadinejad), and hence the Lacanian real in all its terrifying dimension.

Now what is crucial at the formal level is that the film structures the difference between the first fantasmatic part and the second surreal half representing reality deprived of its fantasy frame. The first part of the film, in contrast, produces a scenario in which Nobahar and Arineh can enjoy themselves: they are coming from a party, they're drunk, they laugh and joke around; the mood is light and jovial, comedic, and peaceful; and the first part of the film concludes with them singing the song, "We Are the World." This song itself functions as emblematic of the atmosphere of the first half of the film. This is precisely the fantasy frame that supports the coordinates of their reality in Tehran, without all these fantasmatic elements (such as parties, drinking, smoking drugs, humor, and laughter), reality itself would disintegrate and what we get is a nightmarish world—which is precisely what we get in the second part of the film. It is here that fantasy functions as an ideological category, disguising a deadlock or antagonism in reality, as Žižek states apropos the fantasmatic structure of ideology, "Ideology is not a dreamlike illusion that we build to escape insupportable reality; in its basic dimension it is a phantasy construction which serves as a support for our 'reality' itself; an 'illusion' which structures our effective, real social relations and thereby masks some insupportable, real, impossible kernel…"[27] What this ideology or fantasy construction masks, represented by the first half of the film, is the impossible real kernel embodied in the figure of Toofan (typifying the figure of Ahmadinejad) that appears in the second part of the film, and who stands for the traumatic real kernel of their situation—a situation that Ahmadzadeh wishes to equate with violence and repression in the Islamic Republic and its homology with the dictatorial logic of totalitarianism.

In the film, this separation between the experience of fantasy and reality (and the real of desires) is rendered through changes in the lighting, camera work, editing, and the overall character of the shots between the first and second parts of the film. In the first part, all the shots of the camera are even and the lines are straight and the camera is stable, but in the second part, after the accident scene, already the camera angle becomes skewed, we get a Dutch angle or canted angle shot throughout the scene, gesturing toward the uncanny dimension of the world which we have entered not unlike the world of *film noir*—a world without the support of fantasy and the appearance of the real, the real in all its traumatic dimension. As soon as the mysterious figure of Toofan appears within the frame, the lighting visibly becomes darker and the atmosphere of the film changes. A filter is placed on the camera lens and from this moment onward this world is sufficed with an aura of darkness with dark blue tones. Just before Toofan appears the colors are bright, with lighter tones and bright lighting that bring out the tones in natural colors that accentuate the sense of the light mood and atmosphere in the texture of the first half (happy, boisterous, jovial, etc.). This jovial mood is even gestured to by Nobahar's whistling of the theme song of the cartoon television show that they discussed earlier in the film. But, when the figure of Toofan suddenly leaves the frame, the police appears on the scene of the accident (this disappearance of Toofan at the appearance of the police also suggests a link between the Law and Toofan)—it is as if he represents the obscene underside or double of the police/law, and they cannot be framed together since they represent one entity, which is why after the police leaves Toofan mysteriously reappears again. Strangely the name of the police is also Ahmadzadeh, which is the same as the director's last name: this is a bizarre moment of self-reflexive identification that can only make sense in light of the police's comments to Arineh where he states, "even you guys with your looks are sometimes in agreement with the regime." In this sense, the police stands as Ahmadzadeh's *alter-ego* who also finds himself in agreement with the regime at times, despite their major differences. This is gestured to in the scene where Arineh and Nobahar agree with the police on the stereotypical and demonizing depictions of Iran and Iranians in Hollywood films such as *Argo* (2012). During Toofan's absence, the filter is removed again from the lens, and we get the bright lighting back but when he returns later, the dark filter is placed back on the camera lens and the lighting of the diegetic reality of the world is baptized in darkness.

In the second part of the film, the lighting is not only much darker, but the editing also undergoes a radical shift. For example, in the second part, in an important scene toward the film's end when Arineh runs from the apartment staircase with the camera following her, we get a continuous steady-camera long-take without a cut, which at a formal level, stages the fear and anxiety of Arineh. The same shot is re-doubled when she comes back up the stairs, and the camera follows her in a continuous shot or single take without a cut to the roof. This editing technique suggests that there is an ontological difference between the two worlds of fantasy and reality; and when reality is deprived of its fantasmatic supplement the uncanny dimension of the real manifests itself.

4.3   Ideology and the Structure of Toilets

One of the elementary lessons of cinema studies and film theory is the analysis of the formal structure of the beginning and endings of film.[28] Films often begin with an establishing shot which stages within the *mise-en-scène* some of the motifs that may often play a significant role in the film and can contain key elements that illuminate the film text when read retroactively. Therefore, the proper theoretical question to be asked here is: why does *Atomic Heart* begin early on with a shot of Nobahar sitting on the toilet? Let's examine this first scene in some detail. The film effectively begins with a shot of Nobahar sitting on the toilet. The camera slowly tracks vertically from her shoes, which are incidentally two different colors, one blue and the other red,[29] and finally the camera moves to a close-up of her face. The first thing to be noted about this scene is that it would certainly have been considered inappropriate to the censors, since showing a woman sitting on the toilet is beyond the limits of the modesty system (*hejab*), not least in that we get a close-up of her face in this most private of spaces. It is likely that this scene was among the many scenes the censors found objectionable and for which the film has never been granted permission for screening in Iran. Indeed, the film was denied initial screening in Iran's most prestigious film festival, the Fajr Film Festival. In the semi-official Iranian news agency called *Fars News*, one of the so-called purported objections to the film was its discussion of the nuclear issue.[30]

This scene already adumbrates a number of motifs that runs throughout the film. First, the same toilet scene is repeated in the second part of the film, this time with Arineh sitting on the toilet. Then there is repeated reference and discussion of toilets in the film or the need of the characters (Nobahar and Arineh) to avail themselves of the toilet. But more crucially, the first instance of the dialogue in the film is from Nobahar who exclaims to Arineh, "Whoever invented the Western toilet certainly created the most important invention in human history!" Indeed, this first line of dialogue and the first scene on the toilet takes on added significance later in the first part of the film, where Kami provides the cultural history of the structure of Western toilets and how they were originally Persian in ancient times. Nobahar asks Kami saying, "Kami, do you know who invented Western toilets?" and Kami responds, "The Western toilet was Iranian at first (originally). Then they changed its name." Then Nobahar says in characteristic naivety, "seriously?" And Kami states, "Yes, the ancient Achaemenids really took care of their joints. Because they were mostly warriors and engaged in a lot of physical activities. So, they built a stone platform with a cesspool in the middle. They would sit on it and do their thing. Later, its name was changed to Western toilets." Then Nobahar asks: "My question is why were the [original] Western toilets replaced by the Iranian squat toilets?" Kami replies, "That's because the Mongols attacked Iran. They would shit in a hole and pour soil on it. That's how Iranian – or rather originally Chinese toilets came to be." The obvious point to be noted here is that even though Kami's tone is ironic, even comedic, nonetheless the whole narrative still functions as an instance of nationalist ideology.

It is here that the toilet scene at the beginning of the film can be read retroactively as a comment on the relation between nationalist ideology (fantasy) and the structure of toilets. Here we are confronted with two other objects among the list of the Freudian-Lacanian partial objects, namely the feces and the urinary flow. As noted in previous chapters Lacan links the *objet petit a* to all these partial objects, and the anal *objet a* is the fecal object. The *objet petit a* at its most elementary refers to those anchoring points of the real, or those parts of the body that seem to be attached to an organ or are produced by an organ. They can effectively be detached from the body (feces or urinary flow) and which can be imaginerized as detachable.

In *The Plague of Fantasies*, Žižek has noted that even within the structure of toilets we can find "the exemplary case of how ideology is at work precisely where you don't think you will find it."[31] He goes on to distinguish between the German, French, and Anglo-Saxon (English) versions of toilets as instances of how the most utilitarian objects can often function as unconscious sites of nationalist ideologies. So if we were to add to Žižek's triad of the German, French, and Anglo-Saxon lavatory, the missing fourth Iranian lavatory, we can complete the logical set, or to put it in Aristotelian terms, the Iranian toilet functions as the formal cause of the other three toilets. According to this logic the Iranian lavatory functions as the originary or *Ur*-lavatory that influenced the very form of this triad. In this way, Kami's primordialization of the Iranian toilet that influenced the structure of Western toilets is the Iranian nationalist ideology *par excellence*. In other words, the logic goes something like this: "whatever Western civilization thinks it has accomplished, it is we (Iranians) who invented or achieved it first and this is even evident in the very structure of their toilets, and without it they would be back in the dark ages knee deep in their shit." In this way, the scene of the girl(s) sitting on the toilet stages the fact that we are already knee deep in ideology (as Žižek would have put it). Thus, the cultural history of the structure of toilets in the film functions as the fantasmatic narrative of nationalist ideology.

In his classic text, *The History of Shit* (*Histoire de la merde*) Dominique Laporte provides another theoretical reading of the history of the excremental function that is relevant to Kami's narrative. In his book Laporte conceptualizes a link between the individual and the destiny of human waste, where "the history of shit becomes the history of subjectivity." And as the subtitle of the book suggests, the history of shit functions as a prologue or prolegomena to "a prehistory of modernity and the modern subject."[32] In this sense the cultural history of the structure of Western toilets recounted by Kami is not incidental, since by claiming that Iranians were the first to invent the toilet, which later influenced the structure of Western toilets, it claims for itself the history of the formation of subjectivity (*à la* Laporte) and consequently of modernity itself. According to this logic Persian civilization not only preceded the Euro-American civilization, but even taught them the rudimentary elements of hygiene and gave them the very form of their toilets. The ideology here is one that is related to the history of the influence of Iranian civilization on the culture of Western civilization that is largely unknown or disavowed outside the academy and the scholarly public. However, in this context it is irrelevant whether there has been such a history of influence, which scholars have amply documented; but the important point to note here is the nationalist ideological narrative. It is this sort of nationalist ideology, which is often bordering on racism, and which developed in the early 20th century on certain racist tendencies in Iranian nationalist discourse,[33] which unwittingly aligns middle and upper middle-class Iranians (such as Nobahar, Arineh, and Kami) with the ideology of the Islamic Republic. In this way the older nationalist ideology becomes co-incident with the Islamic community ('*ummat*) of the Islamic Republic, which is why the policeman who gets into the car to question Arineh and Nobahar, says that "even you guys with your looks [presumably modern or Western looks], are at times in agreement with the regime." This emblematizes the paradoxical coming together of Iranian nationalist ideology (exemplified in the pre-revolutionary period by the Pahlavi regime), and the ideology of the Islamic Republic that positions Iran as an "Islamic nation" (*keshvar-e islami*).

This excremental dimension or lavatory logic that pervades both the formal and narrative logic of the film can also be read as a reference to the ideology of the Islamic Republic, which is even interested in the most intimate domains of the life of its citizens, such as in the way (female and male) subjects are to avail themselves of the toilet. Ayatollah Khomeini had composed a jurisprudential treatise (*resaleh*) called *Tawzih al-Masail*, in which he goes into graphic and obsessional detail as to how a Shi'i believer is to properly go to the lavatory (they must not be facing Mecca, they should wash their anus with their left hand and enter the toilet with their right foot, etc.). For example, Khomeini states:

> After urination, one must first wash the anus if it has been soiled by urine; then one must press three times with the middle finger and the base of the penis; then one must put his thumb on top of the penis and his index finger on the bottom and pull the skin forward three times as far as the circumcision ring; and after that three times squeeze the tip of the penis.[34]

Indeed, the writing of a *Tawzih al-Masai* was not peculiar to Khomeini, as many of the Shi'i *'ulama* had their own similar treatises (*resalehs*), much of which pertained to delineating the laws of cleanliness (*taharat*) and impurity (*nejasat*) and formed part of what is called *ahkam-e ab* or commandments of water. It is interesting that just before the 1979 revolution Khomeini had published the treatise with illustrations that describe how to use Western toilets, but after the revolution and the establishment of the Islamic Republic and its anti-western stance, especially toward the US, the publication of this treatise with the reproduction of the images of Western toilets and how to use them ceased.[35] This brings us to the curious fact that in the two scenes where Nobahar and Arineh are sitting on a toilet, the actual toilet is never shown on screen, but only implied. The Western toilet remains invisible throughout both scenes. In this sense, the toilet itself is never shown in the film, likely in order to not fall afoul of the censors. Despite such precautions, the film was never granted screening permission.

Finally, it seems that Ahmadzadeh is symbolically equating the State with the excremental function, with feces and the toilet. Indeed, Laporte in a provocative turn equates the State with the sewer, "Surely, the State is the Sewer. Not just because it spews divine law from its ravenous mouth, but because it reigns as the law of cleanliness above its sewers."[36] Laporte's formulation here can almost isomorphi-cally be mapped onto the theocratic State that is the Islamic Republic, namely that not only does it "spews out divine law," but "it reigns as the law of cleanliness," where every aspect of cleanliness and impurity is enumerated in obsessional detail. Similarly, Sadeq Hedayat had already referred to Iran and its political system during his life under the first Pahlavi regime as a "latrine" (*kala*),[37] and Ahmadzadeh may well be alluding to this excremental dimension of the State and its ruling ideology.

4.4   Repetition or the Double as the Thing (*das Ding*)

In *Atomic Heart*, the double structure of the film is mirrored in the structure of the double in the film. It is apparent in the redoubling or repetition of events and motifs that appear in the first part, and are repeated in the second part, sometimes in their nightmarish traumatic dimension in the second repetition, often representing the dark underside or double of the first part. It is as if the film follows the Freudian logic of the compulsion to repeat or repetition compulsion (*Wiederholungszwang*), where events are repeated in their traumatic dimension. For example, in the first part of the film, the mise-en-scène in the car is staged with Kami in the back seat (background) and the women in the front seats (foreground); the same mise-en-scène is repeated in the second part of the film, but with Toofan taking the place of Kami in the back seat in the same triangular formation. In this formal way the three figures in the car are doubled and the first and second half mirror each other.

   This formal structure suggests a subterranean parallel between the character of Kami and Toofan, where Toofan represents the dark, obscene underside of Kami, his double or doppelgänger. In this sense, what the figure of the double mirrors forth is a spectral obscene dimension in ourselves that we wish to repress or disa-vow. In this way the double always functions as the uncastrated dimension of our-selves, it is the Thing in us more than ourselves. As Žižek notes apropos the double, "…the double embodies the phantom-like Thing in me… the dissymmetry between me and my double is ultimately that between the (ordinary) object and the (sub-lime) Thing. In my double, I don't simply encounter myself (my mirror image), but first of all what is 'in me more than myself': the double is 'myself,'… under the modality of the other, sublime, ethereal body, a pure substance of enjoyment exempted from the circuit of generation and corruption."[38] The figure of the double appears throughout the history of cinema from *The Student of Prague* (*Der Student von Prag*, 1913) up to *Fight Club* (1999). Indeed, this logic of the double is an al-most exact description of the figure of Toofan, a sort of terrifying sublime ethereal body, who drives obscene enjoyment (jouissance) from the anxiety of the two girls and whose existence is beyond the circuit of generation and corruption, where like an atemporal phantom-like Thing he can appear and reappear anywhere, which is why Nobahar and Arineh are unable to escape from him. In the second part of the film, the basic problem of the two girls is how to get rid of Toofan. It is much easier to get rid of a real person, you can evade them or run away from them, which is precisely what the girls try to do (they drive away when Toofan puts the fake

Saddam in the limousine), but it is impossible to get rid of a fantasam, a spectral presence that sticks to you like glue. This inescapability from the fantasmatic figure of Toofan, represents the all-pervasive presence of the State in the life of Iranians.

This logic of repetition or doubling proliferates throughout the film. For instance, the lookout point that they drive to, and which looks over Tehran appears both in the first and the second part of the film, once with Kami where he relates his dream, and then with Toofan when they pick up the figure of Saddam (who himself is referred to by Nobahar as perhaps a body double of the real Saddam). The elevator scene at the beginning of the film has a light and comedic dimension in the first half, but a similar elevator scene appears again in the second part in a more nightmarish and foreboding dimension. In the first part at the beginning of the film, we get a close-up of Nobahar sitting on the toilet, and in the second part we get an exact shot of a close-up of Arineh on the toilet. The motif of C-27 is also repeated twice in the film (the so-called club of those who have died at age 27, which Kami explains to Nobahar in the car, which includes inter alia, Jim Morrison, Jimi Hendrix, Janice Joplin and Amy Winehouse), again with the second repetition becoming more ominous (alluding to an otherworldly place where Toofan is about to take Nobahar).

This structure of the double, which is repeated throughout the film, both at the level of form and narrative, gestures to another characteristic of life in Tehran under the Islamic Republic, namely the double-life led by many of its subjects. This structure of a double-life, where you have to dissimulate the truth in order to survive is part of the technique of *taqiyya* (dissimulation) in Shi'ite doctrine, which has permeated social and political relations in Tehran.[39] In her book *City of Lies: Love, Sex, Death and the Search for Truth in Tehran*, Ramita Navai refers to this structure of a double-life in Tehran and states, "In order to live in Tehran you have to lie. Morals don't come into it: lying in Tehran is about survival."[40]

Due to the strict controls, surveillance, and policing of society by the State apparatus, Iran is a Janus-face society with everyone leading a double-life as a survival strategy. The outward (*zahir*) reality of their lives is never what it seems, and the inner (*batin*) reality is never co-incident with outward appearances. However, this does not mean, as Navai has noted, that "Iranians are congenital liars," but on the contrary that these lies are "a consequence of surviving in an oppressive regime, of being ruled by a government that believes it should be able to interfere in even the most intimate affairs of its citizens."[41] As noted already, this interference extends into the most intimate domains of life such as monitoring (sexual) desires and even the use of toilets. In this sense, the logic of the double in the film is a subtle critique of the way the regime has created a sort of totalitarian nightmare where the people in Tehran lead a double life to keep up appearances before the watchful eye of the big (br)Other (to put it in this Lacanian/Orwellian terms).

4.5 *Che Voui?* or the Desire of the Other

The narrative coherence of the opening section becomes especially pronounced when we contrast it with what follows. The second part of the film is structured around the incessant mystery of desire, around the question of the role of desire and its surveillance in Iran by the State, embodied in the monstrous figure of Toofan (as we shall see in the case of the two female protagonists it is the forbidden same-sex desire). Arineh and Nobahar, as well as the spectator, do not know what Toofan really wants from them, at first it appears that he wants money that he paid on their behalf for the accident, but later at the end of the film in the rooftop scene when Arineh finally gets the money to give to him, he says, "money isn't everything," and Arineh, in visible distress and anxiety, finally states: "what do you want"? This is precisely the logic of desire formulated by Lacan in the famous interrogative in Italian, "*Che voui?*" What do you want? Lacan expanded the psychoanalytic notion of desire in several stages, adding to his earlier formulation "do not compromise with respect to your desire" (discussed in Chapter 3), another famous formulation: *desire is the desire of the Other*. For Lacan, our desires do not emerge spontaneously from some unfathomable abyss of human subjectivity, but rather our desires are learned, we have to learn how to desire. In order for us to desire, for example chocolate ice cream, we must first be properly installed within the symbolic order where chocolate ice cream is already an object of desire. In this sense, our desires emerge through the Other's desire.[42]

In this formulation the subject's desire is not self-generating, it is always constituted through the desire of the Other. The question of desire is not what do I want, but rather, what does the other want from me? What is it that the other sees in me and thereby desires me? As Žižek states, "the desire 'realized' (staged) in fantasy is not the subject's own, but the *other's desire:* fantasy, phantasmic formation, is an answer to the enigma *Che vuoi?*-... The original question of desire is not directly 'What do I want?,' but 'What do *others* want from me? What do they see in me? What am I to others?'"[43] Following this formulation, the desire "realized" or staged in fantasy (the dream/fantasy as the film) is not the desire of the two female characters (Arineh and Nobahar), but rather the Other's desire, namely the desire of Toofan, whom we may equate with the mysterious voice/text that directly addresses the spectator at the beginning of the film. In other words, the dream/film is a fantasy formation where we encounter the desire of the Other in all its traumatic dimension. So, what does the Other, as in Toofan, want? In a sense, what Toofan desires in the two girls is what Lacan calls the *objet petit a*, that illusive unfathomable X in them, that makes them the object of his desire. This is similar to Lacan's formulation: "I love you, but, because inexplicably I love in you something more than you, the *objet petit a*, I mutilate you."[44] This is the destructive passion of the real that seeks to annihilate you in order to get at the real kernel of your being.[45] This is why the encounter with the Other's desire is always traumatic, anxiety inducing; since what the Other (Toofan) desires is this impossible real kernel in them (Nobahar and Arineh), and he is ready to destroy them in order to extract it. Lacan referred to this unfathomable X with the Greek term *agalma*, a luminous and "shining" precious object that was hidden inside Socrates and which functioned as the object cause of Alcibiades' desire.[46]

Conversely, if we read Toofan's behavior as a way to contain the inherent destabilizing dimension of the real of their (same-sex) desire, it can be seen as a reaction to contain and control the revolutionary force of desire as such. Perhaps no one was more aware of this revolutionary dimension of desire than Deleuze and Guattari, as they state, "If desire is repressed, it is because every position of desire... is capable of calling into question the established order of a society: not that desire is asocial, on the contrary. But it is explosive; there is no desiring... without demolishing entire social sectors. Despite what some revolutionaries think about this, desire is revolutionary in its essence..."[47] Here despite the real differences between Deleuze and Guattari and psychoanalytic theory, their formulation of desire as revolutionary is compatible with psychoanalysis, since in psychoanalytic theory there is something always inherently destabilizing or disordering about desire, that can erupt and derail the order of things, which has led to the efforts of its containment or domestication via mechanisms of repression and oppression both psychic and societal. Even Deleuze and Guattari's locution *"real desire,"* recalls the Lacanian formulation of the real of desire, as they state, "no society can tolerate a position of *real desire* without its structures of exploitation, servitude and hierarchy being compromised." [my emphasis][48] Indeed, this insight of Deleuze and Guattari is even more apropos with respect to authoritarian or totalitarian societies, which is precisely how *Atomic Heart* casts the Islamic Republic—as a totalitarian state that represses erotic desire at every turn and not only in its same-sex iteration but desire in all its radical possibilities.

From this perspective, the name Nobahar, becomes a signifier of revolutionary force since in Persian her name means New Spring (it must be recalled the whole rise of the Arab Spring, was preceded by the Iranian Spring which was brutally suppressed), and alludes to the new protest movement, the so-called Green Movement, that erupted in Tehran in June of 2009 after the disputed presidential election of Ahmadinejad, and whose participants were captured via video and photographed by *Basiji* agents of the state dressed in civilian clothing; many of the youth that participated in the protest were subsequently hunted down, beaten, tortured and jailed in the aftermath of the uprising. This is precisely why Toofan wants to take Nobahar to another world. The character of Nobahar or New Spring is sick and dying (she has MS), which symbolizes the sickly and dying condition of the protest movement. Toofan says, "I am here to take you, you are dying anyways."

4.6   The Fright of Real Desires

Apropos the double structure of *Atomic Heart*, there is an important relationship between Ahmadzadeh's two films, *Kami's Party* and *Atomic Heart*, not only in that Kami's character appears in the second film, who was an absent presence throughout the entire duration of the first film, but more crucially, what was only verbally gestured in the first film is visually staged in the second film, namely the existence of same-sex desire in Iran. In this formal sense, the films are two versions of the same film.

In Ahmadzadeh's first film, *Kami's Party*, one of the female characters (which not incidentally happens to be played by the same actress that plays Nobahar in *Atomic Heart*) who has divorced her husband, states that her husband had turned out to be gay, and the male character says in somewhat mock surprise but "we don't have any gays in Iran." This formulation of course is a comedic reference to the (in)famous statement of Mahmud Ahmadinejad in his response to a student question at his talk in Columbia University in 2007, where he stated: "In Iran we don't have homosexuals like you have in your country" (*dar Iran ma methl-e shoma ham-jens baz nadarim*).[49] The female character in the film responds that "yes we have a few," and he protests saying, "no I swear to God we don't have any," and she retorts, "I am telling you we do," have gay people in Iran. In this way, what was initially verbally gestured to in *Kami's Party* is formally staged in the same-sex relationship between Nobahar and Arineh. This disavowal of the existence of homosexuals in Iran is again part of the Janus-faced structure of contemporary Iranian society, where on the face of it, or to keep up the order of appearances, it must be pretended that homosexuals do not exist; but the question is for whom should appearances be maintained since everyone knows very well that homosexuals do exist in Iran? The answer is, to put in Lacanian terms, for the big Other. It is for this virtual big Other as the agency of appearances for whom a façade must be maintained. For example, something is prohibited (homosexuality, alcohol, etc.), but it is not simply enough that it is prohibited, what is important is that it should not exist in the eyes of the big Other, even if we already know that it does exist out there in (social) reality.

As it was demonstrated in Chapter 1 in the analysis of *Daughters of the Sun*, the shaving of the female hair was a strategy that was deployed not only as a technique of unveiling but more importantly as a technology of undecidability for staging same-sex desire or female homoeroticism in the New Iranian Cinema. For instance, through shaving the head and cross-dressing an ambiguity of gender and sexuality was produced whereby same-sex desire and more specifically lesbian desire could be staged visually. Through the technique of shaving the head it was possible to represent sexual desire in all its radical ambiguity, since all non-heterosexual desire is forbidden and punishable by death in the Islamic Republic,[50] it can never be explicitly staged on screen (recall the trans imagery in *Daughters of the Sun* where it is precisely through the operation of the shaved head that a palpable sense of same-sex desire or female homoeroticism is evoked), they can only be gestured through the technique of shaving the head. But, in the shift away from the older generation of New Iranian Cinema exemplified by *Atomic Heart*, a new formal procedure is enacted to represent same-sex desire outside the semiotics of the shaved head, through other visual and narrative cues, especially through the dialogue, namely through double entendre, in the clever verbal locutions of the young hip upper middle-class Tehranis that are the protagonists of this film.

There are several subtle visual and narrative clues throughout the film that suggest that Arineh and Nobahar are not just close friends who live together but are within a same-sex or lesbian relationship. There is a certain ambiguity operative in the often close nature of female friendships in Iranian society that the film exploits, since female friends can even appear in public spaces holding hands or walk arm in arm, without raising any suspicion as to the possible erotic dimension of their relationship (the same is true for young men who also can be seen to hold hands with their friends or walk arm in arm, though this has become less prevalent in recent years, since there is a more visible pressure on moral policing by the *Basiji*'s of the heterosexuality of male relationships).[51] This ambiguity is explored in an early scene, for instance, when Kami asks Arineh how do you wake up Nobahar in the morning, and Arineh lovingly puts her hand on Nobahar's face and caresses it saying, "I turn and say, wake up my dear ('*azizam*)." In this instance there is a clear reference to them sleeping together in the same bed.

In another reference to Nobahar and Arineh's sexuality, while talking about how girls are more sexually aggressive these days, Kami states, "but at least you two are not dangerous." In other words, signaling that they are a lesbian couple, and therefore pose no danger to him. In the second part of the film as well, we get more clues as to the lesbian relationship of Arineh and Nobahar. While in the car, Toofan in a sort of subtle sexual interrogation of the girls says in a double entendre, "I can tell, you girls must like ice cream cones," suggesting that they like phallic oral copulation or fellatio, and Arineh retorts, "we don't eat ice cream cones – never"; meaning they have never been with men sexually or like to give fellatio to men, in other words they are lesbians. In one of the crucial scenes after Toofan has made evident his sexual interest with each of the girls, he says to Arineh that he likes and wants her friend Nobahar, and Arineh says, "You should know by now that, that is impossible," meaning, you should know very well by now that we are a same-sex couple. The logic here is strictly that of the perverse heterosexual male chauvinist universe in which it is thought that the lesbian couple can be "rehabilitated" or "converted" back into heterosexuality through "normal" heterosexual intercourse: in other words, according to this obscene logic all that lesbians need is heterosexual copulation, after which they would then be "normalized." Juynboll refers to how the subject of lesbian desire is dealt with in Islamic jurisprudence within Muslim societies and provides its meaning: "Lesbian (*sihaka* meaning rubbing). Male authors feel uncomfortable with the subject matter because they lack knowledge about lesbian practices, and thus, it is an alien subject. Usually, they argue in favor of 'converting' these women to normal male-oriented heterosexual behavior and the use of judicial discretion (*ta'zir*) rather than the recommended death penalty."[52] Such is the way Toofan acts toward the two girls, where he consistently terrorizes them; in other words, in this instance the enigma of the Other's desire (Toofan) is that he wants to render them heterosexual by copulating with them.

It is precisely here, that not only the two female protagonists encounter the real of the Other's desire (Toofan) but are also confronted with the deadlock of the real of their own desire, a desire that is unsymbolizable ("illicit," "deviant") within the heterosexual matrix of the Islamic Republic. Thus, the figure of Toofan (in another formulation) stages the real of their forbidden and outlawed erotic desire, he is the materialization of the impossible real of their desire, and since same-sex desire is prohibited in the Islamic Republic, Toofan becomes the very embodiment of this prohibition. This is the fright of real desires: when the traumatic kernel of your innermost desires become manifest.

4.7   The Collapse of the Fantasy and the Lacanian Real

The second half of the film is the collapse of the fantasy and represents reality stripped of its fantasmatic supplement, where the figure of Toofan (Mohammad Reza Golzar) functions as the appearance of the traumatic real and the disintegration of the fantasy exemplified by the first part. In other words what we get in the second part is the appearance of the real in all its horror, where reality becomes deprived of its fantasy support, and we get an irreal or surreal nightmarish universe. This cut between the dimension of fantasy and the world of reality is embodied in the figure of Toofan, who is the materialization of the excess of the traumatic real. The real has gone through several permutations in Lacan's work, but one of the fundamental aspects of the real emerges at the point at which symbolization fails. It is the limit inherent in symbolization itself, where the symbolic malfunctions or breaks down. We come close to encountering the real at moments of trauma, anxiety, aversion, and disorientation.[53]

In the film the real is represented as monstrous: through the (ethically) monstrous figure of Toofan; the eerie and ominous figure who is the embodiment of the patriarchal State or the totalitarian regime of the Islamic Republic. The name Toofan in Persian literally means tornado, which precisely fits in with Lacan's notion of the real and represents one of the forces of nature whose catastrophic and traumatic dimension brings us face to face with the horror of the real. Just as a tornado appears like a sort of monstrosity from the depths of nature destroying everything in its wake, so Toofan also suddenly seems to appear from nowhere, like a monster from the depths of inner space, and begins to terrorize the two girls until the very end of the film. Finally, it should be recalled that in a later scene when Toofan is asked by Arineh about his father, he states, "My father is a monster."

In the second part of the film the traumatic real embodied in the figure of Toofan is not disclosed all at once, but we are confronted with it only gradually. At first Toofan seems to be just a hip, stylish but eccentric character who is full of wit and humor, but slowly we discover that there is a dark and sinister dimension that lurks beneath his apparent humorous façade. This is the logic of the Freudian uncanny (*das Unheimliche*), when at first glance Toofan appears as an eccentric funny nice guy who just wants to help the girls (he pays for their car accident), but upon closer inspection, a more terrifying dimension emerges. It is here that Toofan takes on a dark and sinister aura and turns from a witty and humorous character into one who identifies and associates with dictators (Hitler, Saddam), and incessantly terrorizes the girls and physically abuses them. As Žižek states apropos the notion of the Freudian uncanny, "a perfectly 'natural' and 'familiar' situation is denatured, becomes 'uncanny,' loaded with horror and threatening possibilities, as soon as we add to it a small supplementary feature, a detail that 'does not belong'..."[54] It is in this precise sense, that the same situation and character (Toofan) which at first seemed perfectly ordinary and funny becomes all of a sudden "denatured" and "uncanny" and takes on a horrifying and traumatic dimension. In this way the Freudian uncanny and the Lacanian real are mutually linked since there is always an uncanny dimension to the real. This is also why, as Žižek has noted, there is always an *Unheimliche* dimension to the double, as he states, "the double is 'the same as me,' yet totally strange; his sameness all the more accentuates his uncanniness."[55] In this sense, the double always has the structure of the *Unheimliche*.

If there is a figure in theological terms that personifies the fantasmatic dimension of the real in all its horror, it is the devil. In the film there are several visual and narrative clues that link Toofan with the figure of the devil, not unlike the devil in Bulgakov's novel *The Master and Margerita*. There are a number of Christian or demonological motifs that runs through the film that are significant (from Arineh exclaiming that she is Christian and hence can drink alcohol, up to the scene in the Church where Toofan reappears again mysteriously, including the police asking the girls and Kami, "are you Satan-worshipers?") as they gesture toward the diabolical dimension of Toofan and his supernatural powers; but this supernatural dimension should not deceive us, as this is not a theological devil but a political one, with all the force of the theologico-political role of the totalitarian leader or the State exemplified in Ahmadinejad and the Islamic Republic. In one instance in the car Toofan states, "I am in Syria right now." The two girl's look of puzzlement is mirrored in the confusion of the spectator: How can a person be in two places at once? This reference to the fact that he is in Syria at this moment is an allusion to the entanglement of the Islamic Republic in the politics of Syria. It is one of the most explicit statements in the film that gestures toward the figure of Toofan as being the embodiment of the Iranian State or the Islamic Republic.

Freud in his text called, *A Seventeenth-Century Demonological Neurosis* (1922), analyses the story of Christoph Haizmann the painter, who purportedly had the devil appear to him and where the devil figures in several of his paintings. In his analysis of this case Freud conceives of the devil as a father-substitute, and the evil obverse or double of God as the father figure.[56] In this sense, the devil is one of the Names-of-the-Father in Lacanian parlance (for the Name-of-the-Father, see chapter on *Daughters of the Sun*), and stands for the totalitarian leader or the State. The character of Toofan is in a way representative of what Immanuel Kant called diabolical evil, like the diabolical killer Anton Chigurh played by Javier Bardem in the Coen brothers film *No Country for Old Men* (2007). The only other comparable figure of diabolical evil in cinema is perhaps the sinister figure of Ryunosuke Tsukue (played by the great Tatsuya Nakadai), a diabolically evil samurai and master swordsman in Kihachi Okamoto's *The Sword of Doom* (*Dai-bosatsu Tōge*, 1966). In his reading of *No Country for Old Men*, Žižek equates Bardem's character to the Kantian figure of diabolical evil, especially in how he decides to kill his victims through a flip of a coin.[57] Regarding this figure Žižek states, "the figure of the pathological hired killer played by Javier Bardem - a ruthless killing machine, with an ethics of his own, sticking to his word, [is] a figure of what Kant called diabolical Evil."[58] The key to understanding this figure is that it is not a real-life person "but a fantasy-entity - the embodiment of the pure object-obstacle, that unfathomable Y of blind fate - which always, in a weird mixture of chance and inexorable necessity,... intervenes to undermine the fulfilment of subjects' plans and intentions, guaranteeing that, one way or another, things will always somehow go wrong."[59] Similarly Toofan functions as a fantasy-entity whom, like a weird co-incidence of chance and inexorable destiny, the two girls are unable to escape from.

The scene at the end of *Atomic Heart* on the rooftop is one of the hermeneutic keys to the figure of Toofan. Toofan tells Nobahar to jump with him over the rooftop as it represents one of the gates through which they can enter the other parallel world. Arineh refuses and Toofan states, "okay we will decide by playing rock/paper/scissors, and if I win, we all have to jump and if I lose then I will jump." This image of playing a game of chance such as rock/paper/scissors with the capricious figure of Toofan, a game that will decide the destiny of the girls, is precisely the Kantian figure of diabolical evil, and recalls the character of Bardem (Anton Chigurh) in *No Country for Old Men* (the main difference between the two is Toofan's at times sadistic humor). This is the structure of diabolical evil, where the arbitrary flip of a coin or rock/paper/scissors, will determine who lives or dies. At the end when Toofan loses the rock/paper/scissors game, he sticks to his word (demonstrating an ethics of his own, a diabolical ethics), and does not make the two girls jump off the roof but prepares to jump himself.

4.8   The Enigma of Desire and the Dream within a Dream

Atomic Heart like *Mullholand Drive* is a film that splits the realms of fantasy and desire, where the first part depicts the world of fantasy, and the second part stages desire in all its radical mystery. Through the procedures of clearly distinguishing the visual register of the first part of the film from the visual world of the second part, the filmic text gestures respectively to the two worlds of fantasy and desire that are being posited as it were side by side. Indeed, the film opens a sense of mystery through a direct textual address to the spectator that inaugurates the oneiric world which we are about to enter:

> This film is about one of the most important characters of our time. This film is about me. About one of my *dreams* whose events occur on the night the subsidy payments were being distributed. I will never tell you who I am or what my name is, and you will never find out.

From this direct textual address to the spectator in the prelude before the film, what we get effectively is that the film is one of the *dreams* of this mysterious figure addressing us from the cinematic text, in other words the film is the addresser's inner fantasy space projected onto the cinematic screen. In this way the spectator or addressee is put in the position of a desiring subject, since the textual addresser remains undisclosed and the possibility of knowing who is addressing us from behind the text is foreclosed and our desire is thereby aroused from this sense of mystery. This writing in the screen image is what Michel Chion has termed *athorybos*.[60] We want to know who is this mysterious figure addressing us with this athorybos address, but are left desiring for an answer – as Žižek notes, this is "the perverse art of cinema, it does not give you what you desire, it tells you how to desire."[61] In this sense the film text is the portrayal of a dream and the dream text is the portrayal of the film.

The dream logic of the film comes to the fore when in the first part just before delving into the history of the structure of toilets, Kami recounts a dream (or more precisely a nightmare) to Arineh and Nobahar that he has had the night before, which he remembers in a kind of *déjà vu* while overlooking Tehran with lights of the city stretching into the horizon. Kami says that in the dream he was looking for Omid to light his cigarette when all of a sudden, an atomic bomb destroys the city, and its flames light his cigarette. Then he states that the city was not called Tehran but *Atomic Heart Mother*, a reference to the 1970 Pink Floyd record of the same name. The dream of course alludes to the anxiety over the nuclear program in Iran and the hardline stance on the issue by Ahmadinejad. This is the oneiric logic of the film in which the interpretation of the dream is in the dream within a dream. It is here that a Freudo-Lacanian logic of dreams becomes operative, in which censored material from waking reality return in the dream content as the real. As Žižek states, "The situation is similar to that of the Freudian logic of the dream, in which the Real announces itself in the guise of a dream within a dream."[62] Indeed, the real that discloses itself in the dream within the dream (film) is the real of the atomic bomb and the possibility of nuclear disaster in Tehran. From this perspective a Freudo-Lacanian reading of the film is certainly justified, since the logic of fantasy and dreams structure the entire logic of the film (both of which fall within the theoretical coordinates of psychoanalysis). There is even a reference to Freud himself in the film, when in the car Kami, while making fun of an Iranian diasporic news anchor in the United States, refers to Arineh as "Dr. Freudian." In fact there is a hint that Arineh may be a practicing psychoanalyst, as she is asked by Kami and Nobahar to provide an *interpretation* of Kami's dream, where in good psychoanalytic fashion she corrects them saying "analysis" (borrowed from English) rather than "interpretation" (*ta'bir*), to distinguish psychoanalytic dream interpretation from the older manuals of traditional Islamic dream interpretation, such as Ibn Sirin's book on dreams, that proliferate in Persian translations and are popular among Iranians.[63] The same phenomenon appears in other countries such as Egypt as noted by Elizabeth Sirriyeh in *Dreams and Visions in the World of Islam*.[64] Although Sirriyeh's discussion is regarding Egypt, the same can be said of Iran, where the older Islamic manuals on dream interpretation such as Ibn Sirin's can be found in bookstores in Tehran alongside Freud's *Interpretation of Dreams*.

One of the philosophical lessons of *Atomic Heart*, then, is that reality itself is structured like a dream, a dream/fantasy/fiction that is mistaken for reality but through interpretation the dream character or fantasy support of reality can be revealed. As Žižek states, "The ultimate achievement of film art is not to recreate reality within the narrative fiction, to seduce us into (mis)taking a fiction for reality, but, on the contrary, to make us discern the fictional aspect of reality itself..."[65] Perhaps this is the ultimate achievement of *Atomic Heart* as film art, since it stages the fictional or dreamlike structure of reality *itself*, and not only reality within the coordinates of authoritarianism or totalitarianism, but that reality *itself* would be non-existent without the fictions or dreams that structure it.

4.9   Dreaming of a Nightmare in Tehran

In *Atomic Heart* there is a traumatic real that the film as dream has concealed, and it is not in reality that we may uncover it, but in the dream (as the film) itself. *Atomic Heart* is a film where the fiction—or in this instance the dream—provides the means of accessing this traumatic real instead of functioning as an obstacle to it. Although the film provides a sense of reality, particularly in the first half, this is only to juxtapose it to the second half of the film, where the logic of the dream world is foregrounded and privileged. At the end of the film Ahmadzadeh sets up the possibility that waking up is a way of escaping this traumatic real, rather than confronting it. In his *Seminar XVII, The Other Side of Psychoanalysis*, Lacan provides a perfect illustration of this notion between the desire to wake up and its relation to the traumatic truth. He states, "A dream wakes you up just when it might let the truth drop, so that the only reason one wakes up is so as to continue dreaming—dreaming in the real or, to be more exact, in reality."[66] To explicate the logic of this formulation, Lacan turns to his earlier seminar, *The Four Fundamental Concepts of Psychoanalysis*, where he refers to a famous dream recounted by Freud, where a father dreams that his son is burning and exclaims, "Father don't you see I am burning."[67] This traumatic moment makes the father wake up from his dream but only to discover that the coffin of his deceased son has caught fire by candles. Lacan provides an incisive interpretation of this dream that goes beyond Freud's point that the dreamer is often aware of external reality while still dreaming. For Lacan, the father wakes up precisely at the crucial moment where the dream is about to reveal the horror of his own desire, namely the desire for his son's death. In this way, the father's waking up to the reality of the burning coffin functions as a defense mechanism against the traumatic truth of the horror of his own desire that the dream is about to reveal, and he thereby wakes up in order to escape confronting the traumatic truth of his desire.[68] This escape into reality from the horror of the traumatic truth revealed in the dream provides a sense of relief, since it protects us from the horror of our desire, while the logic of the dream asks us to confront our desire(s), regardless of how traumatic its disclosure may be. We wake up in order to escape the traumatic real of our desires revealed in the dream.

In *The Interpretation of Dreams*, Freud alludes to the nightmare "*Alptraum*" only on two occasions in Chapter 1 and does not develop a full theory of the nightmare. But toward the end of Chapter 7, Freud refers to the nightmare with an interesting term "'*Schreckgespent*', which would be classically linked to the *Alptraum* – 'incubus' or, literally, 'frightful specter'."[69] This frightful specter that emerges from the depths of inner space is precisely the real in all its horror, which once confronted in our dream, the dream quickly turns into a nightmare.[70] It is in the second half of the film that we are confronted with this "frightful specter," the horror of the real in the form of Toofan whose jouissance becomes the cause of the two girls' anxiety, as Lacan states, "... the nightmare's anxiety is felt, properly speaking, as that of the Other's *jouissance*."[71] The Other's jouissance or enjoyment, namely Toofan's enjoyment, is the source of anxiety for the two girls, but their anxiety is precisely the source of his (perverse) enjoyment (jouissance). In *The Pervert's Guide to Cinema*, Žižek provides another name for what remains of reality after fantasy disintegrates, as he states, "When fantasy disintegrates, you don't get reality. You get some nightmarish real, too traumatic to be experienced as ordinary reality. That would be another definition of nightmare."[72] It is often in the dream that turns into a nightmare that we encounter some repressed truth of our desire that appears as the traumatic real in all its horror. In this sense the end of *Atomic Heart* stages the need to wake up back into reality from the horror of the real confronted in the dream, embodied in the figure of Toofan. The logic here is effectively Lacanian, at first you dream in order to escape the unbearable reality, but then what you discover in the dream is (even) more horrifying than reality, hence you escape your dream in order to get back to reality. This is the elementary lesson of the Lacanian insight: we do not only avoid a deadlock in reality by escaping into our dreams (fantasies), but more crucially, we escape into reality from the nightmare of our dreams. But even more crucially, we wake up in order to continue to dream, that is, to continue in our fantasy.

We live in weird and eerie times, not only because we have just emerged from a global pandemic, which palpably rendered the entire world into a weird and eerie space (recall the media images of the streets of famous cities around the world emptied of the human, a quintessential feature of the eerie if there ever was one or an instance of the inertia of the real; or recall the weird images of animals taking over empty cityscapes, etc.), but the global climate catastrophe that is looming large on the horizon, the potential prospect of a disastrous world war with apocalyptic consequences, and not to mention technological and economic disruptions due to unchecked AI systems. If we are experiencing an era of the weird and the eerie globally, it is not without its local instantiations, especially as witnessed in Iran with the recent revolutionary movement called "Woman, Life, Freedom"—a women-led movement of emancipatory proportions that sought to dismantle the entire edifice of the Islamic Republic by demanding the abolition of the veil (*hejab*)—a traumatic point for the Islamic Republic's ideology undergirding the functioning and legitimacy of the State, to which they could not afford to give ground. It is no exaggeration to claim that film's such as Ahmadzadeh's *Atomic Heart* and his recent film *Critical Zone* (*Mantagheye bohrani*, 2023), enact a defiant rebellion against the oppressive nightmare created by the Islamic Republic which eventually led to the "Woman, Life, Freedom" movement, and which herald the future emancipation of a nation and its people.

Notes

1   For this article by Foucault, see Janet Afary and Kevin B. Anderson, *Foucault and the Iranian Revolution: Gender and the Seductions of Islamism* (Chicago: University of Chicago, 2005), 203–9. For a critical reassessment of Afary's and Anderson's reading of

Foucault's involvement in the Iranian Revolution, see Behrooz Ghamari-Tabrizi, *Foucault in Iran: Islamic Revolution After the Enlightenment* (Minnesota: University of Minnesota Press, 2016).

2 Todd McGowan in his reading of Lynch's *Mulholland Drive* (2001) also splits the two parts of the film into the world of fantasy (first part) and the world of desire (second part). See Todd McGowan, *The Impossible David Lynch* (New York: Columbia University Press, 2007), 194–219.

3 Post-screening discussion with Ali Ahmadzadeh, "Iranian Film 'Madare ghalb atomi' ('Atom Heart Mother') @ Berlin Film Festival 2015," accessed October 9, 2016. https://www.youtube.com/watch?v=cxA3wLhVs3E

4 Immanuel Kant, *Critique of Pure Reason*, trans. Paul Guyer and Allen W. Wood (Cambridge: University of Cambridge Press, 1998), 362.

5 Žižek writes, "In order to experience something as part of our reality, it has to fit the frame that determines the coordinates of our reality; Kant's name for this frame is the transcendental scheme, and the psychoanalytic name is fantasy." Slavoj Žižek, *Disparities* (New York/London: Bloomsbury Academic, 2016), 14.

6 Slavoj Žižek, *The Plague of Fantasies* (New York: Verso, 2008), 66.

7 Slavoj Žižek, *A Pervert's Guide to Cinema* (dir. Sophie Fiennes, 2006). Film.

8 Frances Restuccia also considers *Mulholland Drive* (2001) to comprise the same three ontological levels. See Frances Restuccia, *The Blue Box: Kristevan/Lacanian Readings of Contemporary Cinema* (London/New York: Continuum, 2012), 95.

9 Farshid Kazemi, "Interpreter of Desires: Iranian Cinema and Psychoanalysis" (PhD diss., University of Edinburgh, 2019); Farshid Kazemi, *A Girl Walks Home Alone at Night* (Liverpool: Liverpool University Press, 2021).

10 Ahmadzadeh seems to be influenced mostly by Abbas Kiarostami's aesthetics in this respect, especially Kiarostami's *Taste of Cherry* and *Ten* with much of the action set in a car. Another example may be in the way that one film acts as a catalyst for another film, such as Kiarostami's Koker trilogy and Ahmadzadeh's own previous film *Kami's Party* (2013), which acts as a catalyst for *Atomic Heart*.

11 I have drawn a theoretical short-circuit between the two modes of the weird and the eerie theorized by Fisher to their literary counterparts in Perso-Arabic literature called *"ajib wa gharib."* See Kazemi (2021).

12 Mark Fisher, *The Weird and the Eerie* (London: Repeater Books, 2016), 8.

13 Fisher, *The Weird and the Eerie*, 10–11.

14 Ibid, 11.

15 Ibid.

16 Ibid, 15.

17 Ibid.

18 Ibid, 9.

19 Ibid.

20 See Viktor Shklovsky, "Art as Technique," in *Russian Formalist Criticism: Four Essays*, ed. Lee T. Lemon and Marion J. Reis (Lincoln: Nebraska University Press, 1965), 3–24; cf. "Sterne's Tristram Shandy: Stylistic Commentary," in *Russian Formalist Criticism: Four Essays*, ed. Lee T. Lemon and Marion J. Reis, (Lincoln: Nebraska University Press, 1965), 25–59.

21 Fisher, *The Weird and the Eerie*, 11.

22 The London Freud Museum video introduction to psychoanalysis begins with the question: "What is Psychoanalysis? Part 1: Is it Weird?," accessed May 9, 2017. https://www.youtube.com/watch?v=pxaFeP9Ls5c

23 See Kazemi (2019) and (2021).

24 Shohini Chaudhuri, *Crisis Cinema in the Middle East: Creativity and Constraint in Iran and the Arab World* (United Kingdom: Bloomsbury Academic, 2022), 217.

25 Ibid, 217.
26 On these terms see Kazemi (2021).
27 Slavoj Žižek, *The Sublime Object of Ideology* (New York: Verso, 1989) 45.
28 On film endings see *Cinematic Cuts: Theorizing Film Endings*, ed. Shiela Kunkle (New York: State University of New York Press, 2016).
29 Given the oneiric dimension of *Atomic Heart* and references to another parallel world, an allusion to the two pills in *The Matrix* (1999) films is not impossible.
30 "'Qalb-e Atomi' Saranjam Roonamai Shod," *Fars News*, accessed July 9, 2016. http://www.farsnews.com/newstext.php?nn=13931121000045
31 Žižek states, "It is clear that none of these versions [of the toilet] can be accounted for in purely utilitarian terms: a certain ideological perception of how the subject should relate to the unpleasant excrement which comes from within our body is clearly discernible…" Žižek, *The Plague of Fantasies*, 3.
32 Dominique Laporte, *The History of Shit* (Cambridge Massachusetts, MIT Press, 2000), viii. For an earlier forgotten classic on this subject see John G. Bourke, *Scatalogic Rites of All Nations* (Washington, D.C.: W. H. Lowdermilk & Co, 1891). Incidentally Freud wrote an introduction to the German publication of the book and Laporte wrote the forward for the French publication.
33 For this racist dimension in the emergence of Iranian secular nationalist discourse, see Reza Zia-Ebrahimi, *The Emergence of Iranian Nationalism: Race and the Politics of Dislocation* (New York: Columbia University, 2016), especially Chapter 3, "Pre-Islamic Iran and Archaistic Frenzy," Chapter 4, "Of Lizard Eaters and Invasions: The Importance of European Racial Thought," and finally Chapter 6, "Aryanism and Dislocation."
34 Ayatollah Sayyed Ruhollah Mousavi Khomeini, *An Unabridged Translation of Resaleh Towzih al-Masael*, trans. J. Borujerdi, with a Foreword by Michael M. J. Fischer and Mehdi Abedi, (Westview Press/ Boulder and London, 1984), 42.
35 Pamela Karimi, "Secular Domesticities, Shiite Modernities: Khomeini's Illustrated *Tawzih al-Masail*," in *Visual Culture in the Modern Middle East: Rhetoric of the Image*, ed. Christiane Gruber and Sune Haugbolle (Bloomington, Indiana: Indiana University Press, 2013), 39–41.
36 Laporte, *History of Shit*, 57. On the same page, Laporte goes on to quote Lacan and writes, "'Civilization', says Lacan, 'is the spoils: the *cloaca maxima* [Roman sewage system].' We could easily substitute State here for civilization…"
37 Homa Katouzian and Elr, "Sadeq Hedayat," *Encyclopedia Iranica*, accessed March 8, 2016. http://www.iranicaonline.org/articles/hedayat-sadeq-i
38 Žižek, *Enjoy Your Symptom!*, 21.
39 On *taqiyya* in Shi'ism see Etan Kohlberg, "Some Imami-Shi'i Views on Taqiyya," *Journal of the American Oriental Society*, 95, no. 3 (July–September 1975): 395–402; Etan Kohlberg, "Taqiyya in Shi'i Theology and Religion," in *Secrecy and Concealment: Studies in the History of Mediterranean and Near Eastern Religions*, ed. Hans Hans Gerhard Kippenberg, Guy G. Stroumsa (Leiden: Brill, 1995), 345–80. L. Clarke, "The Rise and Decline of Taqiyya in Twelver Shi'ism," in *Reason and Inspiration in Islam: Theology and Inspiration in Islam*, ed. Todd Lawson (London: I.B. Tauris Publishers, 2005), 46–63.
40 Ramita Navai. *City of Lies: Love, Sex, Death, and the Search for Truth in Tehran* (London: Weidenfeld & Nicolson, 2014), 1.
41 Navai, *City of Lies*, 2.
42 Lacan states, "man's desire is the Other's desire, in which the *de*/of/provides what grammarians call a 'subjective determination' – namely, that it is qua/as/Other that man desires. … This is why the Other's question – that comes back to the subject from the place from which he expects an oracular reply – which takes some such form as '*Che vuoi?*', 'What do you want?' is the question that best leads the subject to the path of his own desire." See Lacan, *Écrits: A Selection* (New York: W.W. Norton), 1981.

43 Žižek, *The Plague of Fantasies*, 9.

44 Lacan, *Four Fundamental Concepts*, 263.

45 Slavoj Žižek, *The Puppet and the Dwarf* (Cambridge Massachusetts, MIT Press, 2003), 59.

46 Jacques Lacan, *Transference: The Seminar of Jaques Lacan, Book VIII*, trans. Bruce Fink (London: Polity Press, 2015), 135–48.

47 Deleuze and Guattari, *Anti-Oedipus*, 116. It should be recalled here that Guattari was a student of Lacan and was a practicing psychiatrist as well. For a fruitful encounter staged between psychoanalysis and Deleuze, see Aaron Schuster, *The Trouble With Pleasure: Deleuze and Psychoanalysis* (Cambridge: MIT Press, 2016).

48 Ibid.

49 For Ahmadinejad's reply, please see clip, "Ahmadinejad: No homosexuals in Iran," Talk at Columbia University, YouTube, September 24, 2007, 1 min., 41 sec., accessed April 12, 2016. https://www.youtube.com/watch?v=RUE0tukdr4c

50 In Article 131 of the Islamic penal law, it is written: "If the act of lesbianism is repeated three times and punishment is enforced each time, [the] death sentence will be issued the fourth time." Article 129 states that "the punishment for lesbianism is a hundred lashes for each party." "Islamic Penal Code of the Islamic Republic of Iran – Book One & Book Two," Iran Human Rights Documentation Center, accessed April 12, 2016, https://iranhrdc.org/wp-content/uploads/pdf_en/Iranian_Codes/Islamic_Penal_Code_of_the_Islamic_Republic_of_Iran_212133839.pdf.

51 The Article 112 of Islamic penal law on the sexual relations between men and boys states that: "If a mature man of sound mind commits sexual intercourse with an immature person, the doer will be killed and the passive one will be subject to *ta'azir* of 74 lashes if not under duress." Ibid.

52 G.H.A. Juynboll, "Siḥāḳ," in EI2 IX, pp. 565–67. For an analysis of same-sex relationships in Islamic jurisprudence, see Kecia Ali, *Sexual Ethics and Islam: Feminist Reflections on Qur'an, Hadith and Jurisprudence* (London: Oneworld Publications, 2016), especially Chapter 5, "Don't Ask, Don't Tell: Same Sex Intimacy in Muslim Thought."

53 As Glyn Daly states, "The Real is experienced in terms of the Symbolic (dis)functioning itself. We touch the Real through those points where symbolization fails; through trauma, aversion, dislocation and all those markers of uncertainty where the Symbolic fails to deliver a consistent and coherent reality. While the Real cannot be directly represented... it can nonetheless be *shown* in terms of symbolic failure and can be alluded to through figurative embodiments of horror-excess that threaten disintegration (monsters, forces of nature, disease/viruses and so on)." See Glyn Daly, "Slavoj Žižek: Risking the Impossible," for Lacan.com 2004, accessed November 10, 2016. http://www.lacan.com/zizek-primer.htm

54 Žižek, *Looking* Awry, 55.

55 Ibid., 55.

56 Sigmund Freud, *The Complete Psychological Works Of Sigmund Freud*, The Vol. 19: "The Ego and the Id" and Other Works vol. 19 (London: Vintage Classics, 2001), 69–108.

57 I am using the notion of diabolical evil here within the symbolic economy of the film, since Toofan is equated with the devil. Kant made a distinction between *radical* evil, "an insurmountable wickedness," that lies in the human heart and that human beings are "by no means [able] to wipe out" (66). As for *diabolical* evil, Kant argued that it is evil for the sake of evil itself, not evil in opposition to the moral law, but evil with its own internal moral law or maxim that motivates action. Kant ultimately denied the existence or possibility of diabolical evil in human beings and stated that "diabolical being" is not "applicable to human beings" (35). See Immanuel Kant, *Religion within the Limits of Reason Alone*, trans. Theodore M. Green and Hoyt H. Hudson (New York: Harper and Row, 1960). Žižek takes up this notion and claims that Kant was unable to accept the possibility of diabolical evil. Alenka Zupančič and Joan Copjec, each in their own way, mount a defense of Kant's rejection of diabolical evil. See Alenka Zupančič,

Ethics of the Real: Kant and Lacan (London: Verso, 2000), 90–101; Joan Copjec, *Imagine There's No Woman: Ethics and Sublimation* (Boston, Massachusetts: MIT, 2002), Chapter 5.

58 Žižek, *Less Than Nothing*, 658.

59 Ibid, 658.

60 Chion states, "I have given the name athorybos (Greek privative a- + thorybos, noise) to any object or movement in the image that could–either in reality or in the imagination–produce sound but which is not accompanied by any sound. It is my contention that all the writing we read in a film image that is not accompanied by an utterance or is not the source or 'launchpad' for an utterance, merits this term." Michel Chion, *Words on Screen*, trans. Claudia Gorbman (New York: Columbia University Press, 2017), 60.

61 Žižek, *The Pervert's Guide To Cinema.*

62 Žižek, *Less Than Nothing*, 348.

63 For dreams in Iran, see Hossein Ziai, "Dreams II: In the Persian Tradition," EIr VII: 549–51.

64 Elizabeth Sirriyeh states: "It is not unusual to find sections in bookshops containing works on dream interpretation by psychoanalysts placed next to medieval dream manuals. Sometimes, there are also attempts to claim that oneirocrits such as Ibn Sirin prepared the way for the modern discovery of psychoanalysis. It is also not unusual for the introductions to books of Muslim dream interpretation to contain lists of great authorities on dreams, beginning with the classic Muslim authors and ending with Sigmund Freud's *Interpretation of Dreams*." See Elizabeth Sirriyeh, *Dreams and Visions in the World of Islam* (London/New York: I.B. Tauris, 2017), 183. On the significance of dreams, visions and their interpretation in Islamicate societies including Iran, see Özgen Felek and Alexander D. Knysh, *Dreams and Visions in Islamic Societies* (State University of New York Press, 2012); cf. Henry Corbin, "Visionary Dream in Islamic Spirituality," *The Dream and Human Society*, ed. G.E. von Gurnebaum and Roger Caillois (Berkeley and Los Angeles: University of California Press, 1966); cf. Pierre Lory, *Le rêve et ses interprétations en islam* (Paris: Albin Michel, 2015); cf. Nile Green, "The Religious and Cultural Roles of Dreams and Visions in Islam," *Journal of the Royal Asiatic Society* 13, no. 3 (2003): 287–313.

65 Slavoj Žižek, *The Fright of Real Tears: Krzysztof Kieślowski Between Theory and Post-Theory* (London: The British Film Institute, 1999), 77.

66 Jacques Lacan, *The Seminar of Jacques Lacan, Book XVII: The Other Side of Psychoanalysis*, trans. Russell Grigg, ed. Jacques-Alain Miller (New York: Norton, 2007), 57.

67 Sigmund Freud (1900), *The Interpretation of Dreams* (Part II), in *The Standard Edition*, Volume V. (London: Vintage/Hogarth Press, 2001), pp. 339–627 (p. 509).

68 For Lacan's reading of the father's dream, see Jacques Lacan, *The Four Fundamental Concepts of Psychoanalysis*, Chapter 5.

69 See John Forrester's introduction to the new translation of Freud's text, Sigmund Freud, *Interpreting Dreams*, (London: Penguin Books, 2006). On the psychoanalytic notion of the nightmare, see Ernest Jones, *On the Nightmare*, (London, 1931); also see Jacques Lacan, *Anxiety: The Seminar of Jacques Lacan, Book X*, ed. Jacques-Alain Miller (Cambridge: Polity Press, 2014), 61. For a detailed analysis of the figure of the nightmare in relation to another diasporic Iranian film see Kazemi (2021).

70 On the figure of the nightmare and its relation to the vampire and Iranian myths and folklore, see Kazemi, (2021).

71 Lacan, *Anxiety*, 61.

72 Žižek, *The Pervert's Guide to Cinema.*

Conclusion

The Darkness of Desire and the Desire of Iranian Cinema

There is a remarkable power of fascination in a drawing by the French post-impressionist artist Georges Seurat called, "The veil" (drawn possibly between 1880 and 1883). Fascination in the precise sense of the terms etymology, which derives from the Latin *fascināre*, whose semantic field ranges from "irresistibly attractive influence" and "enchantment" to the archaic meanings of "witchcraft" and "sorcery."[1] In the drawing, a mysterious female figure is depicted in profile partially veiled black, in a medium shot (from the waist up). The veil does not cover the young woman's entire face, but veils over her vision (eyes), with the other half of her face remaining unveiled. The space around this figure is darkened by the conté crayon, with the lower half of the woman drawn a deeper darkness by repeating the movement of black crayon on the paper; it is as if this fragile feminine figure seems to appear, like a partial object, from some nether region, from an abyss of darkness. The question to be asked here is: why does this veiled woman exert such a power of fascination upon the viewer? In her analysis of this drawing, Annie Le Brun proposes that this darkness which like a center of energy surrounds the space around this frail female figure "symbolizes the darkness of desire that seems to entirely consume this young woman." Le Brun states that what fascinates her in this drawing "is the unwavering aspect of human desire that Seurat seems to have captured here…" and calls attention to the fact that the drawing "took place almost 20 years before Freud highlighted its [desire's] critical importance."[2] Indeed, from a Lacanian perspective, there is always a darkness to desire, desire is often obscure and opaque to the subject itself, but also the "Other's desire" is "obscure and opaque"[3] to the subject; our desires are never transparent to ourselves, desires have to be interpreted, we need an interpretation of desires. If this veiled female figure in Seruat's drawing may be seen as a metaphor for post-revolutionary Iranian cinema, it is a metaphor for the way in which not only vision is to be circumscribed by the command of the modesty system but the way in which desire itself becomes inscribed in the formal logic of post-revolutionary Iranian cinema due to the logic of the veil. This is precisely what renders this cinema into the cinema of desire. In this quite formal sense, as Alexander Kojève puts it, "desire is the presence of an *absence*…"[4]

DOI: 10.4324/9781003531029-8

Post-revolutionary Iranian cinema began with a problemtics of what to show and what not to show, what to reveal and what to conceal, especially in relation to representing female bodies on screen, which would have to abide by the logic of the veil (*hejab*) or the system of modesty in the broadest sense. This *problématique* as it were, was first articulated by none other than the spiritual and political leader of the Islamic Republic, Ayatollah Ruhollah Khomeini, for whom, as Mottahedeh puts it, "women's bodies marked the site of contamination."[5] Therefore, the problem that post-revolutionary Iranian cinema grappled with was how to represent women's bodies so as not to arouse the desire of the (heterosexual) male subject, especially the "male gaze," and how not to render women into what Mulvey termed "to-be-looked-at-ness." This procedure of imposing the system of modesty on the cinema often had an obverse consequence to its intended effect, especially in relation to the veil, where the secret of the veil raises the fascination of the gaze to imagine what lies behind it, wherein resides the elementary lesson of "fantasy": to fantasize what remains hidden from the visual field. The process of veiling the audio-visual sensorium thus functions as the Lacanian *object petit a*, or the object-cause of desire, a virtual or invisible element that propels desire. In this precise sense, despite the censorship of aurality and visuality implemented by the state apparatus, which inscribes the logic of the "averted gaze" onto the screen image, the system of modesty in Iranian cinema inadvertently created a new filmic grammar that rendered Iranian cinema into the cinema of desire.

Perhaps one of the great auteurs of New Iranian Cinema, Abbas Kiarostami's (d. 2016) cinematic oeuvre left an indelible mark on post-revolutionary Iranian cinema and influenced many filmmakers and spawned many imitators. Indeed, many of the strategies that were part of Kiarostami's formal style of filmmaking became part of the recognizable cinematic grammar of post-revolutionary Iranian cinema (location shooting, rural settings, non-professional actors, the play with reality and fiction etc.), but perhaps none more so than Kiarostami's play with absences, with the possibilities of what may be termed *un-showing*, with what remains hidden or unseen in the screen image—a formal strategy that had a profound impact in the way Iranian cinema became the cinema of desire. As Kiarostami states, "How much can you make visible without actually showing anything? I want to create the kind of cinema that shows by not showing. Some films reveal so much that there is no room for the audience's imagination to intervene."[6] For instance, the first 16 minutes of the film *Dah* (*Ten,* 2002) in which the camera withholds a view of the mother and we only hear her (acousmatic) voice, is a formal strategy that makes "audiences become increasingly curious about who she is, [and] what she looks like." As Kiarostami states, "we can't get this woman out of our minds, or the *desire* to see her [emphasis added]."[7] It is this play with absences, with the invisible in the visible and the unseen in the seen, which evokes and provokes the desire of the viewer that renders Kiarostami's films into the cinema of desire, and the cinema of all those filmmakers that were influenced by him.

Throughout this book I have variously demonstrated that desire like a spectral presence haunts the cinematic landscape of post-revolutionary Iranian cinema.

Indeed, the shadow of the 1979 revolution and its censorship codes hovers over Iranian cinema, much as the shadow of (repressed) desire hovers over its cinematic production. This is what in Lacanian terms would be called "the structuring absence," an absence that structures the entire formal logic of this cinema. In Freudo-Lacanian theory, desire and eroticism are co-extensive. Lacan makes this connection between eros and desire in the seminar on *The Four Fundamental Concepts of Psychoanalysis* while referring to Socrates stating, "… it is said that Socrates never claimed to know anything, except on the subject of Eros, that is to say, desire."[8] What eros and eroticism signify in psychoanalysis is not the common notion of the erotic in popular culture which is often blurred or confused with pornography; for eroticism to be eroticism proper, it must remain implicit rather than explicit. It must be implied, suggested, hinted at, rather than shown explicitly. Eroticism is born out of what you can imagine as opposed to what you can see. Eroticism is related to the logic of fantasy, in the absences within and of the image, what you cannot see explicitly on the screen (the moment of sexual intimacy, etc.), the imagination fills in by providing the fantasmatic supplement. Eroticism is not without secrecy, mystery, and concealment, as Byung Chul-Han puts it, "the erotic is never free of secrecy."[9]

In pornography you see everything, there is little left for the imagination to fill in. This is why Badiou refers to our age as *The Pornographic Age*, in which everything is on display "in the order of the image"[10] within our social mediatic universe and screen saturated societies, where the construction, proliferation, and circulation of images have something of a pornographic logic to them.[11] According to Han, there is a fundamental difference between porn and eroticism. Porn is about revealing, about exhibition, which is contrary to erotic communication, since "exhibition destroys any and all possibilities for erotic communication. A naked face without mystery or expression—reduced simply to being on display—is obscene and pornographic. Capitalism is aggravating the pornographication of society by making everything a commodity and putting it on display. Knowing no other use for sexuality, it profanes eros—into porn."[12] For Han, "Porn is a matter of *bare life on display*," it is the "antagonist of eros, it annihilates even sexuality."[13] Eros is about a play of what is unseen, it is about captivating the imagination, about seduction, but pornography eliminates "erotic seduction, which toys with scenic illusion and deceptive appearances."[14] This is the elementary difference between eroticism and pornography.[15]

This is precisely why many films made outside Iran cannot be categorized as the cinema of desire, in the way that many examples of films that emerge from Iran after the revolution can. For example, a diasporic film called *Tehran Taboo* (2017) directed by Ali Soozande, is a film that deals with the hypocrisies of sexuality in Iran under the Islamic Republic, explicitly gesturing to sexual acts within the diegetic reality of the film, which for obvious reasons, could never be shown in films produced in Iran, and which only a diasporic film such as this could render explicit. It is interesting to note that in *The Interpretation of Dreams*, there is not a single explicitly sexual dream that is mentioned or discussed by Freud,[16] since this would be at the level of the manifest content of the dream, but Freud located the motive force of the dream not in its manifest content but the dream's latent content, and what you discover there is what Freud calls *Wunsch* (wish) and Lacan calls *désir* (desire). The theoretical lesson that must be drawn from this significant absence is clear: *the only truly sexual dreams are non-sexual ones*. Similarly, following this Freudian insight it can be said that the only truly sexual films are non-sexual ones, and hence *Tehran Taboo* cannot be considered a *sexual* film in this strict Freudian sense, since it deals explicitly with sex in Tehran. In this sense, there is nothing properly erotic to the film, as it is all out there in plain sight. Such films, although important in the way in which they reveal the consequences of oppressive measures against desire and sexuality in Iranian society, cannot be formally considered as examples of the cinema of desire.

Here, I would like to return to the question with which I began this book, namely what is at stake today in coupling psychoanalysis and Iranian cinema? If we accept as I have argued that psychoanalytic theory is, at its core, concerned with the structure of desire and its interpretation, it is here then that we can discern that it is in Iranian cinema, perhaps more than any other cinematic universe, that the logic of desire is operative both at the level of cinematic form and content. It is through the encounter between Iranian cinema and Freudo-Lacanian psychoanalytic theory that the interpretation of these (repressed) desires can be brought to light, desires that often undermine the explicit ideology of the Islamic Republic and uncover its hidden libidinal economy.

It is a little puzzling that it has taken this long for psychoanalytic theory to be systematically coupled with Iranian cinema, since as this book has demonstrated, the short-circuiting of Iranian cinema with (Freudo-Lacanian) psychoanalytic theory can bring out theoretical insights that shatter our common perceptions and conceptions of the two in novel ways. Walter Benjamin once used a profoundly counter-intuitive metaphor that is relevant here, he indicated that we must "act as if the classic work is a film for which the appropriate chemical liquid to develop it was invented only later, so that it is only today that we can get the full picture."[17] In this sense, it is perhaps only today that we can get the full picture of the structure of desire operative in Iranian cinema by applying the chemical liquid that is psychoanalytic theory to Iranian films, but also crucially, psychoanalytic theory itself is retroactively transformed by coming into contact with the chemical liquid that is Iranian films.

Although aspects of post-revolutionary Iranian cinema were theorized partially through the prism of psychoanalytic theory before, as we have seen, it was largely through the lens of first-wave psychoanalytic theory or *Screen* theory. This was essentially a *missed encounter* since it missed the essential dimension of this cinema as the cinema of desire; therefore, it is only in its repetition in second-wave psychoanalytic theory that we come to the true encounter between Iranian cinema and psychoanalysis. Here we have a dialectical process by which the first missed or failed encounter, namely between Iranian cinema and first-wave psychoanalytic theory, creates the preconditions by which its truth or its "essence" is realized or posited in the second encounter.

In his magnum opus, *Less Than Nothing*, Žižek strangely claims psychoanalysis only for the Western Judeo-Christian tradition against Islam, by theorizing that it is only the former that endorses the full reality of the objects of desire, whereas for the latter all objects of desire are merely illusory. He states, "This is why psychoanalysis is firmly entrenched in the Western Judeo-Christian tradition, not only against Oriental spirituality but also against Islam, which, like Oriental spirituality, endorses the thesis on *the ultimate vanity and illusory nature of every object of desire* [emphasis added]."[18] Indeed, it is apparent that Žižek is not well equipped in dealing with the nuances, intricacies, and complexities of the study of Islamic thought in relation to desire and sexuality. This book has variously demonstrated that both Sunni and Shi'i Islam acknowledge everywhere the reality and efficacity of (sexual) desire and the erotic, as Bouhdiba states, "In Islam, then, sexuality enjoys a privileged status. Whether in the texts that regulate the exercise of sexuality in social life or in those that allow the dream its full oneiric density, the right to the pleasures of sex is stated forcefully."[19] The reading that claims psychoanalysis only for the Western Judeo-Christian tradition is a disavowal of the profoundly shared cultural and intellectual heritage of these monotheistic "religions of the book" throughout history, a disavowal that is symptomatic of our contemporary era. It is hoped that one of the achievements of this book is to have put to rest such reductive readings, by staging a productive encounter between (Lacanian) psychoanalytic film theory and post-revolutionary Iranian cinema, where the logic of desire inscribed in the formal and narrative structure of this cinema is brought to the fore.

In her epilogue to a collection of articles on *Islamicate Sexualities*, Dina Al-Kassim has noted that "psychoanalytic insight" has not always been accepted in the field of Islamicate sexualities, particularly when such fields have grappled with their own "epistemological frameworks."[20] Al-Kassim states that if she has insisted on "psychoanalytic reflection, it is because the question of how we come to know what desire has been and what it has meant (politically, institutionally, subjectively, rhetorically, juridically, medically, in folk practices, in literature, in translation, in cultural transmission, in heteroglossia of all kinds) requires us to think historically while also attending to the formation of power in the multiple presents sedimented in our archives and our attitudes."[21] To this list we must add *cinema*, in which what desire has been and what it means is policed or formed through the unconscious inscriptions of desire in the filmic text, which form and produce not only spectatorial positions and perceptions that are especially unique to Iranian cinema, but are related to the logic of desire operative in this cinema. Therefore, psychoanalytic insight in the context of studies of sexuality in Iran is profoundly important, "for [psychoanalysis] offers interpretative purchase on the often unconscious inscription of desire in texts."[22] Thus, my own insistence on second-wave psychoanalytic film theory as a productive method for reading Iranian cinema is not to merely argue that "psychoanalysis will afford us a technical language or a ready-made tool of analysis," but, as Al-Kassim argues, "[r]ather, [that] psychoanalysis is a set of reflections on the very objects of our study – desire…"[23]

Finally, it may be asked: what is the desire of Iranian cinema? Here by the "desire" of Iranian cinema I am not referring to the desire within the filmic text or the desire of Iranian filmmakers but rather refer to the "desire" of the Other, the desire of the Islamic Republic and its censorship apparatus (i.e., the Ministry of Culture and Islamic Guidance). It is in the way in which after the revolution the state's "desire" has been to police desire, to drape over the auditory and visual sensorium of Iranian cinema by enveloping it in the system of modesty (*hejab*). In doing so, it has sought to veil over not only the visual and aural sensorium but desire itself—especially female or feminine desire. It is this desire to obscure desire, to conceal it, to veil over it or render it inoperative which has misfired; since it is precisely by seeking to conceal *desire*, and to expel it from the screen image, that it has inadvertently revealed the logic of desire—desire *as* lack, but also simultaneously a sort of excess—this is the dialectic of desire. It is this paradoxical logic which has rendered many instances of post-revolutionary Iranian cinema into the cinema of desire along such movements as Italian Neorealism and the French New Wave. In the final analysis, it is only through an analysis of the darkness of desire and the desire of Iranian cinema, that we may become an *interpreter of desires*.

Notes

1 Mikko Tuhkanen, "Being Fascinated: Toward Blanchotian Film Theory," *Postmodern Culture: Journal of Interdisciplinary Thought On Contemporary Cultures*, 29, no. 2, January 2019, December 3, 2020. https://www.pomoculture.org/2020/12/03/being-fascinated-toward-blanchotian-film-theory/

2 Annie Le Brun, "'The veil' by Georges Seurat," YouTube, September 30, 2019, 3:47–4:44, https://www.youtube.com/watch?v=JfpJetjYUKM

3 Lacan, *Desire and Its Interpretation*, 17.

4 Alexander Kojève, *Introduction to the Reading of Hegel: Lectures on the Phenomenology of Spirit* (Ithaca NY: Cornell University Press, 1980), 134.

5 Mottahedeh, *Displaced Allegories*, 2.

6 Kiarostami, *Lessons with Kiarostami*, 20–21.

7 Ibid., 23–24.

8 Lacan, *The Four Fundamental Concepts*, 232.

9 Chul-Han, *The Agony of Eros*, 32.

10 Alain Badiou, *The Pornographic Age* (London/New York: Bloomsbury Academic, 2020), 2.

11 Ibid., 22.

12 Chul-Han, *The Agony of Eros*, 32.

13 Ibid., 29.

14 Ibid., 33.

15 This of course does not mean that those who are acting in pornography themselves are not in need of fantasy, since the libido is almost always in need of a virtual fantasmatic supplement to sustain itself. See Žižek's reference to a funny episode about a porn actor who while engaging in the sexual act, all of a sudden loses their fantasy support and searches Pornhub to restore it. See Slavoj Žižek, *Surplus-Enjoyment: A Guide for the Non-Preplexed* (London: Bloomsbury Academic, 2022), 4.

16 This is put succinctly in an article on the Freud Museum London website, "If there's anything striking about Freud's dream book, it's the peculiar absence of sex." Why Did Freud Interpret Dreams in a Sexual Way? Freud Museum London, November 12, 2019, https://www.freud.org.uk/2019/11/12/why-did-freud-interpret-dreams-in-a-sexual-way/

17 Slavoj Žižek, *Antigone* (London: Bloomsbury Academic, 2016), introduction, iBooks. See Walter Bejamin, "the Work of Art in the Age of Mechanical Reproduction," in *Illuminations: Essays and Reflections* (New York: Schocken Books, 2007), 220–21.

18 Žižek, *Less Than Nothing*, 132.

19 Bouhdiba, *Sexuality in Islam*, 88.

20 Dina Al-Kassim, "Epilogue: Sexual Epistemologies, East in West," *Islamicate Sexualities: Translations Across Temporal Geographies of Desire*, ed. Kathryn Babayan and Afsaneh Najmabadi (Cambridge, MA: Center for Middle Eastern Studies/Harvard UP, 2008), 332.

21 Ibid.

22 Ibid.

23 Ibid., 333.

Bibliography

Afary, Janet. *Sexual Politics in Modern Iran*. Cambridge: Cambridge University Press, 2009.

Afary, Janet and Kevin B. Anderson. *Foucault and the Iranian Revolution: Gender and the Seductions of Islamism*. Chicago: University of Chicago, 2005.

Ahamdinejad, Mahmud. "In Iran, We Don't Have Homosexuals," YouTube, Sep 24, 2007. https://www.youtube.com/watch?v=U-sC26wpUGQ

Ahmadzadeh, Ali. "Iranian Film "Madare ghalb atomi" ("Atom Heart Mother") @ Berlin Film Festival 2015". https://www.youtube.com/watch?v=cxA3wLhVs3E

Ali, Kecia. *Sexual Ethics and Islam: Feminist Reflections on Qur'an, Hadith and Jurisprudence*. London: Oneworld Publications, 2016.

Althusser, Louis. "Ideology and Ideological State Apparatuses." In *Lenin and Philosophy and Other Essays*, 127–186. Translated by B. Brewster. New York: Monthly Review, 1971.

Amanat, Abbas. *The Pivot of the Universe: Nasir Al-Din Shah Qajar and the Iranian Monarchy, 1831–1896*. London: I.B. Tauris, 2008.

Anderson, Jeffry J. "Rapunzel: The Symbolism of the Cutting of Hair." *Journal of the American Psychoanalytic Association* 28 (1980): 69–88.

Andrew, Geoff. "Kiarostami and the Art of the Invisible." In *DVD Booklet for Shirin*. London: British Film Institute, 2008.

Atwood, Blake. *Reform Cinema in Iran: Film and Political Change in the Islamic Republic*. New York: Columbia University Press, 2016.

Badiou, Alain. *Séminaire Lacan: L'antiphilosophie 3, 1994–1995*. Paris: Fayard, 2013.

Badiou, Alain. *Lacan: Anti-Philosophy 3*. New York: Columbia University Press, 2018.

Barnard, Suzanne and Bruce Fink. *Reading Seminar XX, Lacan's Major Work on Love, Knowledge, and Feminine Sexuality*. Albany: State University of New York Press, 2002.

Barzin, Nader. "La pscychanalyse en Iran." *Topique* 1 (2010): 157–71.

Bashir, Shahzad. *Sufi Bodies: Religion and Society in Medieval Islam*. New York: Columbia University Press, 2011.

Baudry, Jean-Louis. "Ideological Effects of the Basic Cinematographic Apparatus." In *Narrative, Apparatus, Ideology: A Film Theory Reader*, edited by Philip Rosen, 286–98. New York: Columbia University Press, 1986.

Baudry, Jean-Louis. "The Apparatus: Metapsychological Approaches to the Impression of Reality in Cinema." In *Narrative, Apparatus, Ideology: A Film Theory Reader*, edited by Philip Rosen, 299–318. New York: Columbia University Press, 1986.

Behrouzan, Orkideh. *Prozak Diaries: Psychiatry and Generational Memory in Iran*. Stanford, California: Stanford University Press, 2016.

Behrouzan, Orkideh and Michael M. J. Fischer. "Behaves Like a Rooster and Cries Like a [Four Eyed] Canine: The Politics and Poetics of Depression and Psychiatry in Iran."

In *Genocide and Mass Violence: Memory, Symptom, and Recovery*, edited by Devon E. Hinton and Alexander L. Hinton, 105–36. Cambridge: Cambridge University Press, 2014.

Bell-Metereau, Rebecca. *Transgender Cinema*. New Brunswick: Rutgers University Press, 2019.

Benjamin, Walter. *Illuminations: Essays and Reflections*, edited by Hannah Arendt. Translated by Harry Zohn. New York: Schocken Books, 2007.

Benslama, Fethi. *Psychoanalysis and the Challenge of Islam*. Minneapolis: University of Minnesota Press, 2009.

Bergstrom, Janet, ed. *Endless Night: Cinema and Psychoanalysis, Parallel Histories*. Berkeley: University of California Press, 1999.

Beyzaie, Bahram. *Namayesh dar Iran [Drama in Iran]*. Tehran: Roshangaran va motale'at-e zanan, 2001.

Beyzaie, Bahram. *Hezar Afsan Kojast?* [Where is A Thousand Tales?]. Tehran: Roshangaran va motale'at-e zanan, 2011.

Bordwell, David. "The movie looks back at us," Wednesday | April 1, 2009. http://www.davidbordwell.net/blog/2009/04/01/the-movie-looks-back-at-us/

Bouhdiba, Abdelwahab. *La sexualité en Islam*. Paris: Presses Universitaires France, 1975.

Bouhdiba, Abdelwahab, *Sexuality in Islam*. Translated by Alan Sheridan. London: Saqi Books, 2012.

Bourke, John G. *Scatalogic Rites of All Nations*. Washington, D.C: W. H. Lowdermilk & Co, 1891.

Braudy, Leo and Marshall Cohen. *Film Theory and Criticism*. Oxford: Oxford University Press, 2009.

Breton, André. *Manifestoes of Surrealism*. Translated by Richard Seaver and Helen R. Lane. Michigan: The University of Michigan, 2010.

Brown, Vahid. "A Counter-History of Islam: Ibn 'Arabi within the Spiritualn Topography of Henry Corbin." *Journal of Ibn Arabi Society* XXXII (2002): 45–65.

Butler, Judith. *Bodies That Matter*. New York: Routledge, 1993.

Butler, Judith. *The Psychic Life of Power: Theories of Subjection*. New York: Columbia University, 1997.

Butler, Judith. *Gender Trouble*. London: Routledge, 2011.

Cahiers du, Cinéma. "John Ford's Young Mr Lincoln: A Collective Text by the Editors of Cahiers du Cinéma." Translated by Helen Lackner and Diana Matias. *Screen* 13, no. 3 (1972): 5–44.

Carlson, Shanna T. "Transgender Subjectivity and the Logic of Sexual Difference." *Differences* 21, no. 2 (2010): 46–72.

Chaudhuri, Shohini, and Howard Finn. "The Open Image: Poetic Realism and the New Iranian Cinema." *Screen* 44, no. 1 (2003): 38–57.

Chehabi, H. E. "Voices Unveiled: Women Singers in Iran." In *Iran and Beyond*, edited by Rudi Matthee and Beth Baron, 151–66. Costa Mesa, California: Mazda Publishers, 2000.

Chehabi, Houchang E. "The Banning of the Veil and Its Consequences." In *The Making of Modern Iran: State and Society under Riza Shah, 1921–1941*, edited by Stephanie Cronin, 193–210. London: Curzon, 2003.

Chelkowski, Peter. ed. *Ta'ziyeh: Ritual and Drama in Iran*. New York: New York University Press, 1979.

Cheshire, Godfrey. "Abbas Kiarostami: A Cinema of Questions." *Film Comment* 8, no. 6 (1996): 34–43.

Chion, Michel. "The Impossible Embodiment." In *Everything You Always Wanted to Know About Lacan, but Were Afraid to Ask Hitchcock*, edited by Slavoj Žižek. London/New York: Verso, 1992.

Chion, Michel. *The Voice in Cinema*. Translated by Claudia Gorbman. New York: Columbia UP, 1999.

Chion, Michel. *Words on Screen*. Translated by Claudia Gorbman. New York: Columbia University Press, 2017.

Clark, L. "*Hijab* According to the *Hadith*: Text and Interpretation." In *The Muslim Veil in North America*, edited by S.S. Alavi, H. Hoodfar, and S. McDonough, 214–86. Toronto: Women's Press, 2003.

Clark, L. "The Rise and Decline of Taqiyya in Twelver Shi'ism." In *Reason and Inspiration in Islam: Theology and Inspiration in Islam*, edited by Todd Lawson, 46–63. London: I.B. Tauris Publishers, 2005.

Clemens, Justin. *Psychoanalysis is an Antiphilosophy*. Edinburgh: University of Edinburgh, 2013.

Cole, Juan Ricardo, and Nikki R. Keddie eds. *Shi'ism and Social Protest*. New Haven: Yale University Press, 1986.

Comolli, Jean-Louis, and Jean Narboni. "Cinema/Ideology/Criticism (1)." In *Screen Reader 1: Cinema/Ideology/Politics*, edited by John Ellis, 2–11. London: The Society for Education in Film and Television, 1977.

Copjec, Joan. *Read My Desire: Lacan Against the Historicists*. Cambridge, MA: MIT Press, 1994.

Copjec, Joan. *Imagine There's No Woman: Ethics and Sublimation*. Boston, Massachusetts: MIT, 2002.

Copjec, Joan. "The Object-Gaze: Shame, Hejab, Cinema." *Filozofski Vestnik (Ljubljana)* XXVII, no. 2 (2007): 161–83.

Copjec, Joan. "The Censorship of Interiority." *Umbr(a), Islam, A Journal of the Unconscious*. (2009): 165–186. SUNY/Buffalo: The Center for the Study of Psychoanalysis & Culture.

Copjec, Joan. "The Fate of the Image in Church History and the Modern State." *Politica Comun: A Journal of Thought* 1, no. 2 (2012): n.p. Mexico: 17, Instituto de Estudios Criticos/TAMU/Aberdeen/Universita degli Studio Salerno.

Copjec, Joan. "Cinema as Thought Experiment: On Movement and Movements." *Differences* 27, no. 1 (2016): 143–75.

Copjec, Joan. "The Imaginal World and Modern Oblivion: Kiarostami's Zig-Zag." *Filozofski Vestnik* XXXVII, no. 2 (2016): 21–58.

Corbin, Henry. "Visionary Dream in Islamic Spirituality." In *The Dream and Human Society*, edited by G.E. von Gurnebaum and Roger Caillois, 381–408. Berkeley and Los Angeles: University of California Press, 1966.

Corbin, Henry. "*Mundus Imaginalis* or The Imaginary and the Imaginal." Translated by Leonard Fox. In *Swedenborg and Esoteric Islam*. Pennsylvania: Swedenborg Foundation, 1995.

Corbin, Henry, "Mundus imaginalis ou l'imaginaire et l'Imaginal," *Cahiers internationaux du Symbolisme* 6, (1964): 3–26.

Corbin, Henry. *Spiritual Body and Celestial Earth: From Mazdean Iran to Shi'ite Iran*. Trans. Nancy Pearson. 2nd ed. Princeton: Princeton University Press, 1977.

Corbin, Henry. *L'Iran et la philosophie (L'Espace intérieur)*. Paris: Fayard, 1990.

Corbin, Henry. *Alone With the Alone: Creative Imagination in the Sufism of Ibn 'Arabi*. Princeton: University of Princeton Press, 1998.

Creed, Barbra. *The Monstrous-Feminine: Film, Feminism, Psychoanalysis*. London: Routledge, 1993.

Dabashi, Hamid. *Close Up: Iranian Cinema, Past, Present and Future*. London and New York: Verso, 2001.

Dabashi, Hamid. *Masters & Masterpieces of Iranian Cinema*. Washington, DC: Mage Publishers, 2007.

Daly, Glyn. "Slavoj Zizek: Risking the Impossible." lacan.com 2004. http://www.lacan.com/zizek-primer.htm

Daoud, Hassan. "Those Two Heavy Wings of Manhood: On Moustaches." In *Imagined Masculinities: Male Identity and Culture in the Middle East*, edited by Mai Ghoussoub and Emma Sinclair-Webb, 273–80. London: Saqi, 2000.

David, Bordwell, and Noël Carroll eds., *Post-Theory: Reconstructing Film Studies*. Madison: University of Wisconsin Press, 1996.

de Bruijn, J. T. P. "The Qalandariyyat in Persian Mystical Poetry from Sand'i Onwards." In *The Legacy of Mediæval Persian Sufism*, edited by Leonard Lewisohn, 61–75. Oxford: Oneworld, 1992.

Deleuze, Gilles. "Gilles Deleuze on Cinema: What Is the Creative Act, 1987". https://www.youtube.com/watch?v=a_hifamdISs

Deleuze, Gilles. *Masochism: Coldness and Cruelty & Venus in Furs*, Translated from French by Jean McNeil and Aude Willm. New York: Zone Books, 1991.

Deleuze, Gilles, and Guattari Felix. *A Thousand Plateaus*. Translated by Brian Massumi. London and New York: Continuum, 2004.

Deleuze, Gilles, and Guattari Felix. *Anti-Oedipus: Capitalism and Schizophrenia*. Minneapolis: University of Minnesota Press, 2008.

Doane, Mary Ann. "The Voice in the Cinema: The Articulation of Body and Space." *Yale French Studies* 60 (1980): 33–50.

Doane, Mary Ann. *The Desire to Desire: The Women's Films of the 1940s*. Bloomingdale: Indiana University, 1987.

Doane, Mary Ann. *Femmes Fatales: Feminism, Film Theory, Psychoanalysis*. New York: Routledge, 1991.

Doane, Mary Ann. *Bigger Than Life: The Close-Up and Scale in the Cinema*. Durham: Duke University Press, 2021.

Dolar, Mladen. *A Voice and Nothing More*. Cambridge, MA: MIT Press, 2006.

Dolar, Mladen. "Telephone and Psychoanalysis (Walter Benjamin)." *Filozofski Vestnik* 29, no. 1 (2008): 7.

Dolar, Mladen. 'The Object Voice." In *Gaze and Voice as Love Objects*, edited by Renata Salecl, and Slavoj Žižek, 7–31. Duke University Press, 1996.

Dönmez-Colin, Gönül. "Refugees in Love and Life Interview with Majid Majidi by Gonul Donmez-Colin (Film Critic)." (Reprint from Asian Cinema Studies 13, no. 1 (2002). http://www.cinemajidi.com/

Dönmez-Colin, Gönül. *Women, Islam and Cinema*. UK: Reaktion Books, 2004.

Dönmez-Colin, Gönül. *Cinemas of the Other: A Personal Journey with Film-Makers from the Middle East and Central Asia*. Bristol: Intellect, 2006.

During, Jean. "Hal." In *Encyclopaedia Iranica*, Vol. 8, edited by Ehsan Yarshater. New York: Encyclopaedia Iranica Foundation, 2003.

During, Jean, and Zia Mirabdolbaghi. *The Art of Persian Music*. Washington: DC: Mage Publishers, 1991.

El Shakry, Omnia. *The Arabic Freud: Psychoanalysis and Islam in Modern Egypt*. Princeton: Princeton University Press, 2017.

El-Rouayheb, Khaled. *Before Homosexuality in the Arab-Islamic World, 1500–1800*. Chicago: University of Chicago, 2005.

Erfani, Farhang. *Iranian Cinema and Philosophy: Shooting Truth*. Palgrave Macmillan, 2011.

Ernst, Carl W. *Sufism: An Introduction to the Mystical Tradition of Islam*. Boulder, Colorado: Shambhala Publications, 2011.

Esfandiary, Shahab. *Iranian Cinema and Globalization: National, Transnational, and Islamic Dimensions*. University of Chicago: Intellect Ltd. Chicago, 2012.

Fadl, A. El. *Speaking in God's Name: Islamic Law, Authority and Women*. Oxford: Oneworld, 2001.

Fallahzadeh, Mehrdad. *Persian Writing on Music: A Study of Persian Musical Literature from 1000 to 1500 AD*. Studia Iranica Upsaliensia. Stockholm: Uppsala Universitet, 2005.

Farrokhzad, Forough. *Iman biavarim be aghaz-e faṣl-e sard [Let Us Believe in the Cold Season]*. Tehran: Morvarid, 1963.

Felek, Özgen and Alexander D. Knysh. *Dreams and Visions in Islamic Societies*. State University of New York Press, 2012.

Ferdowsi, Abolqasem. *Shahnameh: The Persian Book of Kings*. Translated by Dick Davis. London: Penguin Classics, 2016.

Fink, Bruce. *The Lacanian Subject*. Princeton: Princeton University Press, 1995.

Fisher, Mark. *The Weird and the Eerie*. London: Repeater Books, 2016.

Floor, Willem. *A Social History of Sexual Relations in Iran*. Washington, DC: Mage Publishers, 2008.

Forrester, John. "Introduction." In *Sigmund Freud, Interpreting Dreams*. Translated by J. A. Underwood, vii–lviii. London: Penguin Books, 2006.

"Fourteen Films That Have Been Banned in Iran Since 2007." August 21, 2015. https://globalvoices.org/2015/08/21/14-films-that-have-been-banned-in-iran-since-2007/

Foucault, Michel. *The History of Sexuality*. New York: Vintage Books, 1990.

Foucault, Michel. *The Order of Things*. London: Routledge, 2001.

Freud, Sigmund. *The Interpretation of Dreams*, Part 1, SE IV.

Freud, Sigmund. *The Interpretation of Dreams*, Part 2, SE V.

Freud, Sigmund. "The Ego and the Id." In SE XIX, 69108.

Freud, Sigmund. "Repression." In SE XIV, 283397.

Freud, Sigmund. "The 'Uncanny'." In SE XVII, 217–54.

Freud, Sigmund. "Preface to the Third English Edition." In *The Interpretation of Dreams (I)* in *The Standard Edition of the Complete Psychological Works of Sigmund Freud*, Vol. VI, edited and translated by James Strachey, xvii. London: Hogarth, 1953.

Freud Museum London, "What Is Psychoanalysis? Part 1: Is It Weird?" YouTube, October 22, 2015. https://www.youtube.com/watch?v=pxaFeP9Ls5c

Gaffary, Farrokh. "Akkas-Bashi." *Encyclopedia Iranica*, Vol. 1, edited by Ehsan Yarshater, 719. London: Routledge and Kegan Paul, 1985. http://www.iranicaonline.org/articles/akkas-basi-ebrahim

Garber, Marjorie. *Vested Interests: Cross-Dressing and Cultural Anxiety*. New York, NY and London: Routledge, 1992.

Ghamari-Tabrizi, Behrooz. *Foucault in Iran: Islamic Revolution after the Enlightenment*. Minnesota: University of Minnesota Press, 2016.

Gherovici, Patricia. *Please Select Your Gender: From the Invention of Hysteria to the Democratizing of Transgenderism*. London: Routledge, 2010.

Gherovici, Patricia. *Transgender Psychoanalysis: A Lacanian Perspective on Sexual Difference*. New York: Routledge, 2017.

Ghorbankarimi, Maryam ed. *ReFocus: The Films of Rakhshan Banietemad*. Edinburgh: Edinburgh University Press, 2021.

Glünz, Michael. "The Sword, the Pen and the Phallus: Metaphors and Metonymies of Male Power and Creativity in Medieval Persian Poetry." *Edebiyat* 6 (1995): 223–243.

Gnoli, Gherardo. "Farr(ah)/xᵛarəənah." *Encyclopaedia Iranica*, IX, 1999, pp. 312–19. www.iranicaonline.org/articles/farrah

Gozlan, Oren. *Transsexuality and the Art of Transitioning: A Lacanian Approach*. New York: Routledge, 2015.

Green, Nile. "The Religious and Cultural Roles of Dreams and Visions in Islam." *Journal of the Royal Asiatic Society* 13, no. 3 (2003): 287–313.

Green, Nile. "Between Heidegger and the Hidden Imam: Reflections on Henry Corbin's Approaches to Mystical Islam." In *Le monde turco-iranien en question, coll. Développements*, edited by M.R. Djalili, A. Monsutti and A. Neubauer, 247–59. Paris, Karthala: Genève, Institut de hautes études internationales et du développement, 2008.

Gutas, Dimitri. *Greek Thought, Arabic Culture: The Graeco-Arabic Translation Movement in Baghdad and Early 'Abbasaid Society (2nd-4th/5th-10th c.)*. London/New York: Routledge, 1998.

Haeri, Shahla. *Questions of Cinema*. Bloomington: Indiana University Press, 1981.

Haeri, Shahla. "Sacred Canopy: Love and Sex under the Veil." *Iranian Studies* 42 (2009): 113–126.

Haeri, Shahla (Revised Ed.). *Law of Desire: Temporary Marriage in Shi'i Iran*. Syracuse University Press, 2014.

Han, Byung-Chul. *The Agony of Eros*. Cambridge, Massachusetts: MIT press, 2017.

Heath, Stephen. "Cinema and Psychoanalysis: Parallel Histories." In *Endless Night: Cinema and Psychoanalysis, Parallel Histories*, edited by Janet Bergstrom, 25–56. Berkeley: University of California Press, 1999.

Hedayat, Sadegh. *The Blind Owl*. Translated by D. P. Costello. New York: Grove Press, 2010.

Hegel, G. W. F. *Phenomenology of Spirit*. Translated by A. V. Miller. Oxford: Oxford University Press, 1977.

Heidegger, Martin. *Being and Time*. Translated by John Macquarrie and Edward Robinson. New York: Harper & Row, 1962.

Hillman, Michael C. *A Lonely Woman: Forugh Farrokhzad and Her Poetry*. Washington, DC: Mage Publishers, 1987.

Homayounpour, Gohar. *Doing Psychoanalysis in Tehran*. Cambridge Massachusetts: MIT Press, 2012.

Hoveyda, Fereydoun, "Self-Criticism ('Autocritique', Cahiers du Cinema 126, December 1961)". In *Cahiers du Cinéma Volume 2. 1960–1968: New Vave, New Cinema, Re-evaluating Hollywood*, edited by Jim Hillier, 257–63. London: Routledge, 1986.

Hoveyda, Fereydoun. *Cinéma vérité*, or Fantastic Realism (Cinéma vérité ou realism fantastique', Cahiers du Cinema 125, November 1961). In *Cahiers du Cinéma*, Vol. 2. 1960–1968, edited by Jim Hillier, 248–56. London: Routledge, 1986.

Hoveyda, Fereydoun. *The Hidden Meaning of Mass Communications: Cinema, Books, and Television in the Age of Computers*. Westport, Connecticut/London: Praeger Publishers, 2000.

Issari, Ali M. *Cinema in Iran 1900–1979*. Metuchen: The Scarecrow Press, 1989.

Izutsu, Toshihiko. *Sufism and Taoism*. Los Angeles, CA: University of California Press, 1983.

Jahed, Parviz. *Directory of World Cinema: Iran 2*. Chicago: Intellect Books, 2017.

Jalal al-Din, Rumi. *The Masnavi, Book One*. Translated by Jawid Mojaddedi. Oxford: Oxford University Press, 2004.

Johnson, Adrian. "This Philosophy Which Is Not One: Jean-Claude Milner, Alain Badiou, and Lacanian Antiphilosophy." *S: Journal of the Jan van Eyck Circle for Lacanian Ideology Critique* 3, no. 3 (2010): 137–158. Special issue: "On Jean-Claude Milner" [ed. Justin Clemens and Sigi Jöttkandt], Spring. https://lineofbeauty.org/index.php/sjournal/article/view/112

Jones, Ernest. *Sigmund Freud: Life and Work*. London: Hogarth Press, 1953.

Jones, Ernest. *On the Nightmare*. London, 1931.

Juynboll, G. H. A. "Siḥāḳ." In *EI2* IX, pp. 56567.

Kadkani, Shafi'i-yi Muhammad Reza. *Qalandariyah dar Tarikh: Digarandisi-ha-yi yek Ide'olozhi*. Tehran: Sokhan, 1386/2007.

Kant, Immanuel. *Critique of Pure Reason*. Translated by Paul Guyer and Allen W. Wood. Cambridge: University of Cambridge Press, 1998.

Karamustafa, Ahmet T. *God's Unruly Friends: Dervish Groups in the Islamic Later Middle Period. 1200-1550*. Salt Lake City: University of Utah Press, 1994.

Karimi, Pamela. "Secular Domesticities, Shiite Modernities: Khomeini's Illustrated *Tawzih al-Masail*." In *Visual Culture in the Modern Middle East: Rhetoric of the Image*, edited by

Christiane Gruber and Sune Haugbolle, 32–56. Bloomington, Indiana: Indiana University Press, 2013.

Kazemi, Farshid. "The Speaking Tree: The Mytho-Poetics of the Female Voice in Bahram Beyzaie's Cinema," paper presented at the symposium, in *Conversation with Bahram Beyzaie*, University of St. Andrews, UK. June 23–24, 2017.

Kazemi, Farshid. "The Object-Voice: The Acousmatic Voice in the New Iranian Cinema." *Camera Obscura: Feminism, Culture, and Media Studies* 33, no. 1 (97) (2018): 57–80.

Kazemi, Farshid. "The Repressed Event of (Shi'i) Islam: Psychoanalysis, the Trauma of Iranian Shi'ism, and Feminine Revolt." In *Psychoanalytic Islam and Islamic Psychoanalysis*, edited by Ian Parker and Sabah Siddiqui, 70–87. London/New York: Routledge, 2018.

Kazemi, Farshid. *A Girl Walks Home Alone at Night*. Liverpool: Liverpool University Press, 2021.

Kazemzadeh, Firuz, *Russia and Britain in Persia, 1864-1914: A Study in Imperialism* Yale University Press, 1968.

Kelley, Ron. *Irangeles: Iranians in Los Angeles*. Los Angeles: University of California Press, 1993.

Kheshti, Roshanak. "Cross-Dressing and Gender (Tres)Passing: The Transgender Move as a Site of Agential Potential in the New Iranian Cinema." *Hypatia* 24, no. 3 (2009): 158–77.

Khodaei, Khatereh. "Shirin as Described by Kiarostami." 13, no. 1 (2009). http://offscreen. com/view/shirin_kiarostami

Khomeini, Ayatollah Ruhollah. *Resaleh-ye novin* [New treatise], trans. 'Abdul Karim Baizar-e Shirazi. Tehran: Ketab, 1982.

Kiarostami, Abbas. *An Unabridged Translation of Resaleh Towzih al-Masael*. Translated by J. Borujerdi, with a Foreword by Michael M. J. Fischer and Mehdi Abedi. London: Routledge, 1984.

Kiarostami, Abbas. *Islam and Revolution: Writings and Declarations*. Translated by Hamid Algar. London: KPI Limited, 1985.

Kiarostami, Abbas. "Foreword." In *Doing Psychoanalysis in Tehran*, edited by Gohar Homayounpour, ix–xxviii. Cambridge Massachusetts: MIT Press, 2012.

Kiarostami, Abbas. *Lessons With Kiarostami*, edited by Paul Cronin. New York: Sticking Place Books, 2015.

Kohlberg, Etan. "Some Imami-Shi'i Views on Taqiyya." *Journal of the American Oriental Society* 95, no. 3 (1975): 395–402.

Kohlberg, Etan. "Taqiyya in Shi'i Theology and Religion." In *Secrecy and Concealment: Studies in the History of Mediterranean and Near Eastern Religions*, edited by Hans Hans Gerhard Kippenberg and Guy G. Stroumsa, 345–80. Leiden: Brill, 1995.

Kojève, Alexander. *Introduction to the Reading of Hegel: Lectures on the Phenomenology of Spirit*. Ithaca NY: Cornell University Press, 1980.

Kozloff, Sarah. *Invisible Storytellers: Voice- Over Narration in American Fiction Film*. Berkeley: University of California Press, 1988.

Kravis, Nathan. *On the Couch: A Repressed History of the Analytic Couch from Plato to Freud*. Cambridge, Mass: MIT Press, 2017.

Krips, Henry. Fetish: An Erotics of Culture. New York: Cornell University Press, 1999.

Krips, Henry. "The Politics of the Gaze: Foucault, Lacan and Žižek." Culture Unbound 2 (2010): 91–102.

Kristeva, Julia. "On the Melancholic Imaginary." *New Formations New Formations* 3 (1987): 5–18.

Kristeva, Julia. *Revolt, She Said*. Translated by Brian O'Keeffe. Massachusetts: Semiotext(e) Foreign Agents, 2002.

Kristeva, Julia. *Melanie Klein*. Translated by Ross Guberman. New York: Columbia University Press, 2004.

Lacan, Jacques. *l'Objet de la Psychanalyse*, Seminar XIII (1965–66). Unpublished manuscript. http://www.valas.fr/Jacques-Lacan-l-objet-de-la-psychanalyse,258

Lacan, Jacques. Seminar XIII *The Object of Psychoanalysis* (1965–66). Translated by Cormac Gallagher. http://www.lacaninireland.com/web/wp-content/uploads/2010/06/13-The-Object-of-Psychoanalysis1.pdf

Lacan, Jacques. *Logique du Fantasme*, Seminar XIV (1966–1967). Unpublished manuscript. http://www.valas.fr/IMG/pdf/S14_LOGIQUE.pdf

Lacan, Jacques. *The Logic of Fantasy,* Seminar XIV (1966–1967). Translated by Cormac Gallagher. http://www.lacaninireland.com/web/wp-content/uploads/2010/06/14-Logic-of-Phantasy-Complete.pdf

Lacan, Jacques. *Les non-dupes errent*, lesson 11 (April 9, 1974). Unpublished manuscript. http://www.valas.fr/Jacques-Lacan-les-non-dupes-errent-1973-1974,322?lang=fr

Lacan, Jacques. *The Seminar of Jacques Lacan, Book XI: The Four Fundamental Concepts of Psychoanalysis 1964*, edited by Jacques-Alain Miller, translated by Alan Sheridan. London: Norton, 1977.

Lacan, Jacques. *Television: A Challenge to the Psychoanalytic Establishment*, edited by Joan Copjec, translated by Dennis Hollier, Rosalind Krauss and Annette Michelson. New York: Norton, 1990.

Lacan, Jacques. *The Seminar of Jacques Lacan, Book I: Freud's Papers on Technique 1953–1954*, edited by Jacques-Alain Miller, translated by John Forrester. London: Norton, 1991.

Lacan, Jacques. "*The Ethics of Psychoanalysis*." In *1959–1960, The Seminar of Jacques Translated with Notes by Dennis Porter*, edited by Jacques-Alain Miller. London: Routledge, 1992.

Lacan, Jacques. *The Seminar of Jacques Lacan, Book III: The Psychoses 1955–56*, edited by Jacques-Alain Miller, translated by Russell Grigg. London: Routledge, 1993.

Lacan, Jacques. "The Seminar of Jacques Lacan." In *Book XX: On Feminine Sexuality, the Limits of Love & Knowledge 1972–73: Encore*, edited by Miller and Fink. London: Norton, 1998.

Lacan, Jacques. *Écrits: The First Complete Edition in English*. Translated by Bruce Fink. New York: Norton and Company, 2006.

Lacan, Jacques. *The Seminar of Jacques Lacan, Book XVII: The Other Side of Psychoanalysis 1969–70*, edited by Jacques-Alain Miller, translated by Russell Grigg. London: Norton, 2007.

Lacan, Jacques. *My Teaching*. Translated by David Macey. London: Verso, 2008.

Lacan, Jacques. *Le séminaire: Livre VI, Le Désir et son interpretation*. Paris: Editions de la Martinière, 2013.

Lacan, Jacques. *Anxiety: The Seminar of Jacques Lacan, Book X*. Translated by A. R. Price. Cambridge: Polity, 2014.

Lacan, Jacques. *Transference, The Seminar of Jacques Lacan Book VIII*, ed. Jacques-Alain Miller. Translated by Bruce Fink. Cambridge: Polity Press, 2015.

Lacan, Jacques. *...or Worse: The Seminar of Jacques Lacan Book XIX*. Translated by A. R. Price. Cambridge: Polity Press, 2018.

Lacan, Jacques. *Écrits*. Paris: Seuil, 1966.

Lang, Robert. "An Interview With Fereydoun Hoveyda." *Screen* 34, no. 4 (1993): 392–400.

Laplanche, Jean, and J. B Pontalis. "Fantasy and the Origins of Sexuality." *International Journal of Psychoanalysis* 49, no. 1 (1968): 1–18.

Laporte, Dominique. *The History of Shit*. Cambridge Massachusetts: MIT Press, 2000.

Lawrence, Amy. *Echo and Narcissus: Women's Voices in Classical Hollywood Cinema*. Berkeley: University of California Press, 1991.

Lear, Andrew, and Eva Cantarella. *Images of Pederasty: Boys Were Their Gods*. London and New York: 2008.

Lebeau, Vicky. *Psychoanalysis and Cinema: The Play of Shadows*. New York: Wallflower Press, 2002.

Lewis, Franklin, *Rumi: Past and Present, East and West. The Life Teachings and Poetry of Jalâl Al-Din Rumi*. Foreword by Julie Meisami. Oxford: Oneworld Publications, 2007.

Lewis, Franklin. *Rumi: Swallowing the Sun*. Translated by Franklin Lewis. Oxford: Oneworld, 2008.

Lewisohn, Leonard. "The Sacred Music of Islam: Samā' in the Persian Sufi Tradition." *British Journal of Ethnomusicology* 6 (1997): 1–33.

Lloyd, Ridgeon ed. *Religion and Politics in Modern Iran: A Reader*. London/New York: I.B. Tauris, 2005.

Lory, Pierre. *Le Rêve et Ses Interprétations en Islam*. Paris: Albin Michel, 2015.

Marx, Karl. *The Portable Karl Marx*, edited by Eugene Kamenka. Harmondsworth: Penguin, 1983.

McGowan, Todd. *The Real Gaze: Film Theory after Lacan*. Albany: SUNY Press, 2007.

McGowan, Todd. *The Impossible David Lynch*. New York: Columbia UP, 2007.

McGowan, Todd. *Psychoanalytic Film Theory and the Rules of the Game*. New York: Bloomsbury, 2015.

McGowan, Todd, and Sheila Kunkle, eds. *Lacan and Contemporary Film*. New York: Other Press, 2004.

Mehrabi, Massoud. *Tarikh-e sinema-yi Iran: Az aghaz ta sal-e 1357 [The History of Iranian Cinema: From the Beginning to 1979]*. Tehran: Film Publication, 1988.

Mernissi, Fatima. *Beyond the Veil: Male-Female Dynamics in the Modern Muslim Society* (rev. ed.). Translated by Mary Jo Lakeland. Bloomington: Indiana University Press, 1987.

Metz, Christian. *Film Language: A Semiotics of the Cinema*. Translated by Michael Taylor. New York: Oxford UP, 1974.

Metz, Christian. *The Imaginary Signifier: Psychoanalysis and the Cinema*. Translated by Ben Brewster, Celia Britton and Annwyl Williams. Bloomington, IN: Indiana UP, 1982.

Metz, Christian. *Impersonal Enunciation, or the Place of Film*. Translated with an Introduction by Cormac Deane. New York: Columbia University Press, 2016.

Milani, Abbas. "Hoveyda, Amir-Abbas." *Encyclopaedia Iranica*, XII, no. 5: 543–550. http://www.iranicaonline.org/articles/hoveyda-amir-abbas

Milani, Abbas. *The Persian Sphinx: Amir-Abbas Hoveyda and the Riddle of the Iranian Revolution*. Washington DC: Mage Publishers, 2000.

Milani, Farzaneh. *Veils and Words: The Emerging Voices of Iranian Women Writers*. Syracuse, NY: Syracuse University Press, 1992.

Miller, Elaine P. *Head Cases: Julia Kristeva on Philosophy and Art in Depressed Times*. New York: Columbia University Press, 2014/.

Mitchell, Juliet, and Jaqueline Rose eds., *Feminine Sexuality: Jaques Lacan and the école freudienne*. New York/London: W.W. Norton & Company, Inc, 1985.

Moallem, Minoo. *Between Warrior Brother and Veiled Sister: Islamic Fundamentalism and the Politics of Patriarchy in Iran*. Berkeley: University of California Press, 2005.

Moallem, Minoo. *Persian Carpets: The Nation as a Transnational Commodity*. London/New York: Routledge, 2018.

Mokhtabad, Mostafa. "Kiarostami's Unfinished Cinema and Its Postmodern Reflections." *International Journal of the Humanities* 17, no. 2 (2010): 23–37.

Moraweji, Ayatollah Ali. *Sinama dar ayine-ye fiqh* [Cinema in the Mirror of Jurisprudence], ed. by Mohammad Reza Jabbaran. Tehran: Pazhuhishgah-e arhang va honar-e Islami, 1999.

Morrison, James Douglas. *The Collected Works of Jim Morrison: Poetry, Journals, Transcripts, and Lyrics*. New York: HarperColins/Harper Design, 2021.

Mottahedeh, Negar. "Ta'ziyeh: Karbala Drag Kings and Queens." *The Drama Review* 49, no. 4 (1988, (Winter, 2005): 73–85.

Mottahedeh, Negar. "Scheduled For Judgment Day: The Ta'ziyeh Performance in Qajar Persia and Walter Benjamin's Dramatic Vision of History." *Theatre InSight* 8, no. 1 (1997): 12–20.

Mottahedeh, Negar. "Bahram Bayzai's *Maybe ... Some Other Time*: The Un-Present-Able Iran." *Camera Obscura* 15, no. 1 (43) (2000): 163–191.

Mottahedeh, Negar. "'Life Is Color!' Toward a Transnational Feminist Analysis of Mohsen Makhmalbaf's *Gabbeh*", *Signs*, no. 30, 2004, pp. 1403–1428.

Mottahedeh, Negar. *Representing the Unpresentable: Images of Reform from the Qajars to the Islamic Republic of Iran*. Syracuse: Syracuse University Press, 2008.

Mottahedeh, Negar. *Displaced Allegories: Post-Revolutionary Iranian Cinema*. Duke University Press, 2009.

Mozafari, Parmis. "Carving a Space for Female Solo Singing in Post-Revolution Iran." In *Resistance in Contemporary Middle Eastern Cultures: Literature, Cinema and Music*, edited by Karima Laachir and Saeed Talajooy, 262–278. New York/London: Routledge, 2013.

Mullarkey, John. *Refractions of Reality: Philosophy and the Moving Image*. London: Palgrave Macmillan, 2009.

Mulvey, Laura. "Visual Pleasure and Narrative Cinema." *Screen* 16, no. 3 (1975): 6–18.

Mulvey, Laura. "Afterthoughts on 'Visual Pleasure and Narrative Cinema' Inspired by *Duel in the Sun*." In *Feminism and Film Theory*, edited by Constance Penley, 69–79. New York: Routledge, 1988.

Mulvey, Laura. "Kiarostami's Uncertainty Principle." *Sight and Sound*, June 1998, pp. 24–27.

Mulvey, Laura. *Death 24x a Second: Stillness and the Moving Image*. London: Reaktion Book, 2006.

Mulvey, Laura. "Afterword." In *The New Iranian Cinema: Politics, Representation and Identity*, edited by Richard Tapper. London/New York: I.B. Tauris, 2006.

Mulvey, Laura. *Afterimages: On Cinema, Women and Changing Times*. London: Reaktion Books, 2019.

Naficy, Hamid. "The Averted Gaze in Iranian Postrevolutionary Cinema." *Public Culture* 3, no. 2 (1991): 29–40.

Naficy, Hamid. "Veiled vision/powerful Presences: Women in Post-Revolutionary Iranian Cinema." In *Life and Art: The New Iranian Cinema*, edited by R. Issa and S. Whitaker, 44–65. London: National Film Theatre, 1999.

Naficy, Hamid. "Veiled Voice and Vision in Iranian Cinema: The Evolution of Rakhshan Banietemad's Films." *SOCIAL RESEARCH* 67, no. 2 (2000): 559–567.

Naficy, Hamid. *An Accented Cinema: Exilic and Diasporic Filmmaking*. Princeton: Princeton University Press, 2001.

Naficy, Hamid. "The Islamization of Film Culture in Iran." In *The New Iranian Cinema: Politics, Representation and Identity*, edited by Richard Tapper, 26–65. London/New York: I.B. Tauris, 2006.

Naficy, Hamid. *A Social History of Iranian Cinema*, Vol. 4. Durham: Duke University Press, 2011–2012.

Naficy, Hamid. *A Social History of Iranian Cinema Volume 1: The Artisanal Era, 1897–1941*. Durham: Duke University Press, 2011.

Najmabadi, Afsaneh. *Women With Mustaches and Men Without Beards: Gender and Sexual Anxieties of Iranian Modernity*. Berkeley: University of California Press, 2005.

Najmabadi, Afsaneh. *Professing Selves: Transsexuality and Same-Sex Desire in Contemporary Iran*. Durham and London: Duke University Press, 2014.

Najmabadi, Afsaneh, and Kathryn Babayan eds. *Islamicate Sexualities: Translations Across Temporal Geographies of Desire*. Cambridge: Harvard University Press, 2008.

Nancy, Jean-Luc, *L'Évidence du film. Abbas Kiarostami [The Evidence of Film: Abbas Kiarostami]*. Bruxelles: Yves Gevaert Éditeur, 2001),

Naraghi, Nazanine. 'Tehrangeles,' CA: The Aesthetics of Shame." In *Psychoanalytic Geographies*, edited by Paul Kingsbury and Steve Pile, 165–180. London/New York: Routledge, 2016.

Navai, Ramita. *City of Lies: Love, Sex, Death, and the Search for Truth in Tehran*. London: Weidenfeld & Nicolson, 2104.

Nicholson, Reynold. *The Tarjumán al-Ashwáq: A Collection of Mystical Odes by Muhyiddīn Ibn al-ʿArabī*. London: Royal Asiatic Society, 1981. Oriental Translation Series, New Series xx, reprinted by the Theosophical Publishing House, Wheaton, Illinois.

Novak, Ivana, Dolar Mladen, and Jela Krečič eds. *Lubitsch Can't Wait: A Collection of Ten Philosophical Discussions on Ernst Lubitsch's Film Comedy*. Ljubljana: Slovenian Cinematheque, 2014.

Oudart, Jean-Pierre. "Cinema and Suture." Translated by Kari Hanet." *Screen* 18, no. 4 (1977/78): 35–47.

Pak-Shiraz, Nacim. *Shi'i Islam in Iranian Cinema: Religion and Spirituality in Film*. London and New York: I. B. Tauris, 2011.

Pak-Shiraz, Nacim. "Shi'ism in Iranian Cinema." In *The Shi'i World: Pathways in Tradition and Modernity*, edited by Farhad Daftary, Amyn B. Sajoo and Shainool Jiwa, 300–325. New York: I. B. Tauris, 2015.

Phillips, John. *Transgender on Screen*. Basingstoke, UK: Palgrave Macmillan, 2006.

Pittman, Michael. "Majid Majidi and Baran: Iranian Cinematic Poetics and the Spiritual Poverty of Rumi." *Journal of Religion & Film* 15, no. 2 (2011): 1–13.

"'Qalb-e Atomi' Saranjam Roonamai Shod." *Farsnews*, November 21, 2014. http://www.farsnews.com/newstext.php?nn=13931121000045

Rahbaran, Shiva. *Iranian Cinema Uncensored: Contemporary Film-Makers Since the Islamic Revolution*. London: I.B. Tauris, 2015.

Restuccia, Frances L. *The Taming of the Real: Zizek's Missed Encounter with Kieslowski's Insight*." http://www.lacan.com/white.htm

Restuccia, Frances L. *The Blue Box: Kristevan/Lacanian Readings of Contemporary Cinema*. London/New York: Continuum, 2012.

Rose, Jacqueline "Introduction II." In *Feminine Sexuality: Jacques Lacan and the ecole freudienne*, edited by Juliet Mitchell and Jacqueline Rose. New York and London: W. W. Norton, 1982.

Roudinesco, Elisabeth. *Jacques Lacan: An Outline of a Life and History of a System of Thought*. Cambridge: Polity, 1999.

Rowson, E. K. "Homosexuality ii. In Islamic Law." *Encyclopædia Iranica* XII, no. 4: 441–45. http://www.iranicaonline.org/articles/homosexuality-ii

Sadr, Hamid Reza. *Iranian Cinema: A Political History*. London and New York: I. B. Tauris, 2006.

Saeedvafa, Mehrnaz and Jonathan Rosenbaum. *Abbas Kiarostami*. Urbana: University of Illinois Press, 2003.

Saljoughi, Sara. "Seeing, Iranian Style: Women and Collective Vision in Abbas Kiarostami's *Shirin*." *Iranian Studies* 45, no. 4 (2012): 519–35.

Sanati, Mohammad. *Sadegh Hedayat va Haras az Marg*. Tehran, Markaz, 1380.

Sartre, Jean-Paul. *Being and Nothingness: An Essay on Phenomenological Ontology*. Translated by Hazel E. Barnes. London, Methuen, 1958 [1943].

Schimmel, Annemariel. *My Soul Is a Woman: The Feminine in Islam*. London: Continuum, 2003.

Schuster, Aaron. "The Lacan-Foucault Relation: *Las Meninas*, Sexuality, and the Unconscious." 8. *Transcript of a Lecture Delivered at the "Lacan Contra Foucault" conference*. American University of Beirut, December 4, 2015.

al-Saduq, al-Shaykh Abu Ja'far Muhammad b. 'Ali b. al-Husayn b. Babuya al Qummi. *Man la yahduruhu al-faqih*. Vol. 4, accessed December 15, 2015. http://www.alhassanain.org/arabic/?com=book&id=216

Schuster, Aaron. *The Trouble with Pleasure: Deleuze and Psychoanalysis*. Cambridge, Massachusetts: Press, 2016.

Sells, Michael A. *Mystical Languages of Unsaying*. Chicago and London: University of Chicago Press, 1994.

Sells, Michael A. *Stations of Desire: Love Elegies from Ibn al-'Arabī and New Poems* (Jerusalem: Ibis Editions, 2001.

Sells, Michael A. and James Webb. "Lacan and Bion: Psychoanalysis and the Mystical Language of Unsaying." *Theory and Psychology* 5, no. 2 (1995): 195–215.

Shamlu, A. and J. R. Russell, "Al." *Encyclopaedia Iranica*, I, no. 7: 741–42. http://www.iranicaonline.org/articles/al-folkloric-being-that-personifies-puerperal-fever

Silverman, Kaja. "A Voice to Match: The Female Voice in Classic Cinema." *Iris: A Journal of Theory on Image and Sound* 3, no. 1 (1985): 57–69.

Silverman, Kaja. *The Acoustic Mirror: The Female Voice in Psychoanalysis and Cinema*. Bloomington: Indiana UP, 1988.

Silverman, Kaja. *Male Subjectivity at the Margins*. New York: Routledge, 1992.

Silverman, Kaja. *The Threshold of the Visible World*. New York: Routledge, 1996.

Sirriyeh, Elizabeth. *Dreams and Visions in the World of Islam*. London/New York: I.B. Tauris, 2017.

Sjogren, Britta. *Into the Vortex: Female Voice and Paradox in Film*. Urbana and Chicago, IL: University of Illinois Press, 2005.

Slavoj, Žižek and Renata Salecl eds., *Gaze and Voice as Love Objects*. Durham: Duke University Press, 1996.

Stoneman, Richard, Kyle Erickson, and Ian Netton eds., *The Alexander Romance in Persia and the East*. Groningen: Barkhuis Publishing; Groningen University Library, 2012.

Subtelny, Maria E. "History and Religion: The Fallacy of Metaphysical Questions (A Review Article)." *Iranian Studies* 36, no. 1 (2003): 91–101.

Tabarraee, Babak "Silence Studies in the Cinema and the Case of Abbas Kiarostami" Unpublished Master's thesis, University of British Columbia, 2013.

Tabarraee, Babak. "Rationalizing the Irrational: Reza Attaran's Popularity, Stardom, and the Recent Cycle of Iranian Absurd Films." *Iranian Studies* 51, no. 4 (2018): 613–32.

Tapper, Richard. *The New Iranian Cinema: Politics, Representation, and Identity*. London: I. B. Tauris, 2004.

Terman, Rochelle. "Trans[ition] in Iran." *World Policy Journal* 31, no. 1 (2014): 28–38.

Tourage, Mahdi. *Rumi and the Hermeneutics of Eroticism*. Leiden: Brill, 2007.

Tourage, Mahdi. "Lacan and Sufism: Paths for Moving Beyond Pre- and Postmodern Subjectivities." In *Esoteric Lacan*, edited by Philipp Valentini and Mahdi Tourage, 59–76. London, New York: Rowman and Littlefield, 2019.

Tseëlon, Efrat. "On Women and Clothes and Carnival Fools." In *Masquerade and Identities: Essays on Gender, Sexuality and Marginality*, edited by Efrat Tseëlon. London/New York: Routledge, 2001.

Valentini, Philipp, and Mahdi Tourage. *Esoteric Lacan*. London, New York: Rowman and Littlefield, 2019.

Vanzan, Anna. "The LGBTQ Question in Iranian Cinema: a Proxy Discourse?" *DEP* 25, (2014), 47–48.

Vejdani, Farzin. *Making History in Iran: Education, Nationalism, and Print Culture*. Stanford California: Stanford University Press, 2014.

Vejdani, Farzin. "Hair and Hat Ritual Shaming Punishments in Nineteenth-Century Iran." *Iranian Studies* 56, no. 4 (October 2023): 1–23.

Verhaeghe, Paul. *Beyond Gender: From Subject to Drive*. New York: Other Press, 2001.

Walter, Andrews and Mehmet Kalpaklı. *The Age of Beloveds: Love and the Beloved in Early-Modern Ottoman and European Culture and Society*. Durham and London: Duke University Press, 2005.

Warner, Marina. "Freud's Couch: A Case History." *Raritan* 31, no. 2 (2011): 146–63.

Warner, Marina. *Stranger Magic: Charmed States and the Arabian Nights*. Boston: The Belknap Press/Harvard University Press, 2012.

Wasserstrom, Steven M. *Religion After Religion: Gershom Scholem, Mircea Eliade, and Henry Corbin at Eranos*. Princeton: Princeton University Press, 1999.

Whitaker, Shiela. "Rakhshan Bani-Etemad." In *Life and Art: The New Iranian Cinema*, edited by Rose Issa and Sheila Whitaker. London: British Film Institute, 1999.

Wild, Oscar. *The Importance of Being Earnest and Other Plays*. New York: Pocket Books, 2005.

Wollen, Peter. "On Gaze Theory," New Left Review 44, March-April 2007, pp. 91–106.

Yeganeh, Nahid, and Nikki R Keddie. "Sexuality and Shi'i Social Protest in Iran." In *Women of Iran: The Conflict With Fundamentalist Islam*, edited by Farah Azari, 108–136. London: Ithaca Press, 1983.

Zargar, Cyrus Ali. "Allegory and Ambiguity in the Films of Majid Majidi: A Theodicy of Meaning." *Journal of Religion & Film*: 20, no. 1 (2016): 1–32.

Zia-Ebrahimi, Reza. *The Emergence of Iranian Nationalism: Race and the Politics of Dislocation*. New York: Columbia University, 2016.

Ziai, Hossein. "Dreams and Dream Interpretation: Dreams II: In the Persian Tradition." *EIr* VII: 549–51. http://www.iranicaonline.org/articles/dreams-and-dream-interpretation

Žižek, Slavoj. *"Love Beyond Law."* http://www.lacan.com/zizlola.htm

Žižek, Slavoj. *The Sublime Object of Ideology*. New York: Verso, 1989.

Žižek, Slavoj. *For They Know Not What They Do: Enjoyment as a Political Factor*. London: Verso, 1991.

Žižek, Slavoj. "The Truth Arises from Misrecognition Part I." In *Lacan and the Subject of Language*, edited by Ellie Ragland-Sullivan and Mark Bracher. New York and London: Routledge, 1991. http://zizek.livejournal.com/3848.html

Žižek, Slavoj. *Looking Awry: An Introduction to Lacan Through Popular Culture*. Cambridge, MA: MIT Press, 1992.

Žižek, Slavoj, ed. *Everything You Always Wanted to Know About Lacan (But Were Afraid to Ask Hitchcock)*. London: Verso, 1992.

Žižek, Slavoj. *Tarrying With the Negative: Kant, Hegel and the Critique of Ideology*. Durham, NC: Duke UP, 1993.

Žižek, Slavoj. *Reflections of Media, of Politics and Cinema*. Interview with Geert Lovink, *InterCommunication* 14, February 27, 1995. http://www.lacan.com/zizek-reflections.htm

Žižek, Slavoj. *The Plague of Fantasies*. London: Verso, 1997.

Žižek, Slavoj. "The Undergrowth of Enjoyment: How Popular Culture Can Serve as an Introduction to Lacan." In *The Žižek Reader*, edited by Elizabeth Wright and Edmond Wright, 11–36. Oxford: Blackwell, 1999.

Žižek, Slavoj. *The Ticklish Subject: The Absent Centre of Political Ontology*. London: Verso, 2000.

Žižek, Slavoj. *Enjoy Your Symptom! Jacques Lacan in Hollywood and Out*. rev. ed. London: Routledge, 2001.

Žižek, Slavoj. *The Fright of Real Tears: Krzysztof Kieślowski between Theory and Post-Theory*. London: BFI, 2001.

Žižek, Slavoj. *The Puppet and the Dwarf*. Cambridge Massachusetts: MIT Press, 2003.

Žižek, Slavoj. "Organs Without Bodies," Thursday 6 November 2003. http://www.aaschool.ac.uk/VIDEO/lecture.php?ID=373

Žižek, Slavoj. *Organs Without Bodies: Deleuze and Consequences*. London: Routledge, 2004.

Žižek, Slavoj. *The Metastases of Enjoyment: Six Essays on Women and Causality*. London: Verso, 2005.

Žižek, Slavoj. *The Parallax View*. Cambridge Massachusetts: MIT Press, 2006.

Žižek, Slavoj. *How to Read Lacan*. London: Granta Books, 2006.

Žižek, Slavoj. "Preface to the New Edition: A Glance at the Archives of Islam", in *The Fragile Absolute or Why the Christian Legacy Is Worth Saving?* London: Verso, 2008.

Žižek, Slavoj. *Less than Nothing: Hegel and the Shadow of Dialectical Materialism*. London: Verso, 2012.

Žižek, Slavoj. *Disparities*. New York/London: Bloomsbury Academic, 2016.

Žižek, Slavoj. "The Obscene Immortality and Its Discontents." *The International Journal of Žižek Studies* 11, no. 2 (2017): 1–14.

Žižek, Slavoj. *The Incontinence of the Void: Economico-Philosphical Spandrels*. Cambridge Massachusetts: MIT Press, 2017.

Žižek, Slavoj. *Surplus-Enjoyment: A Guide for the Non-Preplexed*. London: Bloomsbury Academic, 2022.

Žižek, Slavoj. "The Real of Sexual Difference." In *Reading Seminar XX: Lacan's Major Work on Love, Knowledge, and Feminine Sexuality*, edited by Suzanne Barnard and Bruce Fink, 57–76. Albany, NY: SUNY Press, 2002.

Zupančič, Alenka. *Ethics of the Real: Kant and Lacan*. London: Verso, 2000.

Zupančič, Alenka. *What Is Sex?* Cambridge Massachusetts: MIT Press, 2017.

Filmography

10 (Dah). 2002. Abbas Kiarostami.
24 Frames. 2017. Abbas Kiarostami.
A Moment of Innocence (Nun va goldun). 1996. Mohsen Makhmalbaf.
Atomic Heart (Qalb-e atomi). 2015. Ali Ahmadzadeh.
Baran. 2001. Majid Majidi.
Boys Don't Cry. 1999. Kimberly Peirce.
Chess Game of the Wind (Shatranj-e baad). 1976. Mohammad Reza Aslani.
Close-Up (Nema-ye nazdik). 1990. Abbas Kiarostami.
Critical Zone (Mantagheye bohrani). 2023. Ali Amadzadeh.
Chronicle of a Summer (Chronique d'un été). 1961. Jean Rouch.
Daughters of the Sun (Dokhtaran-e Khorshid). 2000. Mariam Shahriar.
Dead Man. 1995. Jim Jaramusch.
Delshodegan (The Love-Stricken). 1992. Ali Hatami.
Dragon Inn (Long men kezhan). 1967. King Hu.
Facing Mirrors (Aynehaye Rooberoo). 2011. Negar Azarbayjani.
Fight Club. 1999. David Fincher.
Gabbeh. 1996. Mohsen Makhmalbaf.
God Is Near (Khoda nazdik ast). 2006. Ali Vazirian.
Goodbye, Dragon Inn (Bu san). 2003. Tsai Ming-liang.
Kami's Party. 2013. Ali Ahmadzadeh.
Life and Nothing More (Zendegi va digar hich). 1992. Abbas Kiarostami.
Lost Reels (Halqehha-ye Gomshodeh). 2004. Mehrdad Zahedian.
Lost Highway. 1997. David Lynch.
Half Moon (Niwemang). 2006. Bahman Ghobadi.
Mulholland Drive. 2001. David Lynch.
No Country for Old Men. 2007. Ethan Coen and Joel Coen.
Nostalghia. 1983. Andrei Tarkovsky.
Offside (Afsaid). 2006. Jafar Panahi.
Parinaz. 2012. Bahram Bahramian.
Party Girl. 1958. Nicholas Ray.
Psycho. 1960. Alfred Hitchcock.
Rear Window. 1954. Alfred Hitchcock.

Shirin. 2008. Abbas Kiarostami.

Snowman (*Adam barfi*). 1995. Davood Mir-Bagheri.

Taste of Cherry (*Ta'm-e gilas*). 1997. Abbas Kiarostami.

Tehran Taboo. 2017. Ali Soozande.

The Crying Game. 1992. Neil Jordan.

The Day I Became a Woman (*Ruzi ke zan shodam*). 2000. Marzieh Meshkini.

The 400 Blows (*Les quatre cents coups*). 1959. François Truffaut.

The House Is Black (*Khaneh siah ast*). 1962. Forough Farrokhzad.

The Magnificent Ambersons. 1942. Orson Welles.

The May Lady (*Banoo-ye ordibehesht*). 1998. Rakhshan Bani-Etemad.

The Mirror of Lucifer (*Ayneh-ye sheytan*). 2016. Farid Valizadeh.

The Passion of Joan of Arc. 1928. Carl Theodor Dreyer.

The Pervert's Guide to Cinema. 2006. Sophie Fiennes with Slavoj Žižek.

The Pervert's Guide to Ideology. 2012. Sophie Fiennes with Slavoj Žižek.

The Sword of Doom (*Dai-bosatsu Tōge*). 1966. Kihachi Okamoto.

The Student of Prague (*Der Student von* Prag). 1913. Stellan Rye.

The Testament of Dr Mabuse (*Das Testament des Dr Mabuse*). 1933. Fritz Lang.

The Wind Will Carry Us (*Bad ma ra khahad bord*). 1999. Abbas Kiarostami.

Vertigo. 1958. Alfred Hitchcock.

When a Stranger Calls. 1979. Fred Walton.

Women's Prison (*Zendan-e zanan*). 2002. Manijeh Hekmat.

Index

For Product Safety Concerns and Information please contact our EU
representative GPSR@taylorandfrancis.com
Taylor & Francis Verlag GmbH, Kaufingerstraße 24, 80331 München, Germany